# THE DECEPTIVE LURE OF DETENTE

# THE DECEPTIVE LURE OF DETENTE

Dr. Marian Leighton

St. Martin's Press
New York

Scholarly and Reference Division
St. Martin's Press, Inc.
175 Fifth Avenue, New York, NY 10010

First published in the United States of America in 1989

Printed in the United States of America

ISBN 0-312-02801-6

Library of Congress Cataloging-in-Publication Data

Leighton, Marian Kirsch.
    The deceptive lure of detente / Marian Kirsch.
        p.    cm.
    ISBN 0-312-02801-6 : $35.00 (est.)
    1. World politics—1975–1985. 2. World politics—1985–1995.
3. Detente. I. Title.
D849.L327   1989
327.73047—dc19                                          88-31581
                                                            CIP

# Contents

# Acknowledgments

I feel as if the process of bringing this book to fruition has been as protracted as the detente process itself. My debts to colleagues both inside and outside the government who offered me encouragement, helpful comments on the manuscript, and moral support are too numerous to list. Special thanks go to Frank Barnett and Dorothy Nicolosi at the National Strategy Information Center, to Gerry Steibel at Freedom House, and to Devon Gaffney for their multifaceted assistance. My editor, Kermit Hummel, performed wizardry on the manuscript by paring it down from 1,000 pages and considerably sharpening its focus. Finally, I would like to thank my family for its awe-inspiring patience and understanding as I juggled my roles of wife, mother, Sovietologist, and author. Naturally, the views expressed in the book are mine alone and do not necessarily reflect those of any agency of the U.S. government.

# Note on the Author

Dr. Marian Leighton, a specialist on Soviet foreign policy, is an alumna of Barnard College and of the W. Averell Harriman Institute for the Advanced Study of the Soviet Union, at Columbia University. She holds a Ph.D. from Columbia. Among her many published works are *The Soviet Threat to NATO's Northern Flank* (Crane & Russak, 1979) and "Regional Conflicts: Their Impact on Detente" (*Global Affairs*, Spring 1987). Dr. Leighton is currently employed by the U.S. Department of Defense.

## TO MY CHILDREN:

Melanie
Russell
Valerie
Kimberly
Adam

whose love sustained me through this lengthy project.

# 1

# The Background

> Few people remember that the word detente originally meant release of a crossbow bolt, once the world's deadliest weapon. A vast arsenal of infinitely more powerful successors to that arm remains pointed westward. (C.L. Sulzberger, *The New York Times*, 16 June 1973)

Speaking to the World Affairs Council of San Francisco on 3 February 1976, Henry Kissinger, who is generally regarded as the architect of detente, declared:

> We must strive for an equilibrium of power, but we must move beyond it to promote the habits of mutual restraint, coexistence, and ultimately co-operation. We must stabilize a new international order in a vastly dangerous environment, but our ultimate goal must be to transform ideological conflict into constructive participation in building a better world. That is what is meant by the process called detente. . . .

Exactly three weeks later, on 24 February, a speech by Leonid Brezhnev to the 25th Congress of the Communist Party of the Soviet

Union (CPSU) gave the Soviet interpretation of detente. Asserting that detente would not interfere with the other basic items on the Soviet foreign policy agenda—consolidation of the Socialist bloc and support for "national liberation movements"—Brezhnev went on to say that

> Some bourgeois figures express surprise and raise a fuss in regard to the solidarity of the Soviet Communists and the Soviet people with the struggle of other peoples for freedom and progress. This is either naivete or, most likely, a deliberate attempt at befogging of the brains. For it is quite clear that detente and peaceful coexistence are concerned with interstate relations. This means primarily that disputes between countries should not be decided by means of war, use of force or the threat of force. Detente does not in the slightest way abolish, and cannot abolish, the laws of the class struggle. No one should expect that in conditions of detente the Communists will become reconciled to capitalist exploitation or that the monopolists will become supporters of revolution. . . . We do not conceal the fact that we see detente as a way toward the creation of more favorable conditions for peaceful Socialist and Communist construction. . . .[1]

It is painfully obvious from these two representative statements that the superpowers' views of detente diverge in every category from the substantive to the semantic. The Soviet Union has regarded detente primarily as an antidote to nuclear war. At the 20th CPSU Congress, Khrushchev posed the stark alternative of "peaceful coexistence or the most destructive war in history. There is no third way." This formula continues to guide Soviet foreign policy. Under the mantle of detente, however, the United States has gone beyond mere avoidance of nuclear war to think in terms of cooperation with the Soviet Union on a wide variety of fronts. The U.S. conception of detente has involved a commitment to maintain international stability and the status quo; the Russian conception has involved, in the words of *Christian Science Monitor* correspondent David K. Willis, "an easing of the prospects of a global shooting war, so that Moscow can get on with fighting the capitalist states for influence by all other means."

Moscow tends to avoid the word "detente" in favor of *razryadka napryazhennosti*, or lessening of tensions, which it defines as "the state of international relations resulting from the observance of the principles of peaceful coexistence." The Soviet concept of detente is limited, however, to specific players, particular arenas, and a finite historical era. Insofar as Moscow aims only at preventing nuclear war between the superpowers, detente is limited to relations between the USSR and the United States. It extends to Europe, however, because Moscow views detente as creating the preconditions for the disintegration of NATO. The Soviets pursue a "divisible" or "selective" detente, fostering the illusions of those in the NATO countries who believe that Western Europe can remain an oasis of detente in a tumultuous world.

As for the historical confines of detente, the Kremlin has frankly stated since Lenin's time that this is merely a concept applicable to the present historical era in which capitalism continues to exist. The "inevitable triumph of Socialism on a world scale," as the Soviets are fond of saying, will render co-existence obsolete. While Kissinger and other U.S. spokesmen talk in terms of prolonged, even indefinite, Soviet-American co-existence, Soviet officials look upon such coexistence as an expedient tactic designed to bide time until they can establish a *Pax Sovietica*.

Kissinger's San Francisco speech focused on the need to strive for an "equilibrium of power"; but in September 1981 President Reagan sent a letter to Brezhnev expressing concern over "the USSR's unremitting and comprehensive military buildup over the past 15 years, a buildup far exceeding Soviet defensive needs and one which carries disturbing implications of a search . . . for military superiority."[2] The very term "equilibrium of power," which implies a static military balance, is alien to the Soviet outlook. The closest equivalent in the Soviet lexicon is probably "correlation of forces," but this has a dynamic connotation and transcends purely military factors to weigh economic, social and ideological considerations in the balance. Moscow asserts that the "correlation of forces" is shifting inexorably in favor of the USSR. Indeed, it deems such a shift historically inevitable and has moved to abet it by all means short of provoking a general East-West confrontation. When U.S. officials chide the Soviet Union for violating the "code of detente," they are accused of "impeding the march of history," an act as dangerous as it is futile.

Kissinger's expressed intention to transcend equilibrium to foster mutual restraint and cooperation appear similarly out of synch with Soviet objectives. Nowhere has the Soviet disinclination toward mutual restraint been so evident as in the Third World, where U.S. moderation has been met with Soviet actions that indicate a plan to exploit targets of opportunity if not to pursue a determined course of expansionism. As a Radio Moscow broadcast stated on 21 March 1976, in the midst of the Angola crisis,

The opponents of worldwide cooperation like to argue that since the Soviet Union continues to support national liberation movements it is not really sincere about wanting better relations with the United States and is just trying to fool America so as to get what it wants. But the Soviet Union never said, when it set out to reach more understanding with America, that it was ready to give up supporting the struggle of nations for independence or go back on any other of its principles. The Soviet Union has turned its back on confrontation on the world scene. It seeks to prevent a thermonuclear war. That is how it sees its policy of reducing world tension.

In the words of a U.S. commentator, the Soviet Union attempts "to use peaceful coexistence as a shield for warding off nuclear war and to use proletarian internationalism as a sword to move forward in other areas."[3]

Perhaps the most striking aspect of Kissinger's San Francisco statement was the connotation of detente as a "process" (a term implying a degree of regularity and continuity), as opposed to "relaxation of tensions" (which has a tactical and temporary connotation). Moscow views the relaxation of tension as a means of lulling Western suspicions of Soviet intentions and thus easing pressures for increased Western defense expenditures and other measures designed to combat the growth of Soviet military power.

Similarly, arms control has come to be viewed by many in the West as a "process," the continuation of which is presented as good in itself, regardless of the outcome of specific negotiations. While participating in arms control talks, however, the USSR has advanced from a position of marked strategic inferiority vis-a-vis the United States to parity and perhaps beyond. Amidst cries that the USSR has already achieved military preponderance, one can recall Kissinger's statement, "What is strategic superiority? What does one do with it?" The path of detente to date indicates that the shifting strategic balance—strict numbers aside—has enabled the USSR to puncture the nuclear umbrella that provided the raison d'etre of the NATO alliance, as well as to provide a deterrent shield for the Soviet Union's expansion abroad into areas that formerly were Western preserves.

It is ironic that the era of detente has coincided with a period in which the waning ideological appeal of Communism and the growing difficulties of the Soviet economy have led the USSR to use military power as its preferred option for projecting Soviet influence throughout the world. While the commitment of Soviet and proxy troops beyond the Soviet bloc, the massive sale and transfer of Soviet arms abroad, and the stationing of Soviet military advisers in the Third World have been the most visible manifestations of the military option, Soviet military power has been utilized with equal success as an instrument of political intimidation. Nowhere has this trend been more noticeable than in Western Europe, where, according to many commentators, the notorious slogan "Better Red than dead" has resurfaced. Moscow currently is spearheading the most ambitious "peace offensive" that Western Europe has witnessed since World War II and has launched a campaign for the "deepening of detente" and its extension from the political into the military sphere by means of a Helsinki-style conference on disarmament in Europe.

While Western Europe generally continues to subscribe to detente, the mood in the United States has tended to vacillate. The swing of the pendulum from euphoria to disillusionment can be explained partly by specific Soviet actions that belie Moscow's avowed devotion to peace and partly by idealism and an impatience with intractable problems. America's disenchantment with detente is further attributable to the amnesia characteristic of a society that too often exalts the "relevance" of contemporary events at the expense of the lessons of history.

In fact, U.S.-Soviet detente is almost as old as the Soviet Union itself, and it has experienced numerous reincarnations. The most remarkable aspect of the recurrent detentes has been their initiation at a time and in a manner of the USSR's own choosing and their curtailment, likewise at Soviet initiative, after Moscow—acting on the Leninist principle of "two steps forward, one step back"—reaped the maximum benefits deemed possible under the then existing "correlation of forces." The denouement, as a result of Afghanistan, of the most recent episode of detente followed this pattern, insofar as Soviet-American relations had reached such a nadir by the end of 1979 that Moscow evidently believed its reassertion of control over Afghanistan would compensate for the loss of further immediate fruits from detente. The Soviet leadership probably also viewed the securing of a grip on Afghanistan as a further step in altering the "correlation of forces" and thus strengthening the Soviet position for a future round of detente.

The first Soviet-American detente came in the wake of the failure of Lenin's "War Communism." In 1920, with the revolution confined to Russia, the economy in a shambles, and civil war wracking the country, Lenin told the Third All-Russia Congress of Water Transport

Workers that the proletariat "could not retain power by dictatorship, by force, by coercion alone; power can be maintained only by adopting the whole experience of cultured, technically equipped, progressive capitalism and by enlisting the services of all these people." In a speech to the Tenth CPSU Congress the following year, Lenin stressed that "we cannot, on our own, rehabilitate our ruined economy without machinery and technical aid from abroad."

Lenin thus appealed for trade, credits and diplomatic recognition from the very capitalist powers that he claimed were conspiring to encircle and destroy the infant Soviet state. He wrote that

> We must be clever enough, by relying on the peculiarities of the capitalist world and exploiting the greed of the capitalists for raw materials, to extract from it such advantages as will strengthen our economic position—however strange this may appear—among capitalists.[4]

As early as May 1919, Soviet Russia offered concessions to the United States so that it might "participate actively in the exploitation of the marine riches of Eastern Siberia, or coal and other mines. . . . " and the *Sovnarkom* adopted a decree in November 1923 that permitted "the exploitation and development of the natural riches of Russia" by foreign enterprises.[5]

Lenin was vindicated in his conviction that the capitalists would sell Moscow the rope with which it would ultimately hang them (cynics have since suggested that the West even lends the Soviets the money to buy the rope). Lenin's appeal brought a $20-million credit from the Chase Bank, $66.3 million in U.S. government assistance, and quantities of foodstuffs in exchange for Soviet gold. Ford and other major American enterprises dispatched several hundred engineers and technicians to help build dams, power stations, tractor plants, railroads and other heavy industry for the "workers' paradise." Armand Hammer (who recently worked out a multibillion-dollar, 20-year superphosphoric acid-for-ammonia deal with the USSR and still enjoys access to the Kremlin's inner sanctum) contributed a pencil factory and other enterprises during Lenin's "New Economic Policy" (NEP) program. Averell Harriman became involved in a manganese concession, from which he claims to have extracted "a modest profit."

The other Western democracies responded on a corresponding scale to Lenin's urgings. The 1922 Rapallo Treaty between the Soviet Union and Germany was particularly noteworthy. Moreover, the eco-

nomic and trade relationship developed during this time between Bolshevik Russia and Weimar Germany and which came to include
German training and provision of equipment for the Soviet armed
forces can be regarded as an antecedent to West Germany's *Ostpolitik*.

Lenin's NEP was rationalized by many Western observers as
"proof" that the militant phase of the Communist revolution was over
and that Lenin was moving toward the reintegration of Russia into the
international community, if not yet toward the restoration of capitalism inside Russia. Lenin, of course, did nothing to disabuse them of
this notion, insofar as such NEP-related measures as a limited free
market, reduction of forced deliveries of produce by peasants to the
state, and freedom for small businessmen and private entrepreneurs to
resume their activities could be portrayed to the West as creating a
climate favorable for investment. Lenin also proved adept at playing
on competition among would-be investors in the West—a tactic that
remains central to Soviet behavior under detente. George F. Kennan
points to one of the earliest examples of this phenomenon:

> It is a revealing fact that the signing of the Anglo-Russian Trade Agree-
> ment of 1921 is said to have been rushed through on the British side at
> the last moment, after months of hesitation, because word had just
> reached London that the Russians were placing an order for several hun-
> dred locomotives in Germany. Moscow . . . was not entirely wrong in the
> confidence it placed in Western economic rivalry as the one factor which,
> more than any other, would render the capitalist world exploitable in the
> interests of its own undoing.[6]

Accompanying the dollars and the engineers into Lenin's Russia
were the Western intellectuals. In this first detente, Lincoln Steffens
rhapsodized that he "had seen the future, and it works." H.G. Wells
opined that the Lenin terror, which he witnessed firsthand, "did on the
whole kill for a reason and for an end."

The first detente had already petered out by 1928, but Stalin put a
definitive end to it by burying NEP in favor of "Socialism in one country" and the First Five-Year Plan, which aimed at economic autarky
and which unleashed horrors in the Soviet Union that taxed the sym-
pathy of all but Stalin's staunchest Western defenders. In the foreign
policy arena, friendly overtures toward the capitalist powers were
downgraded in favor of the Comintern's new line (adopted at the Sixth
Congress in 1928) of active struggle against established governments
and "bourgeois" parties.

Yet, when rising Nazi power threatened the Soviet Union and Stalin instructed Communist parties abroad to call for a "Popular Front," the West again obliged. The flow of technical assistance, which had never ended completely, accelerated again, and what George Watson called "the pro-Stalinist intellectual hysteria" reached its zenith in 1936-38. Hewlett Johnson wrote *The Socialist Sixth of the World* in 1939, extolling Stalinist society and omitting any reference to the forced labor camps. Beatrice and Sidney Webb and Stephen Spender took note of the brutalities; but the Webbs wrote that "the greatest crime is that against the state," and Spender avowed that repression eventually would be swept away and freedom would reign.

Amidst these justifications, Stalin and Hitler signed a nonaggression pact in August 1939, World War II erupted, and the second detente vanished abruptly. An equally abrupt about-face followed Hitler's invasion of his Soviet "ally" on 22 June 1941. Stalin felt no compunction in seeking renewed capitalist support, which, as on past occasions, was soon forthcoming. Churchill announced that he would team up with the Devil if that personage were fighting Hitler. U.S. Lend-Lease aid flowed to the USSR, and President Roosevelt referred to Stalin as "Uncle Joe." Detente III spawned such grotesque features as the film "Mission to Moscow," in which Walter Huston "explained" why Stalin had to liquidate most of Lenin's co-revolutionists, who had inexplicably turned traitor. In 1943 Vice President Henry Wallace visited Kolyma, site of one of the notorious slave-labor camps in Siberia. He wrote subsequently that "in North Siberia today, Russians have developed urban life comparable in general to that of our own northwestern states and Alaska." In December 1944, *National Geographic* published a lengthy article by Prof. Owen Lattimore, another former Kolyma tourist. He called the camp complex there "a combination of Hudson's Bay Company and the TVA" and praised the Mom-and-Pop team who ran the camp for their "trained and sensitive interest in art and music and a deep sense of civic responsibility."

Detente III disappeared in the Cold War. Rigid bipolarity, soon to be enshrined in the NATO and Warsaw Pact alliance systems, was foreshadowed by Churchill's "Iron Curtain" speech at Fulton, Mo., in 1946 and by Andrei Zhdanov's polemic at Zielona Gora, Poland, during the 1947 inauguration of the Cominform. This period also witnessed the birth of the "revisionist" school of history. In 1952 William Appleman Williams advanced the claim that the United States had deliberately destroyed detente in a bid for global supremacy. Other revisionists, like Gar Alperovitz (*Atomic Diplomacy*), Gabriel Kolko (*The Politics of War*), and David Horowitz (*The Free World Colossus*) argued that American wartime policy was to create an "integrated capitalism" and that President Truman dropped the atomic bomb on Japan to intimidate the Soviet Union in Eastern Europe and Asia.

Detente IV emerged in the wake of de-Stalinization. Just as Lenin's NEP increased the attractiveness of the Soviet regime in the eyes of many Westerners after a period of revolution and civil war, so Khrushchev's criticism of the Stalinist blood purges, relaxation of ideological controls and commitment to "goulash Communism" (i.e., economic reform designed to benefit the Soviet consumer) seemed to portend an auspicious turn in Soviet-American relations. At the same time, detente appeared in the West as the only real alternative to the "rollback" of Communism, a doctrine whose sterility was starkly revealed during the uprisings in East Germany in 1953 and Poland and Hungary in 1956.

The fourth detente, like the three that preceded it, entailed the by-then familiar cycle of hope and disillusionment. Soviet-American summits in 1955 and 1959 gave rise to the "Spirit of Geneva" and the "Spirit of Camp David," in deference to their respective sites. However, the USSR's shipment of arms—via Czechoslovakia—to President Gamal Abdel Nasser of Egypt, its threats to rocket-bomb British cities if the Anglo-French-Israeli campaign in Suez did not halt, its shrill demands to the Allies to withdraw from Berlin, and its shooting down of an American U-2 plane all contributed substantially to the abortion of Detente IV. Khrushchev's shoe-banging exhibition at the United Nations in 1960 symbolized the depths to which U.S.-Soviet relations had sunk by that date.

Nevertheless, at least one facet of the relationship that emerged during the fourth detente was destined to played a key role in the further evolution of Soviet-American relations. This was the role of China as a catalyst or a spoiler (depending on whose perspective is involved) in the relationship. Khrushchev's journey to Camp David to meet with President Eisenhower particularly enraged Beijing, which accused Moscow of betraying the Communist revolution in favor of seeking a condominium with Washington to control the world. China's distrust of Soviet intentions—a distrust exacerbated by Mao's personal animosity toward Khrushchev—was a proximate cause of the Sino-Soviet split that, in turn, paved the way for the Sino-Soviet-American triangle that now conditions so heavily the politics of detente.

Less than a year after the shoe-banging episode, Khrushchev went to the summit at Geneva with newly elected President John F. Kennedy. Khrushchev, however, had meanwhile proclaimed worldwide Soviet support for "wars of national liberation"—a proclamation that was probably directed more at Beijing than at Washington but that soured the atmosphere for renewal of detente. It was the building of the Berlin Wall and, most importantly, the Cuban missile crisis that seemed to portend the final burial of detente, however.

Instead, the missile crisis apparently led both sides to reevaluate their relationship, with the chief concern being avoidance of nuclear confrontation. In his book *Kennedy*, Theodore Sorensen depicted the subsequent search for areas of agreement as "the emerging detente." He wrote that "the breathing spell had become a pause, the pause was becoming a detente, and no one could foresee what further changes lay ahead." Khrushchev declared that the USSR would never again permit itself to be forced into backing down in the face of superior American military power, and his heirs embarked upon an unprecedented buildup in all facets of military power to make good his pledge. The United States, for its part, sought to entice the Soviet Union into a process of nuclear arms control which, in effect, became the leitmotif for Detente V. On 7 October 1966, Lyndon Johnson announced that the United States was moving from "the narrow concept of coexistence to the broader vision of peaceful engagement." Except for a brief pause after the Soviet invasion of Czechoslovakia in 1968, this most recent detente continued almost until the end of the 1970's.

A rare glimpse into Soviet thinking on detente during this period emerged from the debriefing of a Czech defector, Maj. Gen. Jan Sejna. In his capacity as first secretary of the Communist Party in the Czech defense ministry, Sejna reportedly attended a secret meeting in Prague on 22 February 1968 among Brezhnev, the Czech Politburo, and the leaders of the other East European Communist regimes. On this occasion, according to Sejna, East German Communist boss Walter Ulbricht complained that Soviet emphasis on peaceful coexistence was weakening ideological discipline within the bloc. Brezhnev reportedly replied that Soviet weakness in such areas as computers and electronics, submarine warfare techniques, and agricultural productivity militated against a direct confrontation with the West. A policy of relaxations of tensions, said Brezhnev, would be needed during the next 10 to 15 years to facilitate acquisition of the Western credits and technology that would permit the USSR to catch up to the West.[7]

Brezhnev's agenda for the catching-up period acquired concrete shape with the launching of the so-called "peace program" at the 24th CPSU Congress in 1971.

The first event to puncture Detente V was the invasion of Czechoslovakia. U.S. denunciations of the Soviet action were little more than perfunctory, however. According to the *Christian Science Monitor* of 16 September 1968, Secretary of State William Rogers told Soviet Ambassador Anatoly Dobrynin that the United States would not intervene but that detente would be "impaired." Senator Claiborne Pell of Rhode Island called the Soviet invasion and the American response "a second Munich in Europe," for which "the illusory price of detente" was being paid. Professor Zbigniew Brzezinski of Columbia University, however, expressed what turned out to be the prevailing U.S. guideline:

> We must differentiate between our immediate outrage and our immediate retaliatory response to express this outrage, from our long-term policy of building bridges. In the short term, we should react, but in the long run we shouldn't flip.

Washington did not flip. Arms control talks remained in limbo for the last months of the Johnson Administration, but the new Nixon entourage declined to vent its spleen on outrage. It took up arms negotiations with the USSR (which had increased its strategic forces dramatically during the 1960's and by 1969 felt strong enough to enter talks), opened a full range of economic and cultural discussions, and prepared the dramatic journey of Nixon and Kissinger to Beijing in February 1972. Three months later, armed with the "China card," they traveled to Moscow to sign the first strategic arms limitation agreements (SALT I), a 12-point declaration of principles governing Soviet-American relations, and a host of other accords.[8]

Before analyzing the results of the Moscow summit, it is instructive to refer to another of Kissinger's statements. Addressing the National Press Club in Washington just before his term as Secretary of State ended in January 1977, Kissinger alluded to the Vietnam trauma and other events that had sapped America's military strength and political will. He then explained that

> Conscious of our limits, we sought to put in place a foreign policy that depended on the perception of priorities, a feeling for the importance of

nuance and a realization that there could be no terminal date for our efforts.

Stripped of its veneer, this remarkable statement depicted the United States as a nation in retreat that was obliged to conduct its diplomacy in a damage-limiting mode. Kissinger's reference to "our limits" evidently alluded to the national mood of retrenchment resulting from what Daniel Patrick Moynihan subsequently called a "failure of nerve." Kissinger and Nixon apparently decided not to buck that trend but rather to roll with it and salvage the best accommodation possible in America's national interest. Against this backdrop, it is not surprising that Moscow—already predisposed ideologically to expect the inevitable decline of the capitalist system—came to regard the United States as a nation past its prime.

Kissinger's approach to detente as making the best deal possible for an America on the defensive accounts for much of the subsequent "overselling" of detente. Rhetorical flourishes—notably Nixon's heralding a move "from an era of confrontation to an era of negotiation"—concealed, or at least explained away, many of the unilateral advantages that Moscow derived from detente. Of even greater long-term import for U.S. conduct of detente, however, was what Richard Lowenthal called a *propaganda* of illusions

which suggested to the American electorate that East-West negotiations were not merely a means to control the forms and limit the range of an ongoing conflict, but were a promising road for *ending* the conflict and creating a "stable structure of peace."

Lowenthal added that by "selling Detente as a road toward ending the conflict [Nixon and Kissinger] made it more difficult to preserve the electorate's willingness to maintain the balance of strength."[9]

Creation of an illusory optimism regarding detente seems to have been necessitated in large measure by the Nixon-Kissinger decision to end the Vietnam War on conditions unfavorable to the United States. It is of the utmost importance to recall that the gestation of the Paris "peace" on Vietnam can be traced to the Moscow summit. It was there that Kissinger told Soviet Foreign Minister Gromyko of U.S. acquiescence in North Vietnam's longstanding demand for a political as well as a military settlement. From unswerving support of South Vietnamese President Thieu, the United States moved to propose a tripartite commission (which emerged ultimately as the "National

Council of Reconciliation and Concord") to govern postwar South Vietnam. This U.S. concession, which broke the chief logjam in the secret negotiations between Kissinger and Le Duc Tho, was symptomatic of a broader U.S. strategy of giving relations with the USSR (and China) precedence over achieving "peace with honor" in Vietnam.

Verbal commitments to linkage notwithstanding, the Nixon Administration in effect decoupled its interest in Vietnam from its pursuit of detente. The rationale reflected the "mirror imaging" that has bedeviled so much of our policy toward the Soviet Union. It was assumed that Moscow, like Washington, viewed the evolving superpower relationship as too important to allow its disruption by fractious allies in faraway places. One of Kissinger's aides is said to have elaborated on this theme:

> Kissinger always felt that the Vietnam war hurt his relations with China and the Soviet Union. Kissinger impressed us from the beginning with how deeply he thought that war was wrong, that it was fought wrong, that it was dividing our society, and that it should be ended as quickly as possible. He was not interested in saving South Vietnam if it meant impairing relations with China and the Soviet Union. He believed that China, but particulary the Soviet Union, really needed better relations with the United States for economic reasons and that they would not intervene in Vietnam if Washington used greater force to get Hanoi to negotiate seriously.[10]

Aside from the total lack of evidence that the Soviet Union shared this perception, subsequent U.S. policy relieved Moscow of the need to choose. Moscow's belief that the impending U.S. withdrawal would be irreversible—a belief later vindicated by Congressional cutoff of funds for bombing in Cambodia and slashing of economic and military assistance for South Vietnam—enabled it to prod Hanoi toward negotiations, as Kissinger had requested, without foreclosing the Communist aim of seizing power in Saigon. In view of what transpired in 1975, it is clear that Moscow's sole contribution to "peace" in Vietnam was to persuade Hanoi to accord the United States a face-saving exit and a "decent interval" before redeeming a Soviet promise to Hanoi to supply the military equipment necessary for conquest of the South.

Soviet-American relations in the aftermath of the Moscow summit hovered closer to the pole of confrontation than to that of negotiation. U.S. expectations that the USSR would exercise restraint in its international behavior in return for the fruits of the summit were shattered during successive crises in the Middle East (October 1973), Portugal (1974-75), Vietnam (spring 1975), and Angola (1975-76). The impact of Angola, coming on top of the Communist takeovers in Indochina and coinciding with an electoral campaign that pitted the more conservative wing of the Republican Party against President Gerald Ford, led Ford to drop the very word "detente" from his political vocabulary in favor of the formulation "peace through strength."

The heyday of Detente V was over by 1976, not only as a result of Soviet-backed adventurism in the Third World but also because of the deadlock in the SALT negotiations and Moscow's cancellation of the Soviet-American trade agreement after Sen. Henry Jackson and Rep. Charles Vanik pushed through an amendment trying most-favored-nation tariff treatment for the USSR to a liberalization of Soviet emigration. Brezhnev's trip to the United States, scheduled for 1975, was postponed indefinitely.

Nevertheless, Soviet media portrayed the election campaign as a referendum on detente and interpreted the sluggish public support for the candidacies of Henry Jackson and George Wallace and the failure of Ronald Reagan to capture the Republican nomination from Ford as signs that no presidential hopeful who opposed the improvement of Soviet-American relations could carry the electorate.[11] At the October 1976 plenum of the CPSU Central Committee, Brezhnev declared that whoever won the election would be obliged to take into account "the real correlation of forces" that had prompted previous U.S. presidents to pursue detente.[12]

Jimmy Carter came to office with a determination to revamp detente. The revamping took at least three forms. Firstly, the new president downplayed the Soviet threat to U.S. global interests by softpedaling the very notion of a Communist danger. Thus, in his remarkable speech at Notre Dame on 22 May 1977, Carter expressed satisfaction that Americans had shed their "inordinate fear of Communism." Secondly, Carter, evidently under the influence of his national security adviser Brzezinski, down-graded the priority of the Soviet-American relationship as an operational principle of U.S. foreign policy. In his book *Between Two Ages*, Brzezinski argued that the trilateral relationship among the United States, Western Europe and Japan, all of which had entered the postindustrial "technetronic" age of high technology, computers and electronics, should be the foremost concern of American foreign policy. The "North-South" relationship—that between the industrialized states and the so-called less-

developed countries (LDC's)—should have second priority. The Soviet-American relationship was in effect relegated to third place.

Carter, in addition, introduced human rights as a principal tool of
the U.S. foreign policy arsenal. Although his human rights policy involved gestures toward Soviet dissidents and strictures against Moscow's repression of human rights, the chief thrust of the policy was
directed against pro-Western authoritarian regimes throughout the
Third World. The resulting destabilization of many such regimes created a situation in which the USSR and its local allies reaped gratuitous benefits.

Carter's philosophy had a direct bearing on his conduct of detente. If one did not unduly fear Communism, then there was no need
to worry about Soviet-sponsored Communist revolutions in the Third
World—especially when many of the regimes that fell were reputed
violators of human rights. Moreover, Carter's avowed intention to accord precedence to the trilateral relationship led him to underestimate
differences between Washington and West European capitals on how
to deal with Soviet expansionism in the Third World—differences that
had emerged with sharp clarity during the Vietnam War and that continued even after the Soviet invasion of Afghanistan. The Carter Administration seemed inclined toward the view that revolutionary
upheavals from Ethiopia to Nicaragua could be traced solely to indigenous forces (an updated version of the theory that Communism is a
scavenger of the modernization process) and that Communism in the
Third World could best be countered with generous American economic aid and appeals for free elections and political pluralism. This
method of dealing with the Third World paralleled the general belief
among Carter's entourage that the Soviet Union itself could be
"tamed" by enveloping it in a web of economic interactions and diplomatic cooperation with the United States.

Symbolic of Carter's attitude toward the Soviet Union was his appointment in 1979 of former IBM chairman Thomas J. Watson Jr. as
ambassador to Moscow. Watson, who replaced hardlining Malcolm
Toon, was reportedly selected on the recommendation of Averell Harriman, who had enjoyed privileged access to Kremlin leaders since his
own ambassadorial tour in the 1940's. Watson himself served in the
USSR during World War II on the Lend-Lease program and was an
active participant on the American Committee on U.S.-Soviet Relations, which advocated a sharp increase in trade with Moscow.

The underlying assumption during Carter's presidency was to view the USSR as basically a status quo power committed to political, economic and military equality with the West and to the prestige accruing therefrom. Ideology was viewed as a trapping of the Soviet regime with little impact on the conduct of Soviet foreign policy. Carter's commencement address on 7 June 1978 to the U.S. Naval Academy at Annapolis (his alma mater) seemed to adopt a more somber view of Soviet behavior than the president had previously displayed. "The Soviet Union can choose either confrontation or cooperation," he intoned. "The United States is adequately prepared to meet either choice." In the aftermath of the speech, however, many skeptics of detente remained convinced that while Moscow was confronting, Washington was cooperating. Carter, by his own admission, suffered a rude awakening to the nature of Soviet intentions when the USSR invaded Afghanistan. He called Brezhnev a "liar" for misleading him and contended that he had learned more about the nature of the Soviet Union in 24 hours than in the previous three years of his presidency.

Whereas Carter's view of the Communist threat shifted dramatically during his term in office, Ronald Reagan assumed the presidency with a somewhat bifurcated perception of Communism. On the one hand, he viewed the Soviet Union, the fountainhead of Communism, as the greatest and most implacable threat to the United States worldwide. On the other hand, the president professed to regard Communism as a disease—albeit a virulent one—and as an historical aberration that was destined to disappear. Some of Reagan's beliefs seemed to stand Leninism on its head. Lenin depicted capitalism as a system confined to a particular historical era and one that would eventually be consigned to the "dustbin of history." He and his successors, however, sought to hasten the "inevitable" process of capitalism's demise, particularly by depriving it of its colonial sources of markets and raw materials. Similarly, the Reagan Administration evidently hoped to promote the eradication of the Communist "disease" by quarantining it and combating its spread—via Soviet expansionism—to new victims.

Another aspect of Reagan's "Leninism in reverse" is also worth mentioning. Lenin and his heirs expressed confidence in the ultimate demise of "imperialism" but cautioned that the "imperialist" powers, in their death throes, could become exceptionally dangerous and lash out like mortally wounded animals. Similarly, some of the officials of the Reagan Administration, citing resistance to Soviet domination in

Poland and Afghanistan, professed to see the first cracks in the Soviet empire. They expressed concern that Moscow would spark a broader East-West confrontation rather than tolerate loss of its empire and eventual weakening of control over the USSR itself.

Reagan restored Soviet-American relations to the top priority in U.S. foreign policy, and Secretary of State Alexander M. Haig Jr. declared that "this Administration will stress linkage as a fundamental fact of East-West relations."[13] Early Administration initiatives to deprive Ambassador Dobrynin of his unique access to the State Department's underground garage and to the Secretary's private elevator symbolized an effort to make detente more reciprocal. Reagan, however, pursued some peculiar forms of linkage, such as lifting of the grain embargo as an apparent quid pro quo for Soviet nonintervention in Poland rather than withdrawal from Afghanistan (at which the embargo was originally aimed) and the announcement of record grain sales to the USSR on the day after the unveiling of an MX missile program that was designed to meet the Soviet military threat to American ICBM's.

If the United States moved to reassert its power and interests on a global scale, Soviet-American relations would enter a period of maximum danger. For those who believed that a "window of vulnerability" had opened—or was about to open—in the strategic realm, the asymmetrical military balance added immeasurably to the danger. Soviet statements frequently alluded to this peril. An article of 28 June 1980 in the armed forces daily *Red Star*, for example, noted that

> as a result of the vigorous and multifaceted activity of the USSR and the Socialist community, the normalization of the international climate was achieved in the seventies. These positive changes met with fierce resistance from imperialist reaction. . . . The CPSU Central Committee plenum assigned the Politburo the task [of] . . . conservation and development of international detente. . . . At the same time, the plenum pointed out that the intrigues of imperialism and other enemies of peace demand our state's constant vigilance and the all-round consolidation of its defense capability, in order to thwart imperialism's plans for achieving military superiority and implementing world *diktat*.

The August 1980 issue of the CPSU's theoretical journal *Kommunist* asserted that

> . . . Great changes which have taken place in the last decade are now involving the whole globe. The capitalist world is trying desperately to

stop these developments. Its leaders, in the first place those of the USA who don't want to take into account the changed correlation of forces and who stubbornly aim at world domination, are more and more actively moving into a counterattack against all the conquests which the peoples won in the 1970's. But today the times are no longer what they were in the 1940's and 1950's. . . . Detente, however much Washington politicians may try to destroy it, has taken deep roots and there is a real possibility of safeguarding and strengthening this positive process. . . .

At the Central Committee plenum of June 1981, Brezhnev declared that the Soviet Union would spare no effort to preserve detente and "all the good things that the Seventies brought."

For Moscow, the Seventies brought not only trade, technology transfer and credits from the West on an unprecedented scale, but also the virtual abandonment by the United States of a containment policy. Thus, under cover of detente, the Soviet Union moved outward geopolitically from the Eurasian heartland to seek hegemony all along its periphery and beyond into the insular regions of the globe. Moscow's ultimate goal is a reverse of what Lenin called "capitalist encirclement" of the USSR. That goal is to outflank and isolate the West—particularly the United States, which is cast in the role of World Island—by controlling the vital sealanes and sources of raw materials that the industrial democracies need to survive. By demonstrating its ability to control these assets in time of crisis, Moscow could achieve global hegemony without resorting to war.

Insofar as detente was reduced to its irreducible minimum context of avoidance of nuclear war between the superpowers, the dilemma for Washington was whether renewal of "containment" would be sufficient to thwart Soviet expansionist aims. The Reagan Administration decided to proceed a step further and take one of the Soviets' pieces off the international chessboard. This thought underlay the U.S. invasion of Grenada. Moscow was left to ponder whether the invasion constituted a "demonstration effect"—a graphic warning to the Kremlin to stop undermining U.S. strategic interests—or the initial step in a modified "rollback" policy. Hopefully, the invasion not only forced the Soviets to reassess their adventurist policy in the Third World, but also generated serious frictions between Moscow and Havana that could have a lasting impact.

It has been said, with much justification, that in the arms race only one side—the Soviet—was racing. The same was true of the geopolitical rivalry in the Third World. During the Reagan Administration, Moscow encountered a newly vigorous opponent in both spheres. In coming years, Kissinger's warning that "the challenge of our time is to reconcile the reality of competition with the imperative of coexistence" will take on added urgency.[14]

# 2

## Arms Control and "Military Detente"

Arms control—the effort to contain and manage the strategic arms competition between the United States and the Soviet Union—has become the centerpiece of detente. At times, it has stood as the lone pillar of detente's edifice when commercial, cultural and interpersonal relations between Washington and Moscow all but disintegrated. Viewing arms control as the bare bones on the skeleton of detente helps to explain the extraordinary tenacity with which its adherents cling to outworn treaties such as SALT II and dubious precepts such as mutual assured destruction (MAD). In the eyes of these adherents, the skeleton of detente must be maintained at all costs, until a more propitious era arises when the bare bones can be covered with the flesh and blood of new Soviet-American accords. Kenneth L. Adelman, former director of the Arms Control and Disarmament Agency (ACDA), has written that "SALT now stands as the sole remnant of a once-trumpeted network of relations binding together the superpowers' fate and welfare."[1]

The limited nuclear test ban treaty of 1963 ushered in a period of considerable, if temporary, warmth between Washington and Moscow, and the SALT I agreements—consisting of an antiballistic missile (ABM) treaty and a five-year interim accord freezing offensive missiles—were hailed by Nixon and Kissinger as marking the threshold of a "generation of peace." The seemingly logical next step was SALT II, signed in 1979, which placed ceilings on the numbers of strategic missile launchers and set sub-limits on multiple independently targeted reentry vehicles (MIRV's).

In analyzing these arms control agreements, one is struck by the fact that in the course of only 16 years the strategic balance (or what the USSR would regard as the military component of the world "correlation of forces") tilted dramatically away from U.S. superiority. Such superiority was unquestioned at the time of the test ban signing but was already precarious at the time of SALT I's completion—a fact duly reflected in that accord. By the time SALT II reached fruition, alarm was expressed in many Western circles that the U.S. vision of "strategic parity" or "essential equivalence" already had given way to Soviet predominance.

In the United States, arms control advocates refer to arms control as a "process," an ongoing phenomenon that must be carefully nurtured and preserved even—and especially—if Soviet-American tensions in other areas increase. It is of considerable significance that the United States institutionalized arms limitation in 1961 in the form of the Arms Control and Disarmament Agency (ACDA)—a phenomenon that finds no counterpart in the Soviet Union.[2] The existence of such an institution inevitably has created a community of people with a vested interest in arms control, often as an end in itself. This built-in constituency for arms control—a constituency augmented by the ranks of defense intellectuals and academic specialists—has contributed to a momentum in the arms control "process" that is absent in the Soviet Union. Experts moving laterally in and out of government often serve while on the outside as lobbyists on arms-control issues. Scientists who circulate in and out of defense-related jobs are able to contribute their technical expertise to public arms-control discussions. Such discussions are rarely if ever held in the USSR, partly because of the paucity of nongovernmental civilian experts and partly because the extreme secrecy that surrounds all things military has made information useful for debate almost impossible to obtain. Contributions to and discussions of military strategy and theory are confined largely to military journals, many of which have limited circulation. Soviet officials and scholar-advocates who staff the Institutes of the USA and Canada and other Soviet-style "think tanks" are virtually unanimous in their view of the U.S. arms-control community as a potent political force that can be relied upon frequently to articulate opposition to Pentagon weapons-building programs and provide a cutting edge in public and Congressional debate on arms-control issues.

Arms-control policymaking in the Soviet Union seems to be restricted to a small circle in the Politburo (the ruling organ of the Communist party), the highly secretive Defense Council, and the ministries of defense (notably the Chief of the General Staff's entourage) and foreign affairs. Input from "think tanks" and academic institutions, aside from technical experts in the Academy of Sciences, is only peripheral. The elevation of the minister of defense and the foreign minister to membership in the Politburo in 1973 may have reflected Brezhnev's intent to monitor more closely the role of these ministries in arms control and other areas covered by the 1972 summit accords. The ultimate concentration of arms-control policy within the party, coupled with the lengthy tenure in the Soviet hierarchy of many arms-control negotiators (compared with generally less seasoned U.S. negotiators), has greatly bolstered Moscow's position in arms-control talks with the West, above and beyond the nuts and bolts of the issues under discussion.

The first East-West nuclear arms-control measure was the limited nuclear test ban treaty of 1963, which banned nuclear tests in the atmosphere, outer space, and under water. It came in the wake of the Cuban missile crisis—mankind's closest brush to date with Armageddon. Many U.S. officials expressed high hopes for subsequent arms-control accords. Moscow, however, was still in a position of strategic nuclear inferiority and chose to play at detente while proceeding with a military buildup that would permit it to negotiate from greater strength.

When the SALT I negotiations began in 1969, the United States and the Soviet Union were virtually equal in numbers of intercontinental land-based ballistic missiles (ICBM's)—(1,054 to about 1,050), and the United States had 41 Polaris-type submarines for the firing of submarine-launched ballistic missiles (SLBM's), vs. none for the USSR. By the time SALT I was signed in 1972, U.S. building programs for both ICBM's and SLBM's had ceased, while Soviet programs were in full swing. SALT I set the ceiling for land-based intercontinental ballistic missiles at 1,618 for the USSR and 1,054 for the United States.[3] Moreover, the Soviet total was to include 308 so-called heavy missiles (the term "heavy" was never precisely defined), vs. none for the United States, the familiar argument being made that Washington had no plans to produce such missiles.

The principal justification put forth publicly by the Nixon Administration for signing a SALT treaty full of asymmetries was to claim that without the treaty the margin between Soviet and American capabilities might be even greater. This argument implied that the United States lacked the resolve to match Soviet missile programs. Another rationalization that Washington put forth involved the extensive U.S. lead in multiple independently targeted reentry vehicles (MIRV's)—a lead that allegedly would permit the United States to balance an advantage in number of warheads against Soviet advantages in launcher numbers and megatonnage. By early 1974, however, Moscow was testing three new MIRV-capable missiles. These new weapons were fully compatible with SALT I, which limited the number of missile launchers that each signatory could deploy but contained no restrictions on qualitative improvements in missiles, including increased accuracy, or on numbers of warheads that each missile could carry. Each of the USSR's three new missiles was larger than Minuteman 3, the best ICBM in the American arsenal.

Hobbled by SALT I in the deployment of a large-scale ABM system to counter the potential vulnerability of its land-based nuclear missile force, the United States contemplated various options to bolster the force. At the Moscow summit of June 1974, U.S. efforts to rectify the potential imbalance in SALT I encountered Soviet resistance. An American proposal to limit MIRV deployment on both sides was brushed aside by the Soviets.

The agreement that U.S. officials claimed to have sought as a follow-on to SALT I was concluded at a Soviet-American meeting at Vladivostok in November 1974. Although President Gerald Ford and Secretary of State Kissinger advertised the accord as "putting a cap on the arms race," it left nuclear throw-weight (the weight of a payload that a missile can lift and deliver to its target) heavily in the Soviets' favor. The essence of the Vladivostok agreement was placement of a ceiling on land- and sea-based missile launchers and, for the first time, on heavy bombers. The ceilings remained very high at Soviet insistence.

The SALT II accord was signed on 18 June 1979, during the Carter-Brezhnev summit in Vienna, but was never ratified by the Senate. The unequal limits on ICBM and SLBM launchers allotted to each party were carried over from SALT I to SALT II. Moreover, SALT II established a ceiling for each side of 2,250 missile launchers and created several sub-ceilings.

At the time of the signing, the Soviet Union reportedly had 2,504 launchers, divided among 1,398 ICBM's (608 with MIRV's), 950 SLBM's (144 with MIRV's), and 156 bombers. The United States possessed 2,283 launchers: 1,054 ICBM's (550—the triple-warhead Minuteman III—with MIRV's), 656 SLBM's (496 with MIRV's), and 573 bombers (three configured for cruise missiles).[4] Reductions down to the level of 2,250 ICBM and SLBM launchers were to be undertaken by both sides before the end of 1981. The SALT II treaty was to remain in force until 31 December 1985.

Flaws in the SALT II treaty included the fundamental fact that, like SALT I, it counted launchers rather than missiles (or warheads). The term launchers has been interpreted to mean silos, and the treaty focused on silos (holes in the ground) because their numbers can be verified through each signatory's "national technical means." Moreover, nothing in the treaty forbids the Soviet Union from reloading launchers with new missiles and new warheads after existing ones are fired. Soviet missile silos, unlike U.S. ones, are reloadable. Even more importantly, defense analysts generally concede that thousands of Soviet missiles are intended for delivery from launchers other than silos. These include trucks, railroad cars, and, in the case of submarine-borne missiles, underwater launching. In short, "we simply do not know how many missiles the Soviets have or how many launchers, or where they are."[5]

The newer Soviet ICBM's, including the "heavy" SS-18's, are "cold-launched" from their silos, as compared with the "hot launch" for American land-based missiles. The Russians can reload their silos and refire their missiles in as little as two hours from the time of a previous launch. Moreover, unlike the United States, the Soviet Union may have a large number of missiles to use for this purpose. Since the SALT process began, the USSR has removed about 900 "old" missiles (SS-7's, 8's, 9's, and 11's) from their silos and replaced them with more modern weapons. The whereabouts of the "old" missiles, which do not fall under the SALT count, is unknown.

Defenders of SALT II in the United States asserted that the treaty's asymmetries paled in comparison with the fact that it put a cap on the growth and modernization of the superpowers' nuclear forces and laid the groundwork for SALT III, which allegedly would bring about substantial reductions in U.S. and Soviet weapons stockpiles. This contention rings hollow. Rather than stopping the arms race, SALT merely allowed it to proceed under slightly different ground rules. In a favorite expression of the SALT sellers, it "codified" the competition. The SALT II treaty explicitly permitted the acquisition by both superpowers of new weapons that would make future reductions more difficult. SALT II did not impede a single qualitative weapons development on the drawing boards. So much for SALT as a deterrent to nuclear war.

SALT II, like its predecessor, should be regarded above all as a political rather than a military document. The arms-control "process," itself a component of the detente "process," was symbolized most saliently by the SALT treaties. As a West European observer noted during the U.S. debate over ratification, "SALT seems to be carrying almost the entire burden of the superpower dialogue."[6]

Once SALT II was signed, it faced an uphill battle in Congress. The treaty aroused so much controversy that even without the Soviet invasion of Afghanistan it probably could not have won ratification in a Senate controlled by Jimmy Carter's own Democratic Party.[7] Republican Sen. Jake Garn of Utah asserted that "SALT I allowed [the Soviets] to catch up. SALT II will allow them to build as rapidly as their economy will be able to take it."[8] Columnist George Will wrote that "SALT II involves only cosmetic reductions and permits huge increases, including new ICBM's."[9] Sen. Jesse Helms (R.-N.C.) summed up much of the philosophical as well as substantive criticism of the SALT II treaty by declaring that it sanctioned arms escalation rather than arms limitation.

According to some U.S. observers, the unlikelihood of SALT's winning Senate approval may have been cited by those in the Kremlin favoring Soviet military intervention in Afghanistan, on the grounds that U.S.-Soviet relations already had reached a nadir and there was little to lose in further alienating Washington. Whatever the truth of this assumption, the invasion of Afghanistan sounded the death knell for SALT II. Carter reluctantly placed the treaty in abeyance but remained convinced of the need for a return to the negotiating table after a "decent interval." In June 1980, for example, Secretary of State Edmund S. Muskie asserted that the Carter Administration was "committed to the SALT process" and was working actively to reintroduce the SALT treaty in the Senate regardless of the Soviet occupation of Afghanistan.[10] As late as 20 August, Defense Secretary Harold Brown told an audience at the U.S. Naval War College that

> The Soviet invasion of Afghanistan made it necessary, in practical political terms, to defer SALT II ratification while we assessed the Soviet action and implemented the necessary responses. But ratification of the treaty at the earliest feasible time is still important to our national security interest.

Meanwhile, the shadow of SALT continued to overhang weapons decisionmaking in the United States. *Wall Street Journal* editor Robert L. Bartley wrote at the time of the Carter-Brezhnev summit that

> The SALT process has subtly but effectively curtailed American strategic programs. The dynamic is this: arms control mutilates the best options, and the Budget Bureau moves in to kill off the cripples. . . . From the Soviet viewpoint, SALT must seem an excellent way to delay, grind down and eventually kill the most promising U.S. weapons developments. It has kept the U.S. from exploiting its strong card of technology, while the Soviets have rolled along with their strong card of churning out masses of weapons. It has been a lever through which they have manipulated our procurement decisions. [11]

A key example of SALT's insidious repercussions involved the increasing vulnerability of the U.S. land-based missile force in the absence of "active defenses" (i.e., ABM). The remedy for restoring America's counterforce capability seemed to rest with a mobile missile, but one that SALT-conscious planners had to endow with an almost impossible combination of characteristics: concealment to guard against Soviet attack; visibility to permit SALT verification by Soviet satellites; and moderate cost to pass budget muster.

During the late 1970's, significant improvements in Soviet missile accuracy and growing numbers of Soviet nuclear warheads were regarded by many members of the U.S. defense establishment as creating the conditions for a successful knockout blow against the land-based portion of the U.S. nuclear triad. In response to these fears, Carter announced that the United States would undertake full-scale development of the MX (missile experimental), which could destroy Soviet land-based missiles in their silos and also constitute a bargaining lever in arms-control negotiations.

Among the MX basing patterns considered by the Carter Administration was one that posited 200 missiles to be shuttled along surface roadways, or "racetracks," to 4,600 underground shelters—a scheme that would have involved the paving of huge areas of the Nevada and Utah deserts. This "shell game" plan met vociferous opposition on grounds of verification, cost, environmental despoilation, and recognition that the Soviets could overwhelm it simply by building more missiles.[12]

Ronald Reagan's electoral campaign of 1980 focused heavily on the MX and related issues. Jimmy Carter and his defense secretary, Harold Brown, maintained that a state of "essential equivalence" prevailed in the nuclear realm between the superpowers. Candidate Reagan, however, claimed that the United States had lost its "margin of safety" and was faced with a situation of "strategic insufficiency." On arms control, Reagan's stance was unambiguous: SALT II was "fatally flawed" and should be "shelved," while new arms-control negotiations with Moscow should be deferred until some headway could be made toward refurbishing U.S. strategic nuclear forces.

During the presidential campaign, Reagan contended that the growth of Soviet strategic power had reached a point at which a "window of vulnerability" had opened. He expressed concern that Moscow might be tempted to launch a first strike against America's vulnerable land-based missile force before Washington could bring MX and other remedies to bear. The MX, with its augmented striking power and accuracy in comparison with earlier generations of American missiles, was designed to penetrate superhardened targets (including ICBM silos) in the Soviet Union. However, the Reagan Administration proved to be just as hobbled as its predecessor by the constraints that the arms-control "process" placed on MX deployment. Indeed, the MX issue has provided an excellent case study of how blind adherence to arms-control agreements vitiates U.S. efforts to fashion a rational and cost-effective strategic posture. The issue continues to plague the United States to this day.

On 2 October 1981, in conjunction with the unveiling of a five-year, $180-billion plan to modernize U.S. strategic forces,[13] President Reagan and Defense Secretary Caspar Weinberger cancelled Carter's "racetrack" scheme and halved the number of MX missiles to be built to 100—the first 40 of which would be based temporarily in silos occupied by obsolescent Titan rockets that were being phased out. The Senate refused to concur with this plan, on the justifiable ground that placing the new missiles in stationary sites would contradict the essential concept of MX as a mobile, and thus less vulnerable, missile.[14] Reagan's proposal in January 1982 that the first MX missiles be placed in reinforced Minuteman silos in Wyoming did virtually nothing to alleviate the problem; in fact, many knowledgeable observers argued that the MX would be even more vulnerable than the Minuteman it would replace, because the MX is much larger and allows less "rattle space," or room in the silo for absorbing shock.

Under pressure from the Senate to enunciate a feasible permanent basing scheme or forego appropriations for MX development, Reagan adopted in November 1982 the "Dense Pack" scheme. It featured 100 missiles clustered in "superhardened" silos (with a capacity to withstand 5,000 pounds per square inch of blast pressure, compared with some 2,000 for Minuteman) spaced about 2,000 feet apart in a 20-square-mile area of Wyoming. The theory behind Dense Pack was that the initial Soviet ICBM's launched against the MX field would be forced into a narrow funnel and would explode so close together that they would commit "fratricide," deflecting or disabling the warheads that followed. Enough MX missiles thus would survive to mount an effective retaliatory strike against the Soviet Union. The plan seemed relatively uncomplicated and inexpensive and would have created great uncertainties for Soviet nuclear targeteers. In addition, it was politically salable because it would have entailed much less spoilation of the environment in Republican home territory than would a "racetrack" arrangement.

Even before Dense Pack was announced officially, however, it was zapped by a scientific panel that warned the Pentagon of a potential Soviet ability to sow the MX field with nuclear mines timed to explode all at once if the MX's were launched. Aside from possible technical flaws in Dense Pack, deployment of the MX in this mode would have run into the by-now familiar argument that it was a violation of both SALT I and SALT II. Article IV of the SALT II treaty forbids the construction of new ICBM launchers or the relocation of "fixed ICBM launchers"; but existing silos were too far apart for Dense Pact requirements.[15] Thus, Reagan was obliged to forego a promising option "merely because he pledged to abide by a treaty that provides for basing the [MX] missile only in a Rube Goldberg way."[16]

Continuing to seek a survivable, politically acceptable, and SALT-certifiable basing mode for the MX, Reagan appointed the Presidential Commission on Strategic Forces, headed by retired Air Force Lt. Gen. Brent Scowcroft. The commission was composed of a bipartisan array of experts from the past four national Administrations. *The Wall Street Journal* noted wryly that "the commission's mission was to craft some weapon that could survive both Soviet and Congressional attacks. Its prescription was to put the MX in undefended, immobile existing silos. In other words, avoid the survivability problem by ignoring it."[17]

The commission's report, released on 11 April 1983, recommended the deployment of 100 MX missiles in hardened Minuteman silos, the vulnerability of which was declared to be minimal "in the near term."[18] Additionally, the commission recommended the development of a small (15-ton) single-warhead, presumably mobile Midgetman missile to supplement the 100-ton MX in the 1990's and urged Reagan to shift his focus in future arms-control proposals from launchers to warheads that would be roughly equivalent for both superpowers in terms of both numbers and yields. Many of the incongruities in the report can be ascribed to an emphasis on arms control, with a virtual exclusion of other considerations:

> In that report, the MX is presented as a bargaining chip rather than as a weapon. On the basis of that premise, the Scowcroft Commission found it easy to recommend a non-survivable basing mode for the MX.[19]

A permanent home continues to elude the MX, which Congress has funded in driblets. There are about 40 MX missiles (incongruously dubbed "Peacekeepers") deployed in a stationary mode as of this writing.

The Reagan Administration's zigzagging position on MX basing was symbolic of the confusion that has attended the policy of seeking a coherent strategic posture while simultaneously making obeisance to the arms control "process." Reagan found himself under intense pressure from the Kremlin, the Congress, the nuclear freeze movement (which published such breezy primers as Ground Zero's "Nuclear War: What's in It for You?"), and the NATO allies to undertake a new initiative on arms control.

On 31 May 1982, as he was about to embark on a journey to Western Europe, Reagan startled some of his staunchest political supporters by announcing that the United States would "refrain from actions which undercut" previous arms control agreements (read: SALT II) "so long as the Soviet Union shows equal restraint."[20] Reagan also advocated a shift of emphasis from SALT (strategic arms limitation) to START (strategic arms reduction).[21]

The START negotiations opened in Geneva on 29 June 1982. Retired Lt. Gen. Edward Rowny was named chief negotiator. He had resigned his military post in order to criticize SALT publicly. The original proposal that Rowny put forward at START was based on a program outlined on 9 May during a speech at Eureka College in Illinois, the President's alma mater. This plan was to reduce the approximately 7,500 warheads that each side was reported to have on its ICBM's and SLBM's to 5,000—of which a maximum of 2,500 could be land-based—and to lower each side's existing force of ICBM's and SLBM's (about 1,700 for the United States and 2,350 for the USSR) to a maximum of 850 over a five-to-ten-year period. In addition, the proposal called on the Soviets to reduce their total of "heavy" missiles (on which they still held a monopoly) from 308 to 110. There were to be equal numbers of bombers at the current American level, which, at more than 300, was roughly double the Soviet bomber fleet.[22]

At the opening of the START negotiations, the USSR possessed (by official U.S. count), 1,398 land-based ICBM'S, carrying more than 5,000 nuclear warheads, vs. 1,052 ICBM'S for the United States, carrying about 2,000 warheads. In addition, the Russians had 989 SLBM'S, deployed on 84 nuclear-powered submarines, compared with a U.S. total of 576 SLBM's on 36 submarines. The Soviet inventory included 308 "heavy" SS-18, ten-warhead missiles, the largest missiles in the Russian arsenal; 330 four-warhead SS-17's, also labeled "medium," for a total of 788. Washington called on Moscow to reduce the total to 210, of which only 110 would consist of SS-18's. (The U.S. Minuteman, incidentally, is characterized as "light".) The American proposals aimed above all at narrowing the Soviet Union's advantage in megatonnage, which stood at approximately 2.5 to 1.[23]

The Soviet Union traditionally has favored using missile launchers rather than warheads as the coin of arms-control negotiations and, moreover, was obviously resistant to shedding the bulk of its land-based nuclear force (about 6,000 of the 7,500 Soviet warheads are on land-based missiles—including more than 3,000 on the 308 SS-18's—vs. some 2,000 for the United States). These factors doomed Reagan's START proposals. In August 1982 the Russians put forth a counter-offer, calling, inter alia, for 1,800 launchers for each side, of which

1,450 would be missiles and the rest long-range bombers. A U.S. official observed that a ceiling of 1,800 launchers, as proposed by the Soviets, "would accommodate the bulk of their forces and phase out some older stuff, while leaving our Minutemen still vulnerable to attack."[24]

By the autumn of 1982, pressure in the United States for arms control reached a fever pitch. The Kennedy-Hatfield amendment introduced in the Senate called for a ban on production as well as deployment of nuclear weapons and delivery systems. Nuclear freeze initiatives appeared on the ballot in several states during the Congressional elections. On the eve of the voting, former Ambassador to Moscow W. Averell Harriman, Washington lawyer and adviser to Democratic presidents Clark Clifford, former CIA director William Colby, and chief SALT II negotiator and former ACDA director Paul Warnke penned a letter to *The New York Times* urging the American people to support these initiatives.[25] Many other influential figures lent their voices in favor of the nuclear freeze. The Soviets, having played a conspicuous part in the huge U.N. rally for disarmament on 12 June in New York, plied their "peace" propaganda relentlessly in the Western media. Commenting on the Soviet "peace offensive," *New York Times* columnist William Safire wrote: "Having tipped the balance in their favor in strategic missiles, and having taken a major jump ahead in European theater missiles, the new [Soviet] leadership is now ready for a deal that will lock in its current advantages."[26]

To add insult to injury, the Soviet Union, having perfunctorily rebuffed all of Washington's START proposals, refused to set a date for the resumption of negotiations after the last scheduled meeting took place on 8 December 1983. The reason for the walkout lay primarily with events occurring in Western Europe, where the United States was poised to deploy 572 new medium-range missiles. No matter how flexible Washington was willing to be in the arena of START, Moscow was determined to hold agreements on offensive strategic arms hostage to prior accords on medium-range weapons.

With SALT progress at a standstill, arms control advocates had turned their attention to Western Europe, where the question of modernizing NATO's nuclear arsenal became a major preoccupation. As of the mid-1970's, there were intermediate-range (1,000- to 2,000-mile) SS-4 and SS-5 tactical nuclear missiles deployed in the western USSR. The United States had emplaced nuclear-capable fighter-bombers throughout Western Europe and had allocated about 400 submarine-launched Poseidon missile warheads to NATO. Pershing I missiles, with a 400-mile range, were deployed in West Germany, while the French bolstered their nuclear *force de frappe*. The balance thus established prevailed until the Soviets began to deploy mobile, triple-warhead SS-20's in 1977.[27]

Detente remained much in vogue on the Continent in the afterglow of the 1975 Helsinki Conference on Security and Cooperation in Europe (CSCE). In the United States, by contrast, detente already had fallen into disfavor—to the extent that President Ford banished the term from his political vocabulary. In view of the pro-detente mood in Western Europe, Moscow's introduction in 1977 of the highly accurate, solid-fueled SS-20 missile should not be viewed as a response to a heightened military threat from NATO, but rather as a blatant attempt to intimidate the Western allies and drive wedges between America and her transatlantic partners.

Prior to the introduction of the SS-20, NATO's qualitative superiority in military forces offset the Soviet Union's quantitative lead in intermediate-range nuclear weapons. The Soviet weapons, moreover, lacked the accuracy to hit military targets in most of Western Europe and were useful mainly against cities. The Warsaw Pact's quantitative edge over NATO in the European theater also was tolerable so long as the United States possessed strategic nuclear superiority over the USSR, thus deterring a Soviet attack by the threat of escalation. The Soviet Union's attainment of strategic nuclear parity with the United States and the modernization of the Soviet theater nuclear force with SS-20 missiles, along with the Warsaw Pact's superiority over NATO in conventional weapons, tilted the European balance strongly against the West and undermined the credibility of the U.S. nuclear umbrella over Western Europe. As then-ACDA director Eugene Rostow stated, "the real risk is not so much nuclear war as nuclear blackmail—what we're witnessing in Europe."[28]

The 3,100-mile-range SS-20 did not fall under SALT limitations. It belonged to a "gray area" category between intercontinental and theater nuclear weapons and was the first Soviet ground-based system capable of deep-penetration strikes into virtually all of Western Europe.[29] The Soviets have two missiles for each SS-20 launcher; each missile, in turn, carries three warheads that can be independently targeted (MIRV'ed). Moreover, each launcher is equipped with a reload capacity of three additional warheads. Thus, for example, 300 SS-20 launchers would pack a total of 600 missiles with three warheads apiece, or 1,800 warheads in all.

NATO had no system comparable to the SS-20 but decided to offset the Soviet deployments by stationing 108 Pershing II ballistic missiles, with a 1,125-mile (1,800-km) range, and 464 Tomahawk ground-launched cruise missiles (GLCM's), with a 1,500-mile (2,500-km) range, in Western Europe. The "Euromissiles," as these U.S.-made weapons came to be called, constituted the expedient for NATO's intermediate nuclear force (INF) modernization program aimed at countering the new Soviet threat. The initiative for this program actually came from West German Chancellor Helmut Schmidt, who told President Carter at a Western summit in Guadeloupe in January 1979 that his country would accept deployment of the Euromissiles on its soil if at least one other European NATO member made a similar commitment.

It was agreed that all the Pershing II's would be based in West Germany, from where they could reach Soviet territory in six to eight minutes from launch.[30] These highly accurate missiles could target key Soviet command, control and communications nodes facing Western Europe.[31] According to a former high ACDA official,

> The Kremlin's preoccupation with the Pershing II was due to its high speed, mobility, ballistic trajectory, and great accuracy. These characteristics made it virtually unstoppable by existing defenses and, except for the number of warheads, a true counterpart in capability to the larger SS-20. [32]

The cruise missiles, which, like the Pershings, could reach the western USSR, were to be stationed in Britain (160), Italy (112), West Germany (96), Belgium (48), and the Netherlands(48). The cruises, which are mounted four to each launcher, would take at least half an hour to reach targets in the Soviet Union and would be far more vulnerable against Soviet defenses than would the Pershing II. Despite the planned missile deployments, the United States displayed its much-vaunted restraint in the name of arms control. The total number of missiles—572—was not high enough to pose the threat of a first strike on the Soviet Union, and the Carter Administration deliberately limited the range of the Pershing II to 1,125 miles so that it could not quite reach Moscow from West German soil.[33]

Fearing that the United States and the Soviet Union would spare each other's homelands and wage a nuclear war in Europe alone, the NATO allies insisted that Euromissile deployments be accompanied by superpower efforts to negotiate a reduction in the overall level of medium-range nuclear weapons on the Continent. Jimmy Carter hammered out the so-called dual track decision (the deployment track and the negotiating track) with the European NATO nations on 12 December 1979. The thrust of the arrangement was that the Europeans would permit deployment of Pershing II's and cruise missiles if good-faith negotiations on the part of Washington failed to yield an acceptable INF agreement with the Soviet Union. Moreover, in deference to a SALT protocol, deployment of the new Euromissiles was postponed until December 1983 (ensuring, inter alia, a long lead-time for the Kremlin to put its anti-INF propaganda machine into high gear).

The question of INF modernization presents an interesting case study of how single-minded devotion to arms control skewed the entire strategic debate. Aside from the specific need to counter Moscow's SS-20's, INF deployments were intended to put the onus on the Soviet Union for initiating strategic nuclear warfare in response to attacks on its territory by the new Euromissiles. Thus, the new missiles (especially the Pershing II's) were designed to maintain "extended deterrence" by raising the stakes for Moscow of attacking Western Europe. Far from wishing to confine a nuclear war to European soil, the United States was "re-coupling" the allies to its own nuclear deterrent, which many NATO countries had feared was eroding because of the Soviet attainment of strategic parity. As one perceptive analyst pointed out,

> NATO governments justified INF requirements largely in terms of Soviet SS-20 deployment, rather than by reference to NATO's changing force needs in the age of strategic nuclear parity. . . . This fostered the mistaken belief that arms control could serve as a substitute for new NATO missiles: if only Soviet SS-20's were removed, NATO could renounce its own deployment. Moreover, by restricting the agenda to Soviet SS-20's, NATO laid the intellectual foundation for its ill-fated zero-option. . . . [34]

Moscow flatly rejected Jimmy Carter's initial offer in October 1980 to negotiate on INF and demanded that NATO rescind its plan to deploy Euromissiles as a precondition for any arms-control talks. This intransigence was typical of the Soviet mood at the time of the invasion of Afghanistan. In the view of veteran Kremlinologist Richard Lowenthal, both the rejection of arms negotiations and the move into Afghanistan

> were the expression of an arrogant over-confidence which no longer seemed to care for preserving a negotiating relationship with the West—a relationship which, in the Soviet view, had brought no substantive benefits and seemed no longer needed to forestall substantive dangers. Without doing so in so many words, both in fact served notice on detente, because the Soviet leaders appeared to feel strong enough to overthrow what was left of the eroded balance [of power].[35]

In July 1981, however, Brezhnev offered during a visit to Moscow by Chancellor Helmut Schmidt to enter INF talks with the United States without prior cancellation of the deployment side of NATO's two-track decision. The Kremlin evidently realized that its obstinate stance was tarnishing its "peace" offensive in Western Europe.

The talks opened in Geneva on 30 November 1981. Representing the American side was Paul Nitze, a founder in 1976 of the Committee for the Present Danger, which played an important role in rallying opposition to the SALT II treaty. The chief Soviet negotiator was Yuli Kvitsinsky, the German-speaking number-two man at the Soviet embassy in Bonn. His appointment was particularly significant, insofar as public opinion in West Germany, the designated site for the Pershing II's, was the chief target audience in Moscow's anti-INF campaign.[36]

The opening salvo for the United States at the INF negotiations was President Reagan's "zero option," which called for the cancellation of plans to deploy the new Euromissiles in return for the dismantling of the 300-odd Soviet SS-20 and 300 SS-4 and SS-5 missile launchers already on station. However, the "zero option" proposal ran up against the inherent difficulty of trading off prospective systems for those already in place. Moreover, the total number of proposed new Euromissiles was only 572—against the more than 1,500 on the Soviet Union's SS-20 launchers alone.[37]

Moscow wasted little time in responding to Reagan's proposal. On 22 November, during a visit to West Germany, Brezhnev introduced what he labeled "genuine zero option."[38] He called for a freeze on INF deployment by the Soviet Union and the United States, preparatory to an agreement at Geneva in which, he said, the Soviets would be ready to reduce medium-range ballistic missiles "not by dozens but by hundreds of units."[39] He didn't specify, however, whether he was referring to SS-20's or to the older SS-4's and SS-5's that the Soviets already were phasing out.

Washington's "zero option" proposal was formally tabled at the Geneva negotiations on 2 February 1982. The following day, Brezhnev elaborated on the Soviet counterproposals.[40] He stated that each side should be permitted to have 300 intermediate-range systems, which, on the Western side, would include the 162 British and French nuclear missiles already deployed on submarines.[41] The Soviets put forth as their rationale the fact that the British and French weapons could reach Soviet territory, whereas the SS-20's could not reach the United States. Aside from rejecting a formula that would have poised 300 highly accurate and sophisticated SS-20's against older, less accurate and slower-moving British and French missiles, the United States argued that it could not negotiate on behalf of its allies. Moreover, the Soviet proposal addressed only the SS-20's in the European part of the USSR, thus allowing an increase in SS-20 deployments in Asia and leaving open the possibility that these launchers could be transported quickly into the western regions. The Kremlin repeatedly refused to include its Asian-based missiles in INF negotiations, claiming that they are needed for the Soviet Union's defense against Chinese missiles and against the planned U.S. deployment of nuclear cruise missiles on surface ships and submarines in the Pacific.

Much of Moscow's propaganda offensive against the Euromissiles revolved around its assertion that NATO has an unfair advantage because of its "forward-based systems"—U.S. and British nuclear-capable fighter-bombers based in Europe, bombers based aboard aircraft carriers off European shores, submarine-launched missiles assigned to NATO, British nuclear forces, and the French *force de frappe*. However, the Russians have avoided mention of some of their most powerful weapons directed at the European theater—notably the Backfire bomber, a long-range plane that can be armed with "stand off" nuclear missiles fired from outside the European battle zone. The U.S. "forward-based" aircraft are virtually incapable of reaching most targets on Soviet territory except on one-way suicide missions and are intended primarily for attacks against Soviet forces in the event of an invasion of Western Europe. Even more importantly, from an arms control standpoint, the British and French nuclear arsenals, along with the American "forward-based systems" in Europe and elsewhere, were excluded from SALT restrictions in exchange for Moscow's being allowed to exclude its "Backfire" bomber and to retain it's 308 "heavy" ICBM's.

On 16 March 1982 Brezhnev announced a unilateral moratorium on the deployment of intermediate-range muclear weapons in the European USSR until U.S.-Soviet negotiations yielded an agreement on a reduction in INF systems in Europe or until the United States embarked on "practical preparations" for the deployment of its "Euromissiles. Specifically, the moratorium was to take the form of a freeze on the replacement of SS-4 and SS-5 missiles with SS-20's. Brezhnev also stated that the Soviet Union would withdraw "a certain number" of its European-based medium-range missiles during 1982 if there was no "new aggravation" in the international situation.[42] At the same time, however, he threatened retaliatory measures if NATO carried out its Euromissile deployments. At the time of Brezhnev's proposal, the USSR had deployed 297 SS-20's, of which 207 (on both sides of the Urals) could reach Western Europe.

These observations aside, however, the moratorium involved less than met the eye. It evidently was meant to be a propaganda gesture at a time when the Soviet Union's planned level of SS-20 deployment was competed or underway, while U.S. deployments were not scheduled until December 1983. The Soviets hoped to generate pressure on the NATO governments through Western public opinion and the anti-nuclear movement to cancel the Euromissile deployments. Furthermore, the moratorium did not apply to to the SS-20's stationed east of the Urals that were targeted on U.S. allies in Asia—notably Japan.[43]

Brezhnev's moratorium statement was coupled with a blistering attack on the Reagan Administration's arms-control policy. He threatened to place the United States in "an analogous position" if it deployed the Pershing II and cruise missiles. On 20 March 1983 *Pravda* elaborated on this issue by stating that the Soviet Union might put nuclear arms in Cuba if the United States installed its Euromissiles. Entitled "There Can Be No Double Standard," the article neatly sidestepped the fact that the Euromissile deployments were in response to the Kremlin's own INF modernization program in the form of the SS-20's.

Overshadowing the moratorium issue was the now-famous "walk in the woods" proposal. On 16 July 1982 Paul Nitze made an unofficial offer to his counterpart, Yuli Kvitsinsky, while the two were strolling near the site of the Geneva arms control meeting. In an apparent effort to move the arms talks away from Reagan's "zero option," the two negotiators proposed informally that the United States would forego deployment of the Pershing II's (the weapon most feared by the Russians) and would restrict cruise missile deployment in Western Europe to 300 warheads aboard 75 GLCM launchers; the USSR, in turn, would cut back to 75 the number of triple-warhead SS-20's aimed at Western Europe and would freeze at 90 the SS-20's targeted on Asia. In addition, each side would retain 150 medium-range aircraft with nuclear weapons. The agreement was rebuffed at the highest levels in both Moscow and Washington.

It is virtually inconceivable that Kvitsinsky could have engineered an accord with the Americans without specific instructions from the Kremlin, but it is possible that rival factions were jockeying for position there in the waning months of Brezhnev's life and that policy (including arms control) questions became entwined in the struggle.[44] On the U.S. side, meanwhile, a senior State Department official was quoted as saying that "a mythology may be created in Europe about all this that somehow Rostow and Nitze negotiated a breakthrough that Neanderthals in Washington blocked."[45] Rostow reportedly received a sharp rebuke from the White House, and this episode helped pave the way for his dismissal as ACDA chief in January 1983. The entire affair illustrated once again how political considerations overshadowed military-strategic ones in evaluating the merits of an arms-control proposal. In fact, the Nitze-Kvitsinsky proposal (dubbed by former Secretary of State and NATO Commander Alexander Haig as "a stumble in the woods.") would have created a highly unfavorable situation for the West, insofar as it envisaged 300 swift and accurate Soviet SS-20 missile launchers arrayed against 300 much slower and less sophisticated NATO cruise missile launchers.

In December 1982, Yuri V. Andropov, the new general secretary of the Soviet Communist party, stated that in return for U.S. abandonment of plans to deploy Pershing II's in Europe, the Soviet Union would reduce the number of its intermediate-range missiles in Europe to "only as many missiles as are kept there by Britain and France—and not a single one more."[46] Aside from the fact that 162 SS-20's remaining in Europe would be more than a match against the older and slower British and French missiles, Andropov made no reference to dismantling "the dozens of SS-20's" that supposedly would be removed from Europe. Most likely, they would be trundled several hundred miles eastward, poised to return to the European theater on short notice or to strike European targets from east of the Urals. Andropov's proposal would assure the Soviet Union a virtual monopoly of land-based mobile missiles in Europe. Secretary of State George Shultz termed Andropov's proposal an example of "giving away the sleeves from your vest."[47] Other U.S. officials opined that Andropov's offer "was intended to produce a negotiation on the editorial pages of the U.S. and its allies."[48]

Washington's immediate response to Andropov's proposals was "an open letter to the people of Europe" from President Reagan, who offered to meet with Andropov "wherever and whenever he wants in order to sign an agreement banning U.S. and Soviet intermediate-range, land-based nuclear missile weapons from the face of the earth."[49] The U.S.-Soviet contest for West European public opinion continued to gain momentum as 1983, the "Year of the Euromissile," opened. The first major event on the 1983 Euro-calendar was the West German election of 6 March. Christian Democratic Chancellor Helmut Kohl faced stiff competition from the Social Democratic Party, the architect of *Ostpolitik* (Eastern Policy). A possible coalition of the Social Democrats and the antinuclear "Greens" loomed. Moscow's clumsy efforts to influence the election backfired and contributed to Kohl's victory.

On 30 March President Reagan veered away publicly for the first time from the 16-month-old "zero option." The President urged the Soviet Union to negotiate an "interim agreement," by which the United States would reduce "substantially" the level of its planned Pershing II and cruise missile deployments in exchange for the Soviet Union's reduction of the number of warheads on its intermediate-range nuclear missiles to an equal level on a global basis (i.e., in Asia as well as Europe). "Interim solution" became the newest buzzword in the arms control community. Moscow rejected the proposal because it did not take into account U.S. "forward-based systems" or British and French missiles. However, the concept itself was seriously deficient:

> . . . . All this follows a familiar historical pattern. The U.S. makes an arms control proposal, the Soviets reject it, and we rush to find something more pleasing to Moscow. Rather than negotiating with the Soviets, we wind up negotiating with ourselves. . . .
>
> The Soviets certainly have no reason to move until they see whether the alliance actually has the will to begin deployment. . . . With an "interim solution," we will be handing the Soviets an invitation to drag on negotia-

tions for an indefinite time, leaving them in their position of superiority and hamstrainging our own efforts to make Western Europe's defenses credible. . . .

Most versions of a so-called interim solution . . . are also flawed on technical grounds. For a variety of reasons, for example, it would be far more difficult to verify an agreement allowing some missiles than an agreement banning missiles altogether—assuming any verification of what goes on in a closed society is possible in the first place. . . . [50]

By summer, arms control frenzy was rife among the American liberal establishment, and unreciprocated concessions to the Russians were by no means ruled out. *New York Times* columnist Tom Wicker wrote that

If Ronald Reagan wants to insure his re-election in 1984, his best policy would be an agreement with Moscow to limit deployment of medium-range missiles in Europe. . . . For Ronald Reagan, an arms control success would largely destroy his warmonger image and give him the kind of solid foreign policy accomplishment that does not otherwise appear available. . . . [51]

On 26 August, with the scheduled deployment of the Euromissiles only months away, Andropov was cited in *Pravda* as offering to "liquidate" any SS-20's eliminated under a U.S.-Soviet INF accord. Although this position compared favorably with previous Soviet indications that any banned missiles would simply be shuttled from Europe to Asia, Andropov remained adamant about cancellation of the Euromissile deployments and about counting British and French missiles in the Western total. Moreover, he gave no hint about how NATO could verify "liquidation" of the SS-20's. Andropov's proposal was watered down further with the "clarification" that it entailed the destruction of the SS-20 launchers only—not of the missiles themselves. Reagan's growing frustrations with Moscow were reflected in his comment to a group of news reporters and editors that the Soviets continued to deploy a new SS-20 every week and we cannot "negotiate forever with ourselves."[52]

On 26 September 1983 the President delivered a major speech on East-West relations to the U.N. General Assembly. Citing the recent Soviet shootdown of a KAL jetliner as "a timely reminder of just how different the Soviets' concept of truth and international cooperation is from the rest of the world," Reagan went on to concede superiority to the Soviets in the number of intermediate-range missiles in the European theater by agreeing not to offset the deployments on a tit-for-tat basis. In return, Reagan called upon the USSR to agree to reductions of missiles on a global level. While most delegations heartily applauded the President's address, the Soviets sat in stony silence. Soviet pique aside, however, Reagan's proposals constituted little more than a fine-tuning of earlier offerings. Most importantly, the United States had never exhibited any determination to match Soviet missiles targeted against Western Europe with an equal quantity of Euromissiles or warheads on NATO territory.

On 3 October, *Pravda* editorialized that Reagan's new proposals were unacceptable because they failed to address two key Soviet demands: that the United States forego its Euromissile deployments altogether; and that British and French nuclear forces be counted in any INF balance. The Kremlin sent Foreign Minister Gromyko to West Germany in October to "reason" with his counterpart about the Euromissiles, while Col. Gen. Nikolai Chervov of the Soviet General Staff told the West German magazine *Stern* that Soviet troops in East Germany were equipped with tactical nuclear weapons having a 60-mile range.[53]

On 24 October, Moscow formally threatened to deploy new nuclear missiles in East Germany and Czechoslovakia if West Germany accepted Euromissiles on its territory.[54] On 19 November, *Pravda* published a vituperative article by Defense Minister Dmitri Ustinov on INF that evidently was intended to sway the impending vote in the West German Bundestag (parliament) on the Euromissiles. Andropov added to the pressure by sending a warning letter to Chancellor Kohl.[55] Nevertheless, the Bundestag voted on 22 November in favor of deployment. The following day, the first components of the Pershing II missiles arrived in West Germany, and the Soviets walked out of the INF negotiations in Geneva, announcing at the same time the cancellation of the moratorium on SS-20 deployments in Europe that allegedly had been in effect since March 1982. Assistant Secretary of State Richard Burt noted that "the United States pursued the negotiations while the Soviet Union deployed. But the Soviet Union suspended its participation in the negotiations when the United States began to deploy."[56]

On 8 December 1983 the Soviets scuttled the START talks by declining to set a date for a new round after the Christmas season recess. Similarly, the Soviet bloc nations declined to set a date for the resumption of the talks in Vienna on Mutual Balanced Force Reduction (MBFR)—talks aimed at lowering the number of ground forces on the European central front. Thus, every facet of the arms control "process" had run aground.

As originally conceived, MBFR was to proceed in tandem with SALT, so that the twin threats of a Soviet conventional blitzkrieg against Western Europe and a knockout blow by Soviet SS-18 and SS-19 "heavy" ICBM's against the United States could be mitigated. Moscow, however, insisted on percentage cuts in East-West force levels, thus leaving intact the Warsaw Pact's numerical advantage (and taking the "B" out of MBFR). Its next ploy was to countenance numerical reductions while understating by an many as 200,000 the number of Warsaw Pact troops and thus the size of the reduction that would be required.

Despite periodic gestures, the Soviets remain resistant to asymmetrical troop reductions that would erode the Warsaw Pact's numerical preponderance. Moreover, the USSR regards its troops in Eastern Europe not only as combat forces in a potential war, but also as instruments for maintaining political control over the Soviet bloc and as psychological props for intimidating the NATO countries.

After its walkout from the INF negotiations, the Soviet Union moved rapidly to deploy three types of short-range surface-to-surface ballistic missiles in Eastern Europe: the SS-21, with a 100-km range, in East Germany and Czechoslovakia; the solid-fueled, mobile SS-12 (Scaleboard), with a 900-km range, in East Germany and Czechoslovakia; and the SS-23, with a range of 500-km, in East Germany. These missiles can deliver nuclear, conventional, or chemical warheads against such vital targets as nuclear weapons storage sites, airfields, air defense installations, and depots stocked with arms and equipment for troops arriving in Western Europe from the United States.

Negotiations on START and INF remained suspended through 1984. With the arms control "process" hopelessly stalled and U.S.-Soviet relations at their lowest ebb in years, Washington moved to pull Moscow's chestnuts out of the fire by proposing "umbrella talks." The idea was to help the Soviets retrieve the prestige they purportedly lost when they walked out of both the START and the INF negotiations. The "umbrella talks" were to provide a new forum, in which both ICBM's and intermediate-range weapons would be discussed as well as space-based weapons.

Face-saving considerations aside, what eventually brought Moscow back to the negotiating table was not only the beginning of Euromissile deployments, but also President Reagan's Strategic Defense Initiative (SDI), which threatened to neutralize two decades of Soviet investment in nuclear weaponry that could pose a credible first-strike capability against the United States. Reagan's proposed new program shifted the nuclear debate away from the focus of strengthening mutual deterrence (the "balance of terror") to the question of building an effective defense against ballistic missile attack. Thus, SDI held the promise of transcending MAD—the doctrine that has preserved a fragile peace at a terrible psychological and moral price. The President expressed the hope that SDI eventually would render nuclear weapons "impotent and obsolete."[57]

By comparison with SDI, the INF modernization issue was a minor bone of contention in East-West relations. From the time that Reagan inaugurated SDI in a nationally televised speech on 23 March 1983, the Kremlin resolved that it should never get off the drawing board. While "Star Wars" conjured up images in the United States of a project that was politically frivolous and technologically infeasible, the Kremlin declined to relegate "Star Wars" to the realm of science fiction. For example, a Soviet scientific report obtained by a Western journalist stated that much of SDI appears technically do-able, albeit immensely expensive.[58] Certainly the Soviets have greater confidence than do many American military and scientific experts that "Star Wars" will work.

In 1967 Soviet Premier Aleksei Kosygin declared that defensive systems were "not a cause of the arms race, but [were] designed instead to prevent the death of people."[59] At that time, the Soviet decision to deploy an ABM system around Moscow sparked U.S. concern that the USSR might be readying a capability to launch a first strike in some future crisis and constructing a nationwide defensive system that would render it virtually invulnerable to American retaliation. Today, the tables are reversed: Moscow evidently believes that the United States is building a defensive shield, behind which to unsheath its nuclear sword against the USSR. Moreover, the Kremlin appears concerned over a defensive arms race that would tax its economic resources and expose its technological backwardness.

Already, SDI is having a revolutionary impact on the arms control community. It is antithetical to SALT, which severely restricts defensive (ABM) systems while attempting to curb the growth of offensive forces. On a moral plane, SDI rejects the doctrine of offensive retaliation. Moreover, although a thermonuclear reaction would be needed to activate an X-ray component of SDI, the sytem is essentially non-nuclear. Finally, "by drawing on our long suit of advanced technology, it can reverse the process by which we have allowed ourselves to become progressively enfeebled vis-a-vis the Soviets."[60]

Those who contend that SDI will destroy the arms control "process" argue essentially that deployment of an anti-missile shield will encourage the Soviet Union to enlarge its offensive nuclear arsenal in order to overcome the defense.

> The arms control argument against the SDI is based entirely upon the offense-reliant arms control theory that has provided the basis for U.S. policy for almost 20 years. . . . The SDI, as the potential prelude to [ballistic missile defense] BMD deployment, is in direct variance with the policy prescriptions stemming from this traditionalist, offense-dominated theory of arms control. Consequently . . . arms control traditionalists . . . are..critical of the SDI. It threatens their arms control "worldview."[61]

The vigorous criticism of SDI on the part of many luminaries in the American arms control community underscored a continuing reluctance to shed their illusions about Soviet strategic objectives. The assumption that the Soviet Union would be willing to reduce its inventory of offensive nuclear arms in the absence of BMD flew in the face of Soviet actions during the decade after SALT I was signed. The U.S. expectation that the ABM treaty and the SALT-mandated limitations on offensive weapons would lead to permanent reductions in such weapons was shattered by a Soviet buildup that placed special emphasis on counterforce systems. Against this backdrop, the emplacement of a "Star Wars" system can no more subvert the basis for arms control than did the Soviet offensive buildup and may even nudge the Kremlin toward a mutually acceptable approach to arms control based on defense-oriented systems.

Moreover, SDI is eminently compatible with arms control efforts, in that progress on START would lessen the possibility that the Soviets could overwhelm "Star Wars" through an endless flow of new offensive missiles. Sen. Richard Lugar (D.-Ind.), chairman of the Senate Foreign Relations Committee, wrote that

> . . . Strategic defense adds a considerable degree of uncertainty to the survivability of offensive weapons, hence rendering them less useful in any first-strike calculation Moscow could make. On the other hand, the

utility of strategic defense weapons would be enhanced if there were deep, verifiable reductions in offensive weapons. Thus, a good arms reduction agreement and strategic defense go hand-in-hand.[62]

Columnist Charles Krauthammer has called SDI an example of "arms control by (American) *diktat.*"[63]

This book will not attempt a scientific analysis of SDI and its feasibility.[64] Let us simply note that the proposed system has three operational layers, which are designed to intercept and destroy enemy missiles immediately after launch (the boost-phase intercept or defense), during flight (mid-course defense), and just prior to impact on U.S. targets (terminal defense). The general consensus among SDI's proponents in the scientific community appears to be that more than 90% of Soviet ICBM's launched in a first strike against the United States would be obliterated in one or another of the three phases before they could reach their destination. These experts contend that a defense against Soviet missiles that utilizes such exotic technologies as lasers and particle beams and that would be almost 100% effective might become a reality in the late 1990's, but that the off-the-shelf technology of the "smart bullet" could be employed by the turn of the decade to provide 90%-protection. The "smart bullet," requiring only "a relatively modest degree of engineering development of existing hardware," is essentially a projectile containing metal fragments that would be launched from a satellite against a Soviet missile in flight and would disable the detonator mechanism of the nuclear device inside the missile.[65]

The Soviet propaganda barrage against SDI has been all-encompassing. One commentator wrote that "in a way, the SDI as a target of a Soviet public relations crusade can be described as the son of INF."[66] Within three days of SDI's debut on 23 March 1983, Andropov denounced the concept of strategic defense. A few weeks later, 244 members of the Soviet Academy of Sciences—led by Yevgeniy Velikhov, a vice president—warned that SDI "is clearly oriented toward a destabilization of the existing strategic balance. By his statement, the President is creating a more dangerous illusion which may cause an even more threatening spiral of the arms race."[67] How an "illusion" could be so threatening was never adequately explained. A U.S. government report later revealed that Velikhov and a host of other signatories of the letter (including Soviet Nobel laureates Nikolay Basov and Aleksandr Prokhorov) were involved in projects to develop conventional and exotic ballistic missile defense systems. Velikhov was also identified in the report as a "central figure" in Soviet laser and particle-beam weapons research.[68]

Reagan's SDI proposal sparked a bitter debate reminiscent of the one that raged in 1969-70 over whether the United States should build an ABM system. The contention that ABM's don't work and that the offense can always overwhelm the defense was applied to SDI. Opponents of "Star Wars" also dusted off the hypothesis that defensive systems were potentially destabilizing because one party might believe it could launch a first strike and destroy the missiles sent to retaliate. In short, the quest for ballistic missile defense, like an ABM system before it, was judged to be both dangerous and futile. The vehemently anti-nuclear Union of Concerned Scientists, for example, has placed advertisements in newspapers and on television falsely implying that SDI will lead to a nuclear war in space; such ads "objectively" support Soviet propaganda.

Whereas they assail space-based defenses, in which they lag technologically, the Soviets have conducted intensive research and testing on earth-based defenses. The system constructed around Moscow in accordance with the 1972 ABM treaty already has been upgraded twice. Edward Teller, father of the U.S. hydrogen bomb, writes that "with parts prepared in advance, the system deployed around Moscow could be duplicated in other cities and military facilities in a very short time."[69] Many Western experts believe that the components of a countrywide system already are available and that the Soviet Union may be on the threshold of a "break out" from the treaty.

It is difficult to avoid the conclusion that SDI is a thorn in the Kremlin's side not because it contributes to an arms race in space, but rather because it threatens to nullify the enormous progress that the Soviets registered in their terrestrial arms buildup during the time that the United States was barely in the running. Originally, the ABM treaty seemed to make sense because it was designed to go hand in hand with limitations and eventual reductions in offensive arms. The continuing large-scale Soviet buildup in strategic weapons vastly altered this equation, however. Now, with the introduction of SDI, the pendulum shows signs of shifting once again—this time, back in a direction favorable to the United States:

> . . . Why then have the Soviets come running, in near panic, back to Geneva? Why, if their capacity to kill us many times over is a given, are

they so alarmed and desperate about the U.S. Strategic Defense Initiative? Quite simple. Moscow's monster missiles are not aimed at America's cities, but at America's strategic silos, at the submarine and SAC bases that house America's deterrent. . . . The half trillion dollars Moscow ploughed into strategic missiles this past generation was . . . made to purchase . . . a war-fighting and war-winning capability, should deterrence fail. . . .

The Soviets are enraged by "Star Wars" not because it threatens the life of a single Russian citizen, but because it threatens to neutralize . . . the advantage these monstrous first-strike weapons were supposed to give the Soviet Union. . . . If the Soviet Union is not developing first-strike weapons, why should it object to our protecting our deterrent? [70]

As noted above, SDI provided psychological leverage to the United States in arms control negotiations even when the program was only a hypothetical concept in President Reagan's head. A perception was created that Washington would be able to negotiate arms control issues from a position of strength and that time was on its side, rather than on Moscow's:

. . . Since the beginning of SALT negotiations in 1969, the momentum of nuclear programs constantly favored the Soviet Union. Such, at least, was the mutual perception. . . . Now . . . the USSR was getting a bit of its own medicine and found it difficult to swallow. . . . [71]

Therein lay a major reason for the Kremlin's walkout at the end of 1983 from arms control talks. Another key motivating factor evidently was the failure of the USSR's campaign of propaganda and intimidation to prevent the scheduled deployment of the Euromissiles. Other factors contributing to the walkout probably included a Soviet calculation that scuttling the talks would frighten Western public opinion into demanding arms control concessions from the NATO governments. Finally, the Soviets may have decided to bide their time in order to reassess the prospects of Reagan's reelection and what this would mean for arms control.

As late as 16 October 1984, a mere four weeks before the U.S. Presidential election, Soviet General Secretary Konstantin Chernenko declared that arms control negotiations would not be resumed unless the United States consented to a freeze in the nuclear arsenals of both nations; ratified accords limiting underground nuclear explosions that had been signed in the mid-1970's; pledged no-first-use of nuclear weapons; and agreed to prevent the "militarization of outer space." On 17 November 1984 Chernenko made an abrupt volte-face, clearly generated by Reagan's massive electoral mandate, and proposed discussions aimed at resuming arms control negotiations; no preconditions were cited.

Fortunately for the Soviets, Reagan had provided them with a face-saving opportunity to return to Geneva under the guise of beginning brand new talks (the "umbrella" format) rather than resuming the ones they had boycotted. The announcement of the "new" talks came on 23 November 1984—a year to the day after the Soviets walked out of the INF negotiations. On 7 January 1985 Shultz and Gromyko conferred to settle the framework for the revived arms talks. The first negotiating session took place in March, thus ending a 16-month hiatus.

Apostles of arms control generally greeted with enthusiasm the accession to power of Mikhail S. Gorbachev, who symbolized a generational change in the Kremlin leadership. Vice President George Bush traveled to Moscow for Chernenko's funeral and used the occasion to deliver a letter from Ronald Reagan inviting the new General Secretary to a summit meeting.[72] In the arms control arena, however, the Soviets remained inflexible. They ignored Reagan's "umbrella" format by demanding a renunciation of SDI (with the possible exception of laboratory research) as a precondition to agreements on INF and strategic nuclear weapons.

If 1983 was the Year of the Euromissile, 1985 was the Year of the Summit, with arms control as the leitmotif. Reagan pledged on 10 June to "go the extra mile" to seek an arms control accord with the USSR. He announced at the same time that Washington would continue to abide by the unratified SALT II treaty "to the extent that Moscow exercises comparable restraint" and provided that the Soviet Union "actively pursues arms-reduction agreements at the nuclear and space talks in Geneva."[73]

As usual on arms control issues, political rather than military considerations fueled the President's decision. He faced pressures from Congress and from U.S. and West European public opinion, as well as from Moscow. Two major factions within the Administration were said to be battling for Reagan's soul on the SALT compliance issue: a pro-compliance group led by Secretary of State Shultz and National Security Affairs Adviser Robert McFarlane and an anti-SALT contingent headed by Defense Secretary Weinberger and CIA Director William Casey.

As an earnest display of his intentions to abide by SALT II, the

President announced that he would dismantle a Poseidon submarine in the autumn when the USS Alaska, an Ohio-class submarine packing 24 Trident multiple-warhead missiles, was ready for sea trials. Keeping the Poseidon in service would cause the United States to exceed by 14 missiles the ceiling of 1,200 multiple-warhead ICBM's and SLBM's established in the SALT II treaty.[74] A *New York Times* editorial typified the jubilation that Reagan's decision inspired:

> [It] buys six months for arms control negotiations. It also buys the time the President would need to prove that the United States is not primarily to blame if they should fail. Even if the Poseidon dismantling proceeds, the costs would be negligible. . . . To have opted for [a] treaty breakout now would have risked torpedoing the Geneva arms talks, offending the NATO allies, and undermining the President's campaign to call attention to more ambiguous Soviet violations. . . . [75]

George Will contended, however, that

> The award for Most Preposterous Argument of 1985 . . . goes to an argument for continuing U.S. compliance with the unratified SALT II treaty even after December 31, when it would have expired anyway. The argument is: To abrogate SALT II limits would send a bad "signal" to Moscow at a "delicate moment" in the arms-control process. . . . But arms control has become such a virulent superstition that preservation of an unratifiable treaty is considered crucial. . . . [76]

While Washington was grappling with the SALT compliance issue, Moscow continued to portray SDI as the chief impediment to new arms control agreements. As usual, the Soviets received a timely assist from their American friends. For example, Marshall Shulman, Director of the Harriman Institute for Advanced Study of the Soviet Union at Columbia University, asserted—in words that could have issued from Gorbachev's own mouth—"The crucial obstacle to agreement in the Geneva negotiations is the proposed Strategic Defense Initiative."[77] Missing from this analysis is the vital issue of why arms control negotiations remained deadlocked for a decade before SDI made its debut. More relevant is the comment by *The Economist* to the effect that "the Russians seem to have an SDI of their own—a strategic delaying initiative, by which they will decline to do any arms control business with America for the remaining three and a half years of Reagan's rule."[78]

On 6 August 1985 (the 40th anniversary of the U.S. bombing of Hiroshima), Moscow dusted off an old favorite in the Kremlin's propa-

ganda repertory: a moratorium on nuclear testing. The proposal came
at a time when the Soviets had just completed tests of their mobile
land-based ICBM's—the SS-24 and SS-25—while the United States
had not yet begun testing of the mobile Midgetman. Even *The New
York Times*, a consistent advocate of arms control, called the linking of
the moratorium to Hiroshima "a cynical propaganda blast."[79]

On 27 September the new Soviet foreign minister, Eduard Shevardnadze, presented Reagan with a proposal for 50-percent cuts in the
superpowers' nuclear arsenals. Gorbachev elaborated on the plan during an official visit to France a week later. Addressing about 50 members of the French National Assembly, he called for a 50-percent cut in
the "strategic nuclear delivery systems of both superpowers"; he defined "strategic" as "nuclear armaments capable of reaching the territory of the other side." These proposed radical cutbacks were
roughly twice as deep as those that Moscow spurned when Secretary of
State Cyrus Vance proffered them to Brezhnev in 1977, but the real
question became "50 percent of what?" Gorbachev appealed for a ceiling on both sides of 6,000 nuclear "charges," of which a maximum of
60 percent, or 3,600 "charges," would reside in any single category of
weapons—e.g., land-based ICBM's.[80]

The term nuclear "charges" evidently encompassed bombs and
air-launched cruise missiles as well as ballistic missile warheads. The
catchall category of nuclear "charges" equated the obsolescent bombs
on aging U.S. fighter planes with the newest warheads on Russia's
giant ICBM's. Moreover, the term "charges" obfuscated the carefully
constructed categories of weapons systems (based on megatonnage and
range) that Moscow and Washington had worked out in previous arms
control negotiations. Since Gorbachev did not mention throw-weight,
it appeared that the maintenance of the 3-to-1 Soviet advantage in this
category was built into his proposal. As for the stipulation that no
more than 60 percent of each side's nuclear "charges" could emanate
from any single weapons category, it seemed at first glance that Moscow was prepared to reduce its force of "heavy missiles." A closer
look at the arithmetic, however, indicated that even after applying a
60-percent limit for each category of weaponry (e.g., ICBM's,
SLBM's, or bombers), the Soviets could retain 3,600 warheads on the
land-based "silo busters." Such a situation certainly would not alleviate the problem of U.S. Minuteman vulnerability.

In addition, there were three major caveats in the Soviet plan.
First, Moscow predicated negotiations toward a 50-percent cutback on

strategic nuclear arms on "cessation of work" on SDI. Bud McFarlane quipped that "[Gorbachev] is telling us, if you will get rid of your defense, I will get rid of your offense."[81] A second caveat involved Gorbachev's stipulation that the introduction of new types of weapons should be prohibited after a cutoff date to be negotiated. American officials regarded this item as a ploy to ban deployment of MX, Midgetman the Stealth bomber, and D-5 missiles for the Trident submarine (all under development), while permitting the USSR to retain its new mobile SS-24 and SS-25 ICBM's and its Blackjack bombers, on the grounds that deployment of these Soviet systems already had commenced.

Thirdly, the Kremlin proposed to halve only the number of nuclear weapons that could reach the other superpower's territory. Such a definition would encompass all U.S. forward-based nuclear systems in Europe and on carriers offshore, as well as the new Euromissiles, while excluding SS-20's and other Soviet INF systems that could reach the homelands of the European NATO allies but not the United States. *New York Times* columnist James Reston reflected the skepticism generated by the Soviet plan when he wrote that Moscow had proffered "a proposal to play tennis with the net down when Mikhail Gorbachev is serving and to raise it when President Reagan is serving."[82]

During a round of "banquet diplomacy" in Paris, Gorbachev sought to win over European public opinion (and to exploit strains between Washington and its NATO allies) by inviting France and Britain to engage in "a direct dialogue" with the Soviet Union aimed at "a separate agreement" on the INF issue. He also claimed that the USSR had "withdrawn" unilaterally some of its SS-20's "in the European zone" of the country (which he defined as "the zone in which medium-range missiles capable of striking targets on the territory of Western Europe are deployed").

The Soviet proposal ignored the persistent Western concern that SS-20's removed from Europe could be brought back quickly in the event of a crisis. As a State Department official emphasized, the number of SS-20's in the European theater is "irrelevant" and Washington has "always insisted on a global limit" because of the missiles' mobility and 3,000-mile range.[83]

The Kremlin failed utterly to sway West European public opinion with its proposals. France and Britain insisted on retaining their nuclear forces for defense of their homelands. The Netherlands, the last holdout on accepting U.S. cruise missiles on its territory, endured a massive onslaught of Soviet agitprop. As the date for the vote neared, Soviet propagandists appeared on Dutch television to offer a variety of arguments against cruise missile deployment, including a claim that the SS-20 was too large and unwieldy to be regarded as mobile.[84] Moreover, Gorbachev sent Prime Minister Ruud Lubbers two apparently unconvincing letters. The vote to accept the cruise missiles came at the end of October. In February 1986 the parliament gave the final go-ahead by ratifying a U.S.-Dutch treaty allowing 48 GLCM's to be stationed in the Netherlands in 1988.

During the Geneva negotiations in October, the Soviets offered for the first time to freeze SS-20 deployments in the Asian part of the USSR, "provided there is no substantial change in the strategic situation there." They also set forth a modified "walk in the woods" proposal and, for good measure, suggested that the Kremlin would go beyond "national technical means" of verification of arms control agreements when such means are "inadequate" and when "mutually agreed procedures" can be worked out.[85]

The Soviet Union's comprehensive (if essentially unworkable) arms control proposals of the autumn of 1985 evidently put Washington on the defensive in the battle for public opinion. The Reagan Administration reportedly was "pleased to have the proposals but unhappy with much of their content."[86] A senior Administration official said: "The good news is that the Soviets have made an offer at last; the bad news is that it's lousy; the even worse news is that it will look great in the headlines."[87]

A U.S. counterproposal, delivered on 1 November, recommended limiting each side's nuclear warheads to 6,000; but, unlike the Soviet plan, this figure excluded warheads on U.S. Euromissiles or "forward-based systems," whose designation as "strategic" Washington does not accept. There was no mention in the proposal of British and French nuclear forces. Washington proposed a figure of 6,000 warheads (the same as that proposed by Moscow for "nuclear charges"); but the U.S. count encompassed warheads on ICBM's and SLBM's and air-launched cruise missiles—items that reflect the strategic balance more accurately than do the categories in the 6,000-warhead Soviet proposal. The American offer also recommended, inter alia, a limitation on INF deployments by both sides, thus implicitly proposing to terminate deployments before all the Euromissiles were in place. More surprisingly, the United States called for a ban on mobile ICBM's, ostensibly because it was virtually impossible for satellites to verify limits on their numbers but in fact, it appears, because of the unfavorable political and budgetary outlook for funding the Midgetman mobile missile. The Americans offered to trade Soviet SS-24's and SS-25's for not-yet-deployed Midgetmen.[88] (Prospects for a mobile MX had all but evaporated.) Other features of the U.S. proposal included a ban on modernizing non-mobile heavy missiles—a ploy to impede the Soviet plan to upgrade the SS-18 force—and a 50-percent cut in megatonnage—a category consistently omitted from Soviet proposals.

Ironically, implementation of the U.S. proposal not only would restrict drastically the number of land-, sea-, and air-launched warheads that could strike the Soviet Union, but also would endanger the survivability of the remaining American nuclear arsenal. In particular, the plan would prohibit new basing modes that would enhance the mobility and thus lessen the vulnerability of the American land-based ICBM force. Even worse, the proposal, which was a pre-summit initiative timed for maximum public-relations impact, evidently was formulated so hastily that its incompatibility with basic U.S. nuclear doctrine and strategy was totally overlooked:

> . . . the new U.S. arms-reduction plan would likely handicap the U.S. ability to implement its own countervailing strategy of deterrence. . . . The logic behind the countervailing strategy is the assumption that if the United States is capable of retaliating against the things Soviet leaders hold most dear, this will maximize U.S. war-deterrence leverage. . . . Such a strategy requires that U.S. forces are able to put at . . . sure risk such things as Soviet leadership bunkers, their chain of command, and . . . ICBM's). It would be difficult to implement the countervailing strategy with just a few MX missiles and a handful of Trident submarines. . . . [89]

By the time the Reagan-Gorbachev summit took place on 19-20 November 1985, all 108 Pershing 2 missiles in West Germany were operational and the United States had installed 32 of the planned 464 cruise missile launchers (in Britain, Italy, and Germany). Thus, NATO had 140 intermediate-range launchers, each with a single-warhead missile, to counter 441 Soviet triple-warhead SS-20's.

As the summit approached, President Reagan came under the familiar fusillade of pressures from arms control devotees in Congress, the media, academia, and among the West European allies—not to mention the Soviets. The thrust of their arguments was that the White

House must meet Gorbachev more than halfway on his offer—still not fully articulated—to trade off SDI for substantial cutbacks in Soviet offensive nuclear forces. Former Vice President Walter Mondale urged Reagan to use SDI as a bargaining chip at the Geneva summit—even, it would seem, before he knew quite what he was bargaining for. Robert Kleiman, a member of *The New York Times* editorial page staff, stated that Gorbachev was on the threshold of major decision-making about resource allocation on military vs. civilian programs and that Reagan could "influence that decision by convincing Mr. Gorbachev that serious negotiations for a trade-off of SDI programs for offensive missile cuts are possible."[90]

Gerard Smith and Paul Warnke wrote that a tradeoff of SDI for significant reductions in Soviet offensive weaponry contains "the makings of an agreement of historic proportions." They conceded that both governments bore a share of responsibility for lack of progress in arms control but went on to urge Reagan rather than Gorbachev to break the stalemate:

> The last five American Presidents have negotiated arms control agreements with the Soviet Union. It is time for President Reagan to end five years of dangerous stagnation. . . . [91]

Although both sides had made pre-summit bids for a 50-percent cut in their nuclear arsenals, Reagan and Gorbachev could not even agree on a framework for negotiation toward that end."[92] The Joint Statement issued at the end of the summit contained only four short paragraphs on arms control—the first noting merely that the issue had been discussed. The two sides agreed "to accelerate the work" at the ongoing arms control negotiations, with a view toward reaching an agreement "to prevent an arms race in space and to terminate it on earth, to limit and reduce nuclear arms and enhance strategic stability." Gorbachev gave a press conference in Geneva, at which he reiterated that the Soviet Union was "prepared to engage in radical cutbacks in nuclear weapons, provided that the door to unleashing an arms race in outer space be firmly slammed shut."[93]

Capitalizing on the public-relations momentum he achieved at the summit, Gorbachev wrote a letter to Reagan on 5 December inviting U.S. participation in the Soviet moratorium on underground nuclear testing that had been in effect since 6 August and offering, in exchange, to support a program of on-site inspection to ensure compliance. However, the letter was characteristically vague, and it appeared to be a ploy to persuade the United States to forego a new testing cycle at a time when the Soviets had just completed such a cycle. The on-site proposal was conditioned on U.S. adherence to a joint test moratorium through 1986. Reagan sent a return letter that rejected Gorbachev's test ban proposal but offered to discuss on-site inspection of nuclear testing in both countries.[94]

On 23 December, the President formally submitted to Congress a written report claiming that the Soviets had gained militarily through violations of treaties covering nuclear, chemical and biological weapons. Nevertheless, Reagan announced that the United States would continue to abide by SALT II after the treaty's formal expiration on 31 December.

The issue of treaty violations represented another prime illustration of the Reagan Administration's inability and/or unwillingness to break away from a bankrupt arms control policy. A commentator wrote in 1979 that "a pattern of downplaying evidence of possible Soviet cheating [on arms agreements] has been apparent under the Carter Administration—to the point where official U.S. reports about this subject read like legal briefs for the USSR."[95] The GOP platform of 1980 stated boldly that "the Republican Party deplores the attempts of the Carter Administration to cover up Soviet noncompliance with arms control agreements." Reagan's record on this issue, however, appears to reflect a fear that the messenger who brings bad news on arms control compliance will be anathematized in the public opinion polls.

During 1985 the issue of Soviet cheating on arms control became so sensitive in Washington that a virtual taboo was imposed on raising it officially lest Moscow cancel the summit. Even after the Geneva meeting, many American officials hoped to shun the subject of violations for fear of undermining the summit "process"—i.e., the tentative agreement for Gorbachev to visit the United States in 1986 and for Reagan to go to Moscow in 1987. Nevertheless, pressures from arms control skeptics over the Kremlin's poor record of treaty compliance made it impossible to sweep the issue under the rug any longer.

The most egregious violation cited by the Administration concerned construction of a huge phased-array radar at Krasnoyarsk in Siberia that was ideally situated and configured to serve in an ABM "battle management" capacity. Even Gerard Smith et. al. conceded that this violation of the 1972 ABM treaty "raises . . . troublesome questions," but they argued that the radar by itself would not give the

Soviets an ABM capability sufficient to degrade the U.S. deterrent posture. They also noted that, since the radar would not become operational until the late 1980's, "there is no urgency in publicly branding it as an example of Soviet dishonesty, since there is still time to get the Soviets to stop the deployment through private negotiations." Meanwhile, the State Department conceded that the new radar violated the treaty but questioned whether the violation was "pernicious" or relatively harmless![96]

If the Reagan Administration has been reluctant to acknowledge Soviet violations of arms control commitments, it has been even more hesitant to act upon its knowledge. Its "see no evil" approach in this regard has been virtually indistinguishable from that of its predecessors, and its policies reflect the persistent influence in government circles of the arms control lobby, regardless of which party or President is in the White House.

Having contributed to a climate that abetted a natural Soviet inclination to cheat on arms control agreements, Washington has fallen back upon legal niceties in failing to charge Moscow with misdeeds. There has been an endless search for "smoking guns." Reagan told a press conference that "it is difficult to establish . . . hard-and-fast evidence that a treaty has been violated. . . . If you can't get the kind of courtroom evidence that you need, then you can't make the charge of violation."[97]

The reasons for Washington's reticence are essentially political, as is the arms control "process" itself. As one experienced observer has pointed out,

> Once a democracy has committed itself to a major, formal arms control treaty . . . finding a partner in violation of that treaty tends to undermine its own foreign policy. It amounts to an admission of past failure. Violations—and their political as well as their military applications—must be explained to the electorate and one's allies. . . . The violation must be made to go away. It did not occur, or, if it did, it was a passing aberration. . . . At all costs, the process of arms control must be protected."[98]

After taking into account the technical complexities of nuclear weapons systems and the semantic ambiguities in the SALT treaties, one is left with having to make a "judgment call" based on the political repercussions that might arise from public criticism of the Soviet Union.

> There will always be serious problems with the quality of the evidence. Since this is not a courtroom proceeding, witnesses cannot be sub-

poenaed; there is no direct access to evidence; Soviet officials cannot be tried for perjury; there is no impartial judge and jury; and there is no agency to enforce the law other than the parties involved. [99]

In an effort to avoid making a "judgment call," Washington has fallen back upon various rationalizations for inaction. The rationalization most frequently resorted to is the need (nowhere justified) to avoid disruption of the arms control "process." Another common rationalization is that disputes over violations can be ironed out if the Administration is really "serious about arms control; in fact, the disputes are papered over with meaningless jargon about "restraint." Many wishful thinkers concede that Soviet violations have indeed occurred but that they are not strategically significant and/or provide Moscow with only a short-term military advantage. This argument, aside from the contempt that it invites from the Kremlin, overlooks the repeated U.S. failure to take steps to rectify imbalances caused by Soviet cheating.

Finally, those who favor "quiet diplomacy" rather than public confrontation on the violations issue rationalize their choice with reference to the possible compromise of intelligence sources and methods. However, now that the Soviets have reverted to wholesale encoding of the data we need to verify their compliance with SALT, there should be less concern about revealing what we learned in the past than about what we are being denied at present. The violation involving encryption is so "pernicious" (as arms control specialists like to say) that it requires a U.S. demarche in the strongest terms.

As 1986 opened and both superpowers began to maneuver into position for a second summit, a spate of new arms control proposals surfaced. If the proposals of the autumn of 1985 were fanciful, the offerings of the new year were downright utopian. On 15 January, Gorbachev proposed nothing less than the complete elimination of nuclear weapons by the year 2000. This omnibus plan was to be implemented in three stages, beginning with the halving of Soviet and American nuclear weapons that can reach each other's territory. Gorbachev exulted that " . . . by the end of 1999 there will be no nuclear weapons on earth. A universal accord will be drawn up that such weapons should never again come into being."[100]

With Gorbachev's proposal, the Kremlin came full circle, back to its tried-and-true nostrum of General and Complete Disarmament. Unlike previous proposals of this ilk, however, the latest one was spurred by President Reagan's SDI and was predicated upon a prior renunciation of the development, testing and deployment of a "Star Wars" system (Gorbachev did not explicitly foreclose laboratory research). The Soviet leader rationalized that there would be no need for SDI—billed by Reagan as a means of rendering nuclear weapons obsolete—if nuclear arms themselves were eliminated. Defense analyst Colin Gray labeled Gorbachev's proposal "insulting to the intelligence of reasonable people in the West," but he conceded that "many people in the U.S. and in Western Europe likely either are convinced or are convincible that the SDI stands in the way of complete nuclear disarmament—which is, of course, Mr. Gorbachev's objective." Gray also placed Gorbachev's dialectic in proper perspective by pointing out that "complete or even very substantial nuclear disarmament will be tolerable for Western security only if we deploy very effective strategic defenses. The logic is absolutely inexorable."[101]

Speculation abounded in the West about the motives behind Gorbachev's proposals—beyond giving new impetus to his anti-SDI offensive. A particularly cogent analysis appeared in London's *Financial Times* on 3 February 1986 under the by-line of Ian Davidson. Entitled "The Case of the Tongue-Tied Strategists," the article noted that

> At least three possible explanations suggest themselves. In the first place, Moscow may be having second thoughts about the deep cuts in strategic nuclear weapons which it proposed last year; complete nuclear disarmament sounds even more virtuous, but the enlargement of the agenda could confuse and slow down the negotiating process in Geneva. . . . The second hypothesis is that Mr. Gorbachev's new plan is meant to be taken seriously but not literally: This is not a blueprint for negotiation, but a political gesture, the significance of which lies more in the direction of movement than in the result at the end of the road. . . .

> . . . This hypothesis . . . is not incompatible with a third explanation: That in Mr. Gorbachev's vast three-phase plan, only Phase One really counts and should be looked at in isolation. Here the innovations [a 50-percent reduction in strategic nuclear delivery vehicles and a 6,000-warhead ceiling on the remainder] seem entirely directed against the security of Western Europe and the solidarity of the Atlantic alliance. . . . The Geneva negotiations leave room for two nightmares: The first is that Ronald Reagan refuses an equitable arms agreement in order to hang on to "Star Wars"; the second is that he does a deal with Moscow at the expense of the European allies. In neither case will the Europeans sleep easy.

The impact of Gorbachev's proposal on NATO bears further scrutiny. In addition to halving the superpowers' strategic nuclear arsenals,

Phase One of his plan called for the "complete elimination of intermediate-range missiles of the USSR and the USA in the European zone, both ballistic and cruise missiles, as a first step toward ridding the European continent of nuclear weapons." In practice, these measures would have removed the American Pershing II and ground-launched cruise missiles, along with Soviet SS-20's targeted on Europe, while retaining SS-20's in Asia, with their potential for rapid movement into the European USSR.

Gorbachev's proposal was formally tabled in Geneva on 16 January, and reportedly it already was modified to ban even scientific research on "Star Wars." Meanwhile, Moscow unleashed a media blitz hailing the General Secretary's proposal as "a peace initiative of historic significance."[102] With scant regard for history, Reagan hailed the plan for being "different from the things that we have heard in the past from leaders in the Soviet Union. It's just about the first time that anyone has ever proposed actually eliminating nuclear weapons." The President added that "we're very grateful for the offer" and "we're studying it with great care."[103] Secretary of State Shultz noted that the proposals have "a lot of problems" but that "potentially we're in a possibly productive phase" and the Geneva arms talks "may be at a rare moment of opportunity." Kenneth Adelman of ACDA chimed in with the remark that "we're in a better position today for real progress in arms control than we've been in years."[104] In general, the Administration's reactions suggested that Washington had been caught off guard by the sweeping nature of the Soviet proposal and thrown onto the public relations defensive.

Once the initial euphoria wore off, the flaws in Gorbachev's proposal became visible to those starry-eyed optimists who hoped to solve the arms control conundrum by eliminating the arms. First of all, one cannot dispose of all nuclear weapons unless one knows how many there are in the Soviet arsenal and where they are located. Moscow's elaborate program of camouflage, concealment and deception has virtually ensured that reliable information never will be available to the West. Secondly, the unwillingness of other nuclear and would-be nuclear states to jump on the nuclear disarmament wagon should be regarded as a given. Aside from the obvious fact that elimination of the superpowers' nuclear inventories would leave such states in possession of a powerful monopoly, most of the nuclear and threshold-nuclear nations covet atomic weapons for reasons having little to do with the Soviet-American global rivalry.

Perhaps of greatest import is that the implementation of Gorbachev's proposal would create unprecedented dangers for NATO. The military doctrine of the alliance rests on the concept of deterrence through the threat of using nuclear weapons in the face of imminent defeat from a Warsaw Pact invasion. The elimination of nuclear weapons thus would make the world safe for conventional warfare, in which NATO would confront vast Warsaw Pact superiority, and would bring the United States and its European allies face to face for the first time with a choice they have sought to avoid for decades: Do they want a world without nuclear weapons in which they would be confronted with Russian conventional military superiority?

The arms control community unabashedly embraced Gorbachev's proposal. Columnist Mary McGrory lamented that his "amazing offer" had "fallen like a rock to the bottom of a pool." She chided the Reagan Administration for its "insult of silence" toward "a man who probably had to fight the Politburo to make an offer the West could hardly refuse" and expressed concern that "Gorbachev may be at the end of his rope" as a result of recriminations from his Kremlin colleagues.[105] Other commentators were more restrained. The general liberal consensus, however, was reflected by *The New York Times*: "It was at the negotiating table . . . that the overall scheme and its intriguing parts would be . . . explored. Yet it was hard to deny that the ball, in diplomatic parlance, was in Washington's court."[106]

Washington ran with the ball. On 24 February the United States introduced a plan calling for the total elimination of the American Euromissiles and of all Soviet intermediate-range missiles from both the European and Asian parts of the USSR. This plan constituted a virtual replay of Reagan's 1981 "zero option," except that the current offering envisaged a specific timetable for the removal of the INF systems and the United States had gained bargaining leverage with the deployment of 108 Pershing 2's and a substantial number of GLCM's in Western Europe, vs. none in 1981. Reagan's new plan was to be implemented over a three-year period, beginning in 1987.[107] It excluded constraints on the British and French nuclear arsenals, however.

The plan was outlined in a letter that the President sent to Gorbachev on the eve of the Soviet Union's 27th Communist party congress. Reagan's initial enthusiasm for Gorbachev's 15 January proposal had cooled considerably by this time. The President linked "the total elimination of nuclear weapons," as proposed by the Soviet leader, to a number of long-term goals, including reduction of Soviet conventional forces to bring them into balance with Western forces, "full compliance" by the Soviets with existing arms control treaties, "peaceful resolution of regional conflicts," and "a demonstrated commitment by the Soviet Union to peaceful competition."[108]

Despite Reagan's contention that nuclear disarmament was "clearly not appropriate for consideration at this time,"[109] the President was looking forward to a second summit—hopefully before the pressures of the Congressional election campaign engulfed him. Gorbachev declined to set a date for the summit and suggested that progress in arms control negotiations would have to precede a meeting. Using the early February visit to Moscow of Sen. Edward Kennedy (D.-Mass.) as a forum, Gorbachev insisted that such progress was both possible and desirable. He hinted to Kennedy that abandonment of "Star Wars" was not a precondition for the elimination of all Soviet and U.S. intermediate-range nuclear forces from Europe. The only preconditions he set were a promise by Britain and France not to expand or modernize their nuclear arsenals and a commitment by the United States not to transfer strategic or medium-range missiles to its NATO allies.

Gorbachev's use of Kennedy, a liberal Democrat, as a conveyor of Soviet preconditions for a summit evidently was a ploy to embarrass the Reagan Administration to be more forthcoming in arms control negotiations. Kennedy told a Washington press conference upon his return that he was encouraged by Gorbachev's "de-linking" of the INF issue from "Star Wars" or reductions in strategic nuclear systems. However, he emphasized that Gorbachev would not set a summit date unless there was tangible progress toward the signing of an INF agreement and/or a comprehensive nuclear test ban accord.[110]

On 20 February, Moscow formally declared its readiness to accept on-site inspections to monitor a complete ban on nuclear testing. Thus, "Gorbachev demonstrated his skill at public diplomacy . . . by removing at a stroke the Reagan Administration's most convenient excuse for avoiding arms-control agreements."[111] Reagan, however, dipped into his own ample public relations skills by proposing a Soviet-American exchange of inspectors who would conduct an inventory of each other's nuclear weapons and monitor deployment sites and production and assembly plants as part of an on-site inspection plan for verifying the elimination of INF systems. The President also invited Soviet scientists to observe and possibly measure the yield of an underground nuclear test in Nevada. Gorbachev piously rebuffed the invitation to send Soviet observers to a Nevada test, declaring that it would be like "asking a man advocating the abolition of capital punishment to witness an execution."[112] Nevertheless, as a result of Reagan's offers, the ball was returned once again to the Soviets' court.

On 25 February, the 27th Soviet Communist party Congress opened in Moscow—the first Congress under Gorbachev's leadership. Gorbachev used his speech before the delegates to reiterate that a second summit with Reagan "ought to produce practical results in arms control," since "there is no sense in holding empty talks."[113] The General Secretary stated, however, that "the Soviet Union is prepared to resolve the question of intermediate-range missiles in the European zone separately, without a direct link to problems related to strategic armaments and outer space." Gorbachev dismissed Reagan's letter of response to his 15 January disarmament proposals as a "tough and nonconstructive" rehash of previous U.S. positions. Without disclosing details of the letter, Gorbachev rebuffed U.S. suggestions that an INF agreement should hinge on Moscow's acceptance of "Star Wars," a unilateral cutback in Soviet conventional arms, or the weakening of Soviet defenses in the Far East (an apparent reference to Reagan's insistence on SS-20 reductions in the Asian part of the USSR).

On 13 March, the USSR announced an indefinite extension of its seven-month-old moratorium on underground nuclear testing and declared that the Soviet Union would not conduct any tests "until the United States carries out its first nuclear explosion."[114] Reagan adhered to his position that testing was necessary in order to uphold the reliability and credibility of the U.S. nuclear stockpile. On 29 March, Gorbachev proposed a summit in Europe to negotiate a nuclear test ban. Reagan immediately quashed the notion of a single-issue summit.[115]

Shultz remarked that "it's probably a measure of the lack of progress recently that all the actions are through press statements, publicly rather than privately."[116] Flora Lewis wrote that

> Credibility has gone. It can be taken pretty much for granted that when Mikhail Gorbachev proposes abolishing nuclear weapons in 15 years . . . or President Reagan offers to give the Russians a someday space defense against American missiles, they are counting on a swift rejection from the other side. That leaves both free to try to please the crowds without risk of compromise and decision. It is a game where the shuttlecock never

touches the ground of reality, and all the motion brings no useful movement. [117]

In short, the arms control dialogue, such as it was, deteriorated into two monologues.

On 4 April, Rep. Dante B. Fascell (D.-Fla.), chairman of the House Foreign Affairs Committee, and Rep. William S. Broomfield (R.-Mich.), the ranking Republican on the committee, met with Gorbachev in Moscow. Arms control apparently topped the agenda. "It appears to me that the window of opportunity to get a real agreement with respect to arms control and reducing tension is a very narrow window and we'd better grab it right now," said Fascell upon returning to Washington.[118] However, mid-May talks between President Reagan and Foreign Minister Shevardnadze that might have put summit plans into motion were cancelled by the Soviets in the wake of U.S. bombing raids on Libya on 15 April.

Gorbachev used the East German Communist party congress as a platform on 18 April to launch two new arms control proposals. One involved a ban on chemical weapons but failed to include any provisions for inspection. The other involved new initiatives on the stalled Mutual Balanced Force Reduction (MBFR) talks in Vienna. Departing from the established format of seeking troop reductions in West Germany and the Benelux countries on NATO's side and the USSR, East Germany, Poland and Czechoslovakia on the Warsaw Pact's side, Gorbachev proposed an enlargement of the zone to include all of Europe "from the Atlantic to the Urals" (to borrow a phrase from Charles de Gaulle). The Soviets called for a one-on-one reduction in troops, thus disregarding the "B" (for balanced) in MBFR. In addition to manpower cutbacks, Gorbachev proposed reductions in tactical nuclear weapons (nuclear-capable artillery and mines); previous MBFR guidelines on armaments had called only for reductions in conventional weapons.

The daunting task of monitoring and verifying cutbacks in arsenals and among hostile armies in such an immense geographic area and the fact that Gorbachev aired his plan publicly (as part of his peace offensive in Europe) rather than at the negotiating table forced most observers to treat his proposal as merely a publicity stunt. Referring to the lack of progress in the MBFR talks since they opened in 1973, *The Economist* noted wryly that the new Soviet scheme "could keep the Great Vienna Hot Air Factory in business for another 13 years."[119]

On 14 May, Gorbachev delivered a televised speech that evidently was intended both to reassure Soviet citizens about the effects of the accident at the Chernobyl nuclear power plant and to divert attention from that disaster to his campaign for nuclear disarmament. The General Secretary announced an extension of the USSR's unilateral moratorium on nuclear testing until 6 August—the anniversary of Hiroshima—and offered to meet Reagan in Europe or Hiroshima to begin negotiations on a comprehensive nuclear test ban. On 15 May, the Soviet delegation at the Geneva arms talks presented a draft treaty for the elimination of intermediate-range nuclear weapons in Europe. It was essentially a rehash of some of the proposals that Gorbachev had presented on 15 January and did not address U.S. concerns about Soviet SS-20 missiles in the Asian part of the USSR or short-range Soviet missiles deployed in Eastern Europe.

On 27 May, Ronald Reagan bit the bullet on SALT compliance and announced that he would base future strategic decisions on "the nature and magnitude of the [Soviet] threat," and not on "standards" contained in arms control accords. He said that the United States might breach SALT limits by the end of the year.[120] The President, citing "a general patten of Soviet noncompliance,"[121] said that two Poseidon submarines would be dismantled to keep the country within the SALT ceiling for intercontinental ballistic missiles when the newest Trident submarine began sea trials, but that equipping B-52 bombers with air-launched cruise missiles (ALCM's) would continue. When the 131st B-52 was thus outfitted, probably sometime in the autumn, the United States would exceed the SALT limits of 1,320 on total numbers of multiple-warhead launchers. Reagan stated that his decision to dismantle two Poseidons was motivated not by SALT, but rather by the fact that the cost of overhauling them would outweigh their military utility.[122]

The President assured his listeners that he would not breach any SALT limits without giving the Soviet Union an opportunity to clean up its act on treaty violations. He declared that if Moscow would "take the constructive steps to alter the current situation," he would "certainly take this into account." However, he did not indicate what kinds of steps would alleviate his concerns.[123]

Various Administration officials attempted to refine and clarify the President's position but succeeded more often in obfuscating it. Weinberger said that the United States is "no longer bound" to continue adhering to SALT II.[124] Paul Nitze stated that Weinberger's interpretation was "correct" but that the President was committed "to take another look at the matter" if Moscow moved during the next several months to satisfy Washington's concerns about treaty violations.[125] Kenneth Adelman, ACDA's director, declared that "in essence, we're not bound by SALT II anymore" and that Reagan's announcement "in essence changes the President's political commitment"; no further explanation was offered by this normally articulate official.[126] Edward Rowny used the formulation that "SALT is behind us."[127] Shultz told a meeting of NATO foreign ministers in Halifax, Nova Scotia, that the Administration was "shifting gears" by basing its nuclear weapons policies on national security needs rather than on "the technicalities" of SALT II. Shultz faulted the "so-called restraints" in the SALT treaty and declared that the treaty was "obsolete" because it dealt with numbers of launchers instead of the more "correct unit of count," i.e., warheads.[128] This was a position that Weinberger and Perle had long advocated against Shultz's opposition.

On 11 June, Reagan suggested during a nationally televised news conference that his 27 May announcement was not the final word. The following day, however, White House officials emphasized that the President was not signaling a retreat from his original position.[129] On 12 June, presidential spokesman Larry Speakes asserted that Reagan "indicated that we will no longer be bound by the numerical limits" of SALT II; but "we have not violated it yet. We may not go over it in the fall." Speakes noted that "the decisions we make on arms reductions . . . will be based on Soviet behavior. In the meantime, Reagan declared that the SALT limits "no longer exist" and "we are going to try and replace it with a better deal."[130] When a journalist retorted that "Larry Speakes told us very definitively that it [SALT] is dead and yet you won't say it," Reagan replied that "I think you can trust what Larry Speakes said."[131] Shultz subsequently denied that the SALT II treaty was dead or that it had been so characterized by Larry Speakes. Shultz rebuffed those who "keep trying to insert that word, 'dead,' into other people's mouths."[132]

Reagan's failure to bury SALT II outright seems to have encouraged both the Soviets and the Western arms control lobby to believe that concerted pressure could resuscitate the treaty. A massive public relations campaign was unleashed to convince Western audiences that SALT II is the best antidote to a nuclear holocaust. There was a disjunction in the campaign on the American side, however. The SALT sellers contended that allowing the treaty to die would lead the

*Soviets*—not the Reaganite "hawks"—to pursue a military buildup that would shatter the fragile balance of deterrence. Thus, for example, Robert McNamara told a meeting of the Arms Control Association that if Reagan abandoned the policy of restraint, "I guarantee you will see an acceleration of the offensive arms race the likes of which most of you in this room could never even imagine."[133] However, the former defense secretary portrayed only the Soviet side as racing; he suggested that the USSR would retain all its existing "heavy" missiles, even while phasing in its fifth generation of ICBM's (the SS-24 and SS-25). Similarly, Rep. Dante Fascell argued that by abandoning SALT II the United States "would heat up the arms race and give unprecedented opportunities to the *Soviets* to substantially increase their nuclear threat against the United States."[134] Paul Warnke cautioned that the Soviet Union could add more than 10,000 warheads to its arsenal in the absence of SALT restraints.[135]

The political offensive in favor of SALT II brought out a number of opinions that Lenin would have characterized as issuing from "useful idiots." Former SALT negotiator Gerard Smith, for instance, groused that "Reagan had laid down "impossible conditions" to the Soviets in his announcement of 27 May; one wonders why a request to Moscow to slow down its military buildup and cease its violations of SALT in return for continued U.S. adherence to the treaty should be viewed as intolerable.[136] *New York Times* columnist Anthony Lewis wrote that

> Even if he wanted to ignore the *provocative* Reagan tactics, Mr. Gorbachev does not rule alone in these matters. There are hardliners in the Soviet leadership who have always doubted the value of agreements with the United States. Now, strengthened by the Reagan decision, they will press for a new weapons buildup." [137]

*The New York Times* editorialized that

> A breakout from SALT would bring Mr. Reagan no military benefit and add nothing to his bargaining position. His desire to negotiate from strength has surely been achieved already. And . . . Star Wars . . . has impressed the Russians as an ace in the hole. To sweat Mr. Gorbachev a little more . . . flaunts a sense of superiority that has no meaning in the nuclear age and may well turn him inflexible. [138]

Such advocacy of a "no-gloat" policy overlooks the fact that Gorbachev's alleged flexibility exists only in the mind of the beholder.

Meanwhile, a British diplomat worried that Reagan's stance on SALT would rule out the prospects of a new Soviet-American summit. "The Soviets may just decide that the Administration is playing hardball. Gorbachev's internal position may be that he can't give in."[139] Senator Albert Gore Jr. (D.-Tenn.) wrote that "we should consider what changes in *our* behavior might contribute to the kind of strategic outcome the Administration says it wants. . . . "[140]

Few of Reagan's critics disputed the fact that Moscow had committed violations of SALT II; the argument was over how to react. McNamara conceded that "I don't think there is any doubt" about Soviet violations of some SALT provisions, but the President's response is "totally inappropriate"; he did not elaborate.[141] Senator Dale Bumpers declared that "junking SALT would not end these violations—it would only legalize them."[142]

However, it was clear long before Reagan's belated announcement, five months after SALT II's official expiration date, that the treaty had not served either U.S. military or political interests. Militarily, the treaty was expected to lend predictability to the "arms race," thus facilitating American strategic planning. While it placed constraints on certain categories of weapons and required the dismantling of some systems, however, nothing in SALT II prevented the USSR from modernizing its existing nuclear arsenal or building entire new generations of weapons. The United States, of course, had the same options but more often than not failed to exercise them for fear of jeopardizing future arms control accords. Politically, SALT II was intended to facilitate future agreements and to convince U.S. public opinion and the NATO allies that Washington was "serious" about arms control. It seems to have failed on both accounts.

On 29 May, two days after Reagan's announcement about SALT, the Soviet delegation at Geneva offered to begin reductions in strategic nuclear forces if the United States would promise not to withdraw from the 1972 ABM treaty for 15-20 years and would take steps to strengthen the treaty. A Reagan Administration official described the Soviet move as "tantalizing"—a description that was incomprehensible given the fact that strengthening the ABM pact probably would sound the death knell for the President's pet SDI program.[143] As the Geneva negotiations recessed for the summer, the Soviet delegation proposed a 50-percent cut in strategic arms in return for long-term adherence to the ABM treaty and abandonment of SDI. Larry Speakes said the newest Soviet proposals had "merit" and the offer was "not being taken as a propagandistic endeavor."[144]

Despite Reagan's prolonged effort (dating from the opening of the START negotiations in May 1982) to channel the arms control process away from SALT-type ceilings toward genuine reductions, the liberal Establishment seemed unable to relinquish SALT—an old and familiar security blanket, albeit badly frayed. Rep. Henry Hyde (R.-Ill.) called SALT II "a paper pussycat" and said the notion that it restrains the Soviets is "a superstition dear to the hearts of the so-called arms-control intellectuals."[145] Patrick Buchanan pointed out that "the Soviets did not impoverish a whole generation of Russians to build the greatest arsenal . . . the world has ever seen, simply to destroy [it] pursuant to a piece of paper co-signed by . . . the United States."[146]

Even if Washington foreswore SDI, it is questionable whether Moscow would contemplate wholesale reductions in its nuclear inventory. Rather than engage in reciprocal concessions (the so-called "grand compromise" of dramatic reductions in Soviet strategic missiles in return for a radical emasculation of SDI), the Kremlin is likely to place its hopes in Gramm-Rudman-style budget cuts and the inauguration of a new President who is less personally committed than is Reagan to "Star Wars." As of the time of writing, the United States continued to insist that research on SDI was non-negotiable but that development and deployment of any system that might emerge from the laboratory would be preceded by consultations with the USSR. This is an arrangement that the Russians can live with, especially in view of the probability that a research program without a clear objective will lose political momentum and, thus, Congressional appropriations.

Meanwhile, the Soviet military buildup continues unimpeded by public opinion or an obstreperous legislature. In June 1985, portions of a National Intelligence Estimate on Soviet strategic forces were declassified at the request of the White House. The report concluded that the Soviet Union was poised for a major expansion of both offensive nuclear weapons and defensive sytems--an expansion unlikely to be thwarted by domestic economic problems.[147] Already, the Soviets are deploying their fifth-generation ICBM's, notably the road-mobile SS-25 and the rail-mobile SS-24. In addition, the USSR reportedly has tested a modernized version of the SS-18 "heavy" missile, launched from an enlarged silo.[148] Two senior CIA officials told a joint Senate hearing of the Defense Appropriations Subcommittee and the Armed Services

Committee that by 1994 the Soviet Union might possess as many as 21,000 nuclear warheads; such estimates do not even take into account the hundreds or even thousands of warheads that may be hidden throughout the vastness of the USSR.[149] Lawrence Gershwin of the CIA's National Intelligence Council told the same gathering that by the end of the 1980's the Soviet Union will have deployed all the components necessary for a nationwide ABM system, including sophisticated early-warning radars and ballistic missile interceptors.[150] "Our evaluation is that by the 1990's they could have in place a fairly large ABM system," Gershwin reported. "They have provided for that option."[151]

In addition, the Soviets are engaged in extensive modernization of their nuclear submarine force and have moved to challenge the traditional U.S. qualitative lead in sea-based strategic forces. The USSR's new Delta IV ballistic missile submarines carry SS-N-23 SLBM's (the Soviet Union's most advanced sea-based missile), each with ten warheads. The 25,000-ton Typhoon-class submarines, the world's largest, are armed with six to nine MIRV'ed warheads; as many as 8 Typhoons may join the Soviet fleet. The Soviets are moving ahead on still another front—the development of long-range nuclear-strike aircraft. The most important item in this category is the Blackjack intercontinental bomber, a supersonic, swing-wing plane that exceeds America's B-1 in size and payload. The Blackjack, with an initial deployment date of 1988, could pose a serious threat to the United States, which has allowed its air defenses to deteriorate alarmingly. The Soviets have forged ahead in their air-launched cruise missiles (ALCM's) as well, and reportedly have reopened the production line for the Bear bomber, which is an excellent platform for air-launched cruise missiles.[152]

These developments on the Soviet side are not occurring in a vacuum, of course. The Pentagon has made impressive strides in the buildup and modernization of nuclear weaponry. The deployment around 1990 of the long-range, highly accurate D-5 SLBM for the Trident II submarine will enable the United States to strike Soviet land-based ICBM's without having to rely exclusively on its land-based missile force. The Stealth bomber, which is also coming on line, is reputed to be virtually invisible to radar. Less publicized has been the so-called Advanced Cruise Missile (ACM), which incorporates Stealth technology. The United States, in addition, is reportedly creating a new generation of weaponry called nuclear-powered directed-energy weapons (NDEW's). According to scientists at the Lawrence Livermore National Laboratory in California, the new weapons, which would make use of X-rays, microwaves, or gamma rays, "could be used to destroy other missiles, to attack satellites, to incapacitate Soviet mobile missiles on the ground, to disrupt enemy communications, or for uncounted other missions."[153] These weapons are politically vulnerable, however; a comprehensive nuclear test ban treaty, a strengthening of the ABM accord, or a cutback in research funds as part of a curb on SDI could jeopardize the upgrading of the U.S. nuclear arsenal.

Soviet strides in building a sizable land-based mobile ICBM force represent the most threatening new development on the strategic horizon. The SS-24, equipped with a rapid reload and refire capability and with MIRV'ed warheads, is of particular concern to Washington. Pentagon officials stated that the missile could neither be verified for arms control purposes nor targeted by U.S. strategic forces.[154] The SS-25, a Midgetman-style missile, carries a warhead assumed to be accurate enough to knock out hardened U.S. military targets.

With Midgetman's future clouded and with only 50 MX missiles scheduled for deployment (as of the end of 1986), compared with the 200 envisaged by Jimmy Carter, it is not surprising that the Kremlin shunned Wahington's proposal for a ban on mobile missiles. As *The Economist* remarked, "The Russians may have to be convinced that Mr. Reagan can make good his threat to deploy new weapons before they will negotiate away any of their own. And the only way of convincing them may be to deploy some."

Internecine bickering in the U.S. government has undermined weapons programs that could be used as bargaining chips to obtain reciprocal concessions from the Soviets. Moscow not only benefits from the disarray in Washington, but actively contributes to that disarray by unleashing its formidable propaganda assets and its network of sympathizers in the West to influence U.S. arms control debates in its favor. As William Schneider observes,

[Soviet] propaganda thrusts are aimed at undermining the U.S. negotiating position via the "back door" of American public and Congressional opinion. . . . Moscow's aim is to raise public expectations in the United States and allied countries of negotiation outcomes, with the hope of thus generating pressures on the Administration to render the needed concessions in the interest of early results. Meanwhile, the negotiations process itself is expected to work debilitatingly on U.S. defense procurement decisionmaking. The success of such Soviet tactics is conspicuously engraved on arms agreements into which the United States entered in the

1970's, as well as upon a legacy of U.S. weapons programs forsaken, abandoned, or delayed. [155]

Since Gorbachev's accession to power, Soviet spokesmen have fed the illusions of Western opinion molders that the new leader is aching for an improvement in Soviet-American relations but is constrained by "hawks" in the Kremlin. *The Economist* exhibited this mindset when it wrote that " . . . Mr. Gorbachev's . . . own instinct is probably for cuts [in armaments], but his reluctant generals still have powerful allies in the Politburo." Such contentions ignore the fact that Soviet "doves" are, for the most part, in the Gulag. Soviet spokesmen also cater to the widespread belief in the West that Gorbachev cannot afford to allocate scarce resources to nuclear expansion when the Soviet Union is "an economic basket case." Tom Wicker of *The New York Times* portrayed this belief, for example, when he opined that "Mikhail Gorbachev has been sending repeated signals that he's ready for an arms deal, no doubt to allow him to devote resources to a desperately sagging economy."[156] These musings disregard the facts that the Soviet civilian sector always has taken a back seat to the military and that, moreover, economic development *per se* never has been accorded top priority by any Kremlin leader.

Even with the best intentions on both sides, the superpowers would face formidable odds in negotiating mutually acceptable arms control accords:

> Most of the reasons for the comparatively lean accomplishments of 20 years of arms negotiations are built into the structure of Soviet-American competition. Because of the lack of trust, neither side is about to make large concessions or take large risks. The adversaries' forces are asymmetrical, with the Russians dependent mostly on land-based missiles and the Americans preferring a more balanced structure that emphasizes the additional elements of long-range bombers and submarines. Finding major areas of compromise has often been like trading apples and oranges. [157]

Keith Payne, Director of National Security Studies at the National Institute for Public Policy, notes that

> . . . the Soviet Union has demonstrated that it perceives great value in those types of offensive strategic forces with the potential to destroy U.S. retaliatory forces. . . . The Soviet strategic arsenal is composed primarily of large, MIRV'ed ICBM's tailored to this counterforce mission. The Soviet Union has proven most reluctant over the course of negotiations

since 1969 to accept effective constraints on such systems, which is primarily what the United States has tried to achieve. . . . [158]

Ronald Reagan has expressed cautious optimism that his SDI will prod Moscow into concessions on arms control, but his case is weakened by opposition to this program at home. While "hawks" (based largely in the Pentagon) urge the President to focus on strengthening U.S. defenses in the face of a growing Soviet threat, "doves" (nesting most conspicuously in the State Department) place their emphasis on upholding the arms control "process." Other officials, notably former White House chief of staff James Baker III, reportedly advocated arms control because it was attractive to the voters. According to Evans & Novak, this group was called "the populists" because it relied on public opinion polls when formulating foreign policy.[159] Citing all these contradictory tendencies, James Reston noted wryly that "the players seem confused about whether they're trying to protect the country from the Russians or from one another."[160]

Reagan himself often seemed to be caught between the "competing visions" of some of his closest aides. Moreover, the President evidently was sensitive to the charges that he "failed" on the arms control front charges that the 1987 INF treaty did not entirely put to rest.

> Reagan's command of the intricacies of arms control is scant. His intuition . . . drives him in opposite directions. He has never trusted the Soviets nor liked the "fatally flawed" SALT II agreement. . . . At the same time, he recognizes that his Administration will be judged in part on its success in reducing the superpowers' nuclear arsenals. Reagan also prides himself on his skill as a negotiator and understands that SDI gives him negotiating leverage. [161]

The explanation for Reagan's striving for a new arms agreement despite his own internal resistance seems to lie in an impression that, political attractiveness aside, arms control treaties are necessary for the reduction of Soviet-American tensions. He appears to ignore the fact that arms control accords reflect much more than they mold the state of political relations between the superpowers.

Moreover, arms control pacts neither slow down the arms race (which merely takes off in directions not covered by the treaties, as happened after SALT II) nor saves money (to the contrary, millions of dollars were wasted on MX to shape it in a manner consistent with SALT verification procedures but totally inconsistent with strategic realities). As for the contention that arms control agreements are necessary to prevent the outbreak of nuclear war, such reasoning implies that, in the absence of such agreements, the United States and/or the Soviet Union would unleash the bomb. In fact, neither superpower is likely to revert to a first strike (although Soviet use of nuclear superiority for purposes of coercion and blackmail cannot be ruled out) in pursuit of any vital national objective that looms on the horizon.

> It is, then, not hard to fault arms control on its merits. Nevertheless, no U.S. President has come out flatly against arms control. Why? First, arms control is thought to be so politically popular (a notion fanned by the media despite polls which seem to demonstrate deep suspicion on the part of the public) . . . that no one seeking office can afford to oppose it in principle. Secondly, European support of and pressure for arms control must be reckoned with if the U.S. wants a politically viable alliance. Thirdly, no President can possibly take office without feeling the heavy burden placed upon him by the very existence of nuclear weapons. . . .
> 162

Although presidents have disagreed on the specifics of arms control agreements, none seems to have doubted that, given the right formula, Washington and Moscow can forge a mutually acceptable arms pact.

> Are there, then, any conditions that would permit an equitable agreement to limit nuclear arms? Two suggest themselves: first, fundamental Soviet political objectives might change. That is, the Soviets might abandon their quest for the advancement of a "socialist" international order responsive to Moscow. Clearly, this is not a realistic prospect. Second, the U.S. might establish so formidable a level of military power that the Soviet Union would have no other alternative than to seek genuinely equitable agreements. This too seems remote. . . . The notion that the United States might even try to reestablish military superiority . . . is denounced by the U.S. press for reasons which remain obscure. . . . 163

In concluding, we appeal for a curb on "arms-control craving" (to borrow a phrase from Carnes Lord), for a slowdown of the "mad momentum of arms control" (Albert Wohlstetter), and for a recognition that, in Caspar Weinberger's words, "arms control has hardly been a raving success."164 Perhaps most important, we must convey to U.S. voters that the future of arms control appears no brighter than its past. *Wall Street Journal* editor Robert Bartley has observed that

> . . . we find ourselves pondering what psychologists call "denial," the neurotic refusal to admit reality precisely because it is so threatening. . . . Why can't simple truths be uttered? The prospect for meaningful agree-

ment with the Soviets is slim to negligible. . . . Our politicians, including Mr. Reagan, shrink from these truths because they fear the public does not want to hear them. [165]

Here is the syndrome of condemning the messenger who brings bad tidings.

Unfortunately, as we noted in the beginning of this chapter, arms control has become the central pillar of detente, and there is widespread concern that if it collapses the whole edifice will come tumbling down—with consequences as dire as the possible outbreak of a nuclear war. Flora Lewis has written that

> The issue of linkage, of whether arms control should be made to carry the focal burden of Soviet-American rivalry or whether other . . . issues should have equal weight, has been overtaken by events. The arms competition is now the key issue, and no amount of palaver will make it secondary. [166]

This position, however, is closer to that of the Kremlin than of the White House. Reagan has sought to strengthen other pillars of detente's edifice besides arms control—human rights, trade and economic ties, and a joint approach to managing crises in the Third World. As is the case with arms control, however, the Soviets are likely to modify their behavior only if the penalties for misbehaving outweigh the rewards of cooperation with the United States. What Kissinger wrote with regard to arms control has relevance to all other aspects of detente as well:

> Given his necessities, Gorbachev might in time agree to a real, even historic, change of political and strategic relationships and to a serious discussion of the relationship between offense and defense. But he will have no incentive to do so while the West is mesmerized by the most transparent Soviet proposals and arranges periodic respites while the Soviets sort out their domestic problems. [167]

# 3

# The Trade Bridge

Alexander Hamilton once stated that "the spirit of commerce has a tendency to soften the manner of men and to extinguish those inflammable humours which so often have kindled into wars." Two centuries later, the heirs of America's founding fathers are attempting to "mellow" the Soviet Union through trade and persuade it to channel its aggressive tendencies into the realm of peaceful competition with the capitalist world. The United States and its Western allies have proffered trade, credits, loans, and subsidy programs as incentives for Soviet good behavior in the international arena.

During the era of detente, Soviet efforts to acquire Western equipment, technology and production and management expertise have accelerated, but Soviet spokesmen distinguish between Western hardware and the "bourgeois" culture that produced it. To a large extent, this hardware has constituted the "missing dynamic" that helps compensate for the economic stagnation brought on by the rigidities of the Communist system.

Trade with the Soviet Union never has constituted more than a miniscule proportion of the quantity or value of U.S. exports. Moreover, the balance of trade has always favored the United States. Nothing that America imports from the Soviets is remotely as important to it as are American grain and technology to the USSR[1] (wags say that spies are the Soviet Union's chief export). Theoretically, such a situation creates considerable leverage for Washington to pry political concessions from Mosocw in return for increased trade. At least two important constraints affect U.S. leverage, however.

First, the Soviet Union relies on credits to finance its imports from the United States. The flow of credit can be an important source of leverage; but, by the same token, the debt accumulated by the Soviet Union is a potential instrument of counter-leverage. Sen. Strom Thurmond (R.-S.C.) warned Congress that "U.S. policymakers should never lose sight of the fact that these huge outstanding Soviet debts to our banks serve to compromise needed policy decisions for fear of endangering payment." A study by the Heritage Foundation observes that "the only hope the Western banks seem to have of being repaid is to continue to foster East-West trade. The great danger is that a Communist payment failure could start a banking panic in the West."[2] The second major constraint on the United States lies in the political pressure exerted on the White House by both government agencies (especially the State and Commerce departments) and private corporations that have a vested interest in East-West trade. Similar pressures from the NATO allies constitute still another constraint.

As in every other facet of the detente process, the trade and economic sphere contains glaring asymmetries. First of all, foreign trade is a state monopoly in the Soviet Union. It is conducted by state-controlled organizations that exercise political direction and also enjoy exclusive access to statistical and related information. On the American side, by contrast, government agencies help to coordinate and regulate trade and financial matters, particularly vis-a-vis the Soviet bloc; but a plethora of corporations and smaller enterpises in the private sector conduct their own foreign transactions and compete against each other to proffer the most favorable terms to foreign customers. Moreover, information about supply and demand, about the characteristics of items for sale, and about general economic (and political) conditions that bear on export policy are readily available to Soviet and East

European officials—who then may manipulate them to advantage, as in the "Great Grain Robbery" of 1972.

U.S. business representatives cannot stroll through the halls of the Soviet foreign trade ministry or make direct approaches to purchasing agents for Soviet enterprises the way Soviet officials prowl the Congressional corridors in search of contacts and information. "Trying to get a Soviet official on the telphone is hard enough," says one Westerner in Moscow. "'He's not here' can mean he's out for three minues, three hours, or three months—there are no explanations." Another laments that "just finding out the name of the right official to call can be a giant problem."[3] The Soviets have neither a comprehensive, up-to-date telephone book nor a complete listing of the organizations involved in foreign trade. Moreover, Western business representatives and commercial offices in the Soviet capital are kept physically isolated in hotels, offices and apartment complexes reserved for foreigners so that business relationships with Soviet citizens do not shade into friendships. Published Soviet trade statistics are so sparse and appear so irregularly that a U.S. specialist on East-West trade claims to be forced into the realm of "economic archeology" in a search for data.[4]

Ironically, the Soviets frequently rely on Western sources for vital information about their own country. For example, Soviet agricultural officials have difficulty obtaining timely and accurate forecasts of crop yields because the operators of reconnaissance satellites that gather such information are reluctant to disseminate data through non-military channels. Thus, the KGB instructs its agents in the United States who pose as diplomatic and commercial personnel to seek Soviet crop data acquired by U.S. overhead photography![5]

Also of interest is the fact that "the Russians have been extremely reluctant to divulge information on plant operations—let alone to allow American technicians to visit the plants for which they have been asked to design systems."[6] The reason for this hesitancy, aside from the obsession with secrecy that pervades all areas of Soviet society, evidently lies in the fact that virtually every enterprise in the Soviet Union is geared at least partially for military-related production. Miles Costick, head of the Washington-based Institute on Strategic Trade, observed that "it is virtually impossible to identify a single industry in the USSR which manufactures only civilian goods. Every institute, every R&D facility, every educational institution, every factory has its 'first section,' staffed by military and KGB representatives." As far back as 1933, Zara Witkin, an American engineer who supervised construction of some industrial enterprises during the first Soviet Five-Year Plan, told a U.S. Consul in Poland that every tractor plant "is of course a tank factory, and an automobile plant [is] a factory which may at any time produce mobile artillery."[7]

Philosophical and ideological divergencies between Russia and the West constitute still another barrier to the use of trade as a lubricating mechanism for detente. Protectionism notwithstanding, the United States remains committed in principle to the unimpeded flow of trade and to its value in enhancing the vigor of the free enterprise system. The Soviet Union, however, proclaims its commitment to "bury" the capitalist system and is determined to prevent Western imports from becoming wedges to pry apart the Socialist monolith.

From the time of Peter the Great, Russia has sought to import and imitate Western industrial and scientific achievements while screening out the politico-economic milieu that gave impetus to such accomplishments. Peter himself was especially interested in "borrowing" Western equipment and technology to strengthen Russia's military capacity. Later Tsars also sought to import the fruits of the Western industrial and scientific revolution to narrow the gap between Russia and the advanced capitalist countries. During the 1890's, Count Sergei Witte, who served as an adviser to Alexander III and Nicholas II, tested Western willingness to furnish capital and expertise on a giant scale to modernize the Russian economy. The Western countries' response exceeded his wildest expectations. "Why would they create with their own hands an even more terrible rival?" Witte wrote in a memo to Tsar Nicholas, "For me, it is evident that, in giving us capital, foreign countries commit a political error, and my only desire is that their blindness continue for as long as possible."[8]

British, French, Belgian, German and Dutch capital and technology developed the coal, iron, steel, chemical, textile and other industries of pre-war Russia. Among the monuments to their efforts are the Trans-Siberian Railway and the Donets Basin mining and metallurgical complex known as Yuzovka, in honor of John Hughes, its English underwriter. American enterprises that participated in the Russian bonanza included International Harvester, which became the largest manufacturer of agricultural equipment in pre-revolutionary Russia, and the Singer Sewing Machine Co., "which had holdings worth over $100 million and employed a sales force in Russia of more than 27,000 people in 1914."[9] The bulk of Western capital investment, however, flowed into the oil sector. The Nobel brothers of Sweden developed the oilfields of Baku, along the Caspian Sea, that helped to propel Russia into the top spot among the world's oil producers.

In 1918 Lenin wrote in *The Immediate Tasks of the Soviet Government* that "the possibility of building Socialism depends exactly upon our success in combining Soviet power and the Soviet organization of administration with the up-to-date achievements of capitalism." Lenin spent a substantial portion of his life in the West, spoke German and English, and had a far greater insight into the mentality of Western businessmen than of Russian peasants. After the revolution, he exhorted his Bolshevik comrades to "learn to trade" with the West in order to revitalize the Soviet economy. In 1920 Lenin wrote that

> We must be clever enough, by relying on the peculiarities of the capitalist world and exploiting the greed of the capitalists for raw materials, to extract from it such advantages as will strengthen our economic position—however strange this may appear—among capitalists.[10]

In a speech to the AFL-CIO on 30 June 1975, Aleksandr Solzhenitsyn declared that "Lenin foretold this whole process" by which "the Western capitalists would "compete with each other to sell us goods."

> And in a difficult moment, at a party meeting in Moscow Lenin] said: "Comrades, don't panic; when things go very hard for us, we will give a rope to the bourgeoisie, and the bourgeoisie will hang itself." Then, Karl Radek . . . said: "Vladimir Ilyich, but where are we going to get enough rope to hang the whole bourgeoisie?" Lenin effortlessly replied: "They'll supply us with it."

Lenin's dictum that when the time comes to hang the capitalist class, its members will compete with each other to "sell us the rope" may be apocryphal, but the underlying attitude it conveys is manifest. Subsequently, wags have opined that if the Communists could not afford to buy enough rope to hang the entire capitalist class, the capitalists would lend them the requisite money.

That Lenin said "Communism equals Soviet power plus the electrification of the whole country" is not in dispute. Nor is the fact that Western assistance was necessary to transform the dream of "electrification" into reality. Lenin's acknowledgment of this fact was reflected in his injunction that "one cannot be satisfied with the collapse of capitalism. It is necessary to take all its science [and] technology. Without that, we will not be able to build Communism." The immediate objective of the fledgling Bolshevik regime, however, was to "get the country moving again," to borrow a phrase from later American history. War and revolution had left Russia paralyzed. The Allies seized all its gold and foreign reserves; thus, credits were unobtainable. The Communist regime expropriated all Western capital investment and financial assets. The economy simply collapsed. An American observer of the Soviet scene noted that the Bolshevik regime

> had to resort to clandestine sales of art and national treasure to finance its Communist International (Comintern) apparatus and diamond smuggling to support its diplomats. It even permitted its intelligence service to sell secret documents—both phony and real—to anti-Communist exile groups throughout the 1920's. [11]

*In extremis*, Lenin had to make a temporary ideological adjustment and supplant "War Communism" with the New Economic Policy (NEP). A limited private sector was introduced alongside the "commanding heights" of the economy, which remained under state control. During the course of the NEP, from 1921 to 1928, the Soviet Union invited Western enterprises to help develop the economy and promised them substantial profits. In view of Lenin's faith in "electrification," it was appropriate that General Electric became one of the U.S. firms to establish a "concession" in the Soviet Union; it moved rapidly to build power grids and laboratories. Other U.S. recipients of concessions included the Ford Motor Co., which supplied road and agricultural vehicles; the W.A. Harriman Co., which was permitted to seek and mine manganese; and International Barnsdall, which was involved in processing, producing and distributing oil. While these firms, along with European industries, were giving the Soviet economy a new lease on life, Lenin assured his Communist party colleagues that "concessions do not mean peace with capitalism, but [rather] war on a new plane."[12]

Stalin's liquidation of foreign concessions did not dampen the enthusiasm of Western businesses for assistance to the Soviet Union's first Five-Year Plan (1928-33). More than 300 foreign enterprises played a role. American business involvement in this massive industrialization scheme was extraordinary. Stalin later acknowledged during a conversation with Eric Johnston, president of the U.S. Chamber of Commerce, that two-thirds of the large industrial projects in the Soviet Union had been built with American assistance.[13]

. . . By 1933, there were no foreign manufacturing concessions left in the Soviet Union, even though many firms had signed contracts covering periods of 30 and even 50 years. Some of the concessions were closed down by force, but the more common methods were punitive taxation, breach of contract, legal harassment, and disruptions by workers. The largest concession of all, the British mining company Lena Goldfields Ltd. . . . was attacked as a "weed in the socialist system." The OGPU (secret police) raided its units, threw out many of its personnel, and jailed several of its leading technicians on charges of "industrial espionage." [14]

After Stalin's death, in 1953, the Kremlin sought new openings to the West. Nikita Khrushchev emphasized the political as well as the economic benefits that East-West trade could confer on the Soviet Union. "We value trade least for economic reasons and most for political reasons," he said. It was under the Brezhnev regime, however, that commerce between the USSR and the United States reached its apex.

In April 1973, a $20-billion agreement was signed by which the Soviet Union would provide Occidental Petroleum with one million metric tons of ammonia, potash and urea annually in return for phosphate fertilizer. Armand Hammer, the head of Occidental, whose family had business relations with the Soviet Union dating back to Lenin's time, persuaded President Nixon to grant Moscow a low-interest loan to build the factories, storage facilities, and pipelines needed to support his fertilizer project.

Nixon and Kissinger, as noted previously, looked upon detente as a web of interlocking Soviet-American relationships that could give the USSR a vested interest in maintaining global peace. Secretary Kissinger testified before the Senate Foreign Relations Committee that

By acquiring a stake in this network of relationships with the West, the Soviet Union may become more conscious of what it would lose by a return to confrontation . . . . Trade and investment leaven the autarkic tendencies of the Soviet system, invite gradual association of the Soviet economy with the world economy, and foster a degree of interdependence that adds an element of stability. . . .

Since Nixon represented the Republican Party, with its pro-business orientation, he was well placed to promote trade with the Soviets. His longstanding reputation as a warrior against Communism conferred on him special protection against critics who might charge the White House with selling out to the Russians. And his expressed desire for Soviet help in extricating the United States from an unwinnable war in Vietnam constituted an extra incentive for him to pursue all avenues toward detente.

The Johnson Administration had favored the promotion of East-West trade as part of its policy of "building bridges" to the Soviet bloc; but real strides in this direction awaited Nixon, who was undergirded by Kissinger's doctrine of "linkage." In 1969, shortly after Nixon took office, he signed into law the Export Administration Act, which liberalized the Export Control Act of 1949. The new legislation retained a ban on exports that would strengthen the USSR's military potential but omitted the constraints on improving its economic potential.

In 1971 the signing of a quadripartite accord regulating the status of Berlin, progress toward an arms control agreement, and the announcement that Brezhnev would host a superpower summit the following year put a bloom on Soviet-American relations and raised hopes for expanded East-West trade. At the 24th Congress of the Communist Party of the Soviet Union (CPSU), Brezhnev introduced his "peace program," which called for an across-the-board improvement in relations with the United States. This policy was based largely on Moscow's desire to reinvigorate the Soviet economy through the importation of advanced U.S. technology.

In November 1971, Maurice Stans became the first U.S. Secretary of Commerce ever to visit the USSR. He came home to recommend U.S. participation in the construction of a huge Soviet truck factory on the Kama River. The White House approved a large number of licenses for the export of machine tools and other equipment for the Kama River plant. In the spring of 1972, the United States and the USSR concluded a $130-million grain deal—the first between the two countries since 1963.

Trade and economic relations evidently ranked high on the agenda of the Nixon-Brezhnev summit of May 1972, although the arms control agreements signed there captured all the headlines. The two leaders established a Joint Soviet-American Commercial Commission to promote and facilitate future transactions. Total trade turnover at the time was running about $200 million annually—less than 1 percent of total U.S. trade. On 7 July a deal was concluded by which the Soviet Union agreed to purchase from private grain dealers $750 million worth of U.S. grain during the next three years, with $200 million to be bought during the first year. With the exception of the wartime Lend-Lease program, this was the largest Soviet-American commercial arrangement to date. It involved a U.S. commitment to extend credit facilities to the USSR (through the Commodity Credit Corporation) up to the amount of the total purchase, but no more than $500 million would be outstanding at any one time. Interest was pegged at the regular commercial rate of six-and-one-eighth percent.

It is worth noting that, according to Frank Drozek, head of the Seafarers' Union, the Soviets valued the accord less for the grain (for which other suppliers existed) than for the access it provided to 42 U.S. ports. In earlier decades, when Communist Party members played a key role in American dockworkers' unions, the Soviets had been able to foment strikes and agitation along the U.S. waterfront. Although anti-Communist trade unionists had regained control of the waterfront by the 1970's, the Soviets evidently still hoped to use their presence in U.S. ports to disseminate propaganda and perhaps pave the way for future subversion.

Ten days after the conclusion of the grain accord, Secretary of Commerce Peter G. Peterson, co-chairman of the newly established Joint Soviet-American Commercial Commission, led a delegation to Moscow to work out a comprehensive trade pact. Peterson purported to see "great promise" in the creation of joint enterprises to tap Soviet sources of energy and raw materials. He subsequently expressed hope for creating "a vested economic interest in peace" even while ideological rivalry persists.[15]

The "Great Grain Robbery" that the Soviets perpetrated in the summer of 1972 abruptly clouded the post-summit atmosphere and became a campaign issue in Nixon's quest for re-election. Despite the damage that bad weather had visited on their wheat fields, there was no doubt about the government's ability to feed the population adequately. Imports were needed rather to sustain the livestock herds at current levels. Dealing with a handful of American grain trading organizations, each of which was led to believe that it was the sole potential seller, the Soviets purchased more than 17 million metric tons of wheat and corn (worth more than $1 billion) in less than five weeks. Some of the grain was sold at prices subsidized by the U.S. government. When the full scale of the Soviet purchase came to light, grain prices soared and the American consumer suffered.

A number of other highly significant Soviet-American commercial transactions occurred during the early 1970's, involving such strategically valuable items as computers, microelectronic circuitry (an industry that had just come into its own in the United States), precision instruments, and seismic equipment. Items that the Kremlin was unable to obtain through regular commercial channels found their way to the USSR through middlemen (mainly in the United States or Western Europe), dummy corporations, other diversion schemes, or outright theft. For example, Undersecretary of State William Schneider Jr. noted that "the Soviets illegally acquired IBM 360 and 370 mainframe computers from the West in 1972. We have noted to our despair that the Soviet RYAD computer series uses the same repair manuals as the IBM. . . . "[16] The RYAD I and II computers not only perform a number of basic tasks throughout the Soviet economy; they also are believed to be the mainstay of the Warsaw Pact's air defense system.[17] In 1972 Soviet espionage agents at a trade fair in Switzerland stole a sophisticated computer manufactured by the U.S. firm of Hewlett-Packard. A precise replica of the computer reportedly controls the ten MIRV'ed warheads on the Soviet SS-18 "heavy" missile.[18]

West European firms were as eager as their American counterparts to reap the benefits of trade with the Soviet bloc. Datasaab of Sweden, for example, sold the USSR an automated air traffic control system, purportedly for use at Moscow's Vnukovo airport. The system, which contains U.S.-manufactured integrated circuitry, was sent to the Soviets with Commerce Department approval. Pentagon officials opposed the sale, however, because the system can detect any type of airborne object (even if it emits no radio signal), calculate its flight path, and predict its location at a specific moment in the future.[19] West German enterprises have sold the Russians sophisticated machinery to treat titanium, which has been a crucial component of the newer, quieter generation of Soviet submarines—notably the titanium-hulled Typhoon, which is nearly twice as large as the American Trident boats.[20]

Probably the most controversial item in the category of Soviet-American trade during the Carter Administration involved the sale by Dresser Industries of Dallas of a $144-million turnkey plant for the production of deep-well oil drilling equipment. Included in the proposed sale was a computerized electronic beam welding machine for manufacturing drill bits. The welder, however, could also be used in the manufacture of jet aircraft and to make armor-piercing shells. Carter's contention that the Soviet Union could acquire the Dresser technology from other foreign sources was demolished when a Defense Science Board task force headed by J. Fred Bucy, president of Texas Instruments, attested that the technologies involved were "solely concentrated in the United States."[21] Another pro-trade argument held that the Dresser deal could help the Soviets to develop their own energy supplies and thus dampen their alleged temptation to launch an attack against the oil-rich Persian Gulf.

On 3 October 1979 the Carter Administration approved record grain purchases for the USSR. Not long afterward, the Soviets invaded Afghanistan, and Carter announced punitive economic measures. However, they applied to only a fraction of the East-West trade in industrial equipment and technology. The chief sanction was suspension of grain deliveries above the level (6-8 million tons annually) provided for in a five-year grain accord that was then in its fourth year. Thus, 17 million tons that Moscow had ordered in excess of that amount were embargoed The Soviet Union obtained from other suppliers the amount of grain withheld by the United States; but it had to pay higher prices for lower quality (especially from Argentina), and shipping delays created difficulties and necessitated some distress slaughtering of livestock herds.[22] This situation threw a monkey wrench into Brezhnev's plans to improve the Soviet meat supply, which were designed in part to forestall the type of workers' protests against food shortages that Poland had experienced. The 1980 Soviet grain harvest was only 189 million tons, and the prospect of another long, harsh winter for Soviet families loomed. *The Economist* noted that "a combination of Soviet agricultural incompetence and pure bad luck with the weather is giving the American embargo some unexpected muscle, despite the unwillingness of other grain-exporting countries to back it up."[23] On 22 October 1980 Moscow officially reduced its economic growth targets for the next year to 4.1 percent—the smallest planned increase since World War II.

The grain embargo became a campaign issue in the 1980 presidential election. Typical of Republican candidate Ronald Reagan's stance was a speech in the Iowa grain belt in which he said Carter was imperiling the future of the family farm by "grandstanding for the American people at your expense."[24] He also took exception to the embargo on the grounds that U.S. farmers should not be "punished" for Soviet transgressions in Afghanistan. The Reagan Administration duly cancelled the grain embargo in the spring of 1981.

By 1985, the year of Reagan's first summit with the Soviets, the Republican Administration had all but eliminated the sanctions opposed by Jimmy Carter in the aftermath of Afghanistan. Ronald Reagan, belying his "hard-line" image and rhetoric, had presided over the signing of a new long-term U.S.-Soviet grain agreement (with a clause prohibiting embargoes), authorized an increase in nonstrategic trade (loosely defined), renewed Soviet fishing privileges in U.S. territorial waters, and expanded Soviet-American exchanges across the board. He also had rebuffed pressures to declare Poland in default on its international debts and had approved the rescheduling arrangement worked out by Western banks.

The President, in concert with the Coordinating Committee for Multilateral Export Controls (COCOM), to which most of the NATO allies and Japan belonged, managed to curtail the illicit transfer of high-tech computers and other very sophisticated items; but these represented only a "narrow band on the spectrum" of equipment and technology flowing to the Soviet bloc. As for the rest, wrote William Safire, "it was during the Reagan Administration that the floodgates were opened." Safire observed, for example, that Reagan and his fellow "hardliners" had failed to support efforts to move 17 oil and gas exploration items with important strategic applications out of the State Department's lax jurisdiction onto the Defense Department's national security export-control list. The upshot of the Reagan Administration's policy, wrote Safire, "is not merely 'business as usual' with the Russians, but 'better business than ever.'"[25]

In May 1985 the Joint Governmental Commercial Commission met for the first time in seven years. The meeting occurred not long after Soviet military personnel shot Maj. Arthur D. Nicholson Jr., a member of the U.S. liaison unit in East Germany, and let him bleed to death. Defense Secretary Weinberger's pleas to cancel the trade talks were to no avail. Commerce Secretary Baldrige met in the Kremlin with Gorbachev, who declared that it was "high time to defrost the potential of Soviet-American cooperation." [26]

In June 1985 Undersecretary of Commerce Lionel Olmer led a delegation to Moscow to reopen high-level trade talks between the United States and the USSR, which had been suspended since the Soviet invasion of Afghanistan. The Americans sought to partake of the lucrative contracts that the Kremlin was dangling in front of Western businessmen in connection with the upcoming 1986-90 Five-Year Plan. According to the report issued upon Olmer's return, "the Soviet delegation believed that a very large incrase in trade could take place if the United States would grant MFN and credits, limit its export controls, and guarantee contract sanctity."[27] The American delegation, evidently ready to leap at the chance to give away the store, exclaimed that "the Soviet interest is particularly striking in that the Soviets remained positive and non-polemical despite the blunt U.S. statements on the need for human rights improvements."[28]

In August 1985 Secretary of Agriculture Block traveled to Moscow on a weeklong mission to promote Soviet purchases of U.S. farm products. Reagan authorized the journey despite recent disclosures that the Soviet secret police had dusted U.S. diplomats in the USSR with a "potentially harmful" chemical powder in order to keep track of their movements and contacts. On the eve of his departure from Washington, Block took note of the "spy dust" scandal but demurred that it would "probably not be appropriate" for an agricultural official to raise it during his discussions in the Soviet Union.[29] State Department spokesman Charles E. Redman conceded that the Soviet use of chemical tracing agents was "a serious issue," but he expressed hope that it would not jeopardize "mutually beneficial bilateral cooperation."[30]

There was no concrete progress on the trade issue (or any other) during the long-awaited Reagan-Gorbachev summit in November, but the day after it ended Gorbachev called for U.S. business investment in the Soviet Union. He told journalists that "we should appreciate the importance of economics in our relationship. If we trade with each other more, we will depend on each other more."[31] A month afterward, American advocates of increased trade seized the impetus that the new "spirit of Geneva's" brief afterglow provided. On 8 December the "Clipper Business Summit," a chartered Pan Am jumbo jet, landed in Moscow with members of the US-USSR Trade and Economic Council aboard. This was the largest such group ever to participate in Soviet-American trade talks. The plane's arrival was symbolic in itself, for direct flights between the countries had been suspended after the Soviets shot down a South Korean jetliner with 269 passengers (including many Americans) in 1983. Baldrige led the delegation, which was composed of more than 400 businessmen constituting a virtual Who's Who of chief executive officers. Among the companies represented were Dow Chemical, General Electric, IBM, Du Pont, Armco, Dresser Industries, Pepsi, Coke, Monsanto, Occidental Petroleum,Ralston Purina, and Salomon Brothers. Mayor Dianne Feinstein of San Francisco also attended; her city houses a Soviet consulate, which cultivates the high-tech denizens of Silicon Valley.

James H. Giffen, president of Mercator Corp. (a New York banking and trading company) and of the US-USSR Trade and Economic Council, declared that "there is a great trade potential. The question is how the hell you spring it loose."[32] Gorbachev offered some suggestions. Addressing a banquet in honor of the delegation, he declared that the United States would have to resume Ex-Im Bank credits and restore MFN status to the Soviet Union, as well as loosen restrictions on the sale of non-military technology, if it wanted trade to expand. He also denounced Washington for resorting to sanctions and trade embargoes. "In our dangerous world, we simply cannot afford to neglect, nor have we the right to do so, the stabilizing factors in relations, such as trade and economic, scientific and technolocigal ties," said Gorbachev.[33] He asserted that a removal of the abovementioned "political obstacles" to improved commercial ties would enable U.S. enterprises to compete for sizable, long-term contracts in Soviet energy development, agribusiness, and overall industrial modernization. However, the General Secretary cautioned that "we are not going to beg the United States for anything."[34]

Gorbachev held a private meeting with Baldrige, who reminded him that the 1985 Export Act had strengthened the inviolability of contracts and that the Reagan Administration had removed certain categories of high-technology items from its list of restricted exports. The Commerce Secretary also hinted that the Reagan Administration was amenable to a revision of the Jackson-Vanik Amendment, which links increased trade and credits to more liberal Soviet emigration policies, but "we couldn't get it through Congress" at the present time.[35] The American members of the Council evidently believed that Washington should be more forthcoming, however. During a press conference in Moscow on 9 December, Giffen declared that "many of us are asking whether we have used the stick long enough and whether we should start to use the carrot. After all, ten years [of restrictions] have not got us much."[36] Giffen contended that the Soviets still regarded the United States as an unreliable trade partner that was likely to resort to future embargoes. However, *Pravda* averred that better Soviet-American trade relations would create the "material fabric . . . for building up an atmosphere of trust."[37]

As Washington was preparing for the summit, *The Wall Street Journal* reported from the grain trading capital of Chicago that "the Soviet Union has violated a long-term grain agreement with the United States for the first time since such agreements were initiated in 1975."[38] During the fiscal year ending on 1 October 1985, the Soviets purchased a record 18.6 million metric tons of corn—nearly four times the amount mandated by the agreement—but it fell short by 1.1 million metric tons in wheat purchases. American wheat farmers lost $100 million from the Soviet default, but the U.S. government failed to censure Moscow.

As the end of the 1986 fiscal year approached, the USSR again indulged in grain maneuvers, apparently trying to coax the United States into lowering wheat prices. American wheat farmers lost about $500 million as a result of a new Soviet default. Reagan, under pressure from grain-state Congressmen in a crucial election involving control of the Senate, took action. Not only did he disavow the injunction of the longshoremen's union chief Teddy Gleason that "you can't fight them and feed them"; he allowed them to partake of a subsidy program. By means of the Bonus Incentive Commodity Export Program (Bicep), the United States gives foreign buyers a bonus shipment from stockpiles of government-owned surplus grain as an inducement to make commercial purchases. The President had used his discretionary authority to exclude Communist countries, however. Senate Majority Leader Robert Dole (R.-Kan.) took the initiative in legislation to lift the ban on subsidized agricultural sales to the USSR and China ("Soviets on the Dole," exclaimed a *Wall Street Journal* editorial). The legislation, in the form of an amendment to a bill on the Export-Import Bank, cleared the Senate in late July and was approved by President Reagan on 1 August.

Reagan defended his approval for subsidized sales of four million metric tons of wheat to the Soviet Union (the minimum required under the long-term grain accord) by claiming that the alternative was to stockpile the grain and hurt the American farmer by depressing prices. Shultz, however, called the subsidy "ridiculous" and declared that the Soviets "must be chortling" and "scratching their heads" over obtaining U.S.-produced food for less than American housewives would have to pay.[38] Shultz also opposed undermining friendly competitors, such as Australia, Canada and Argentina, in the sale of grain to the Russians. Amid the furor, *The Wall Street Journal* cautioned that " . . . the Soviet tactics in exploiting the U.S. . . . should not go unnoticed. The Soviets once again have reneged on a contract obligation when it suited their purpose, a habit we cannot remind arms-control fanatics of often enough."[40]

In their commercial transactions with the capitalist world, the Soviets have kept the faith with Lenin's dictum that "when you live among wolves, you must howl like a wolf." Marshall Goldman of Harvard University's Russian Research Center once asked the director of the Soviet central bank how officials are trained to carry on foreigh trade. "It's very simple," the bank official replied. "We tell them to do exactly the opposite of what they do at home."[41]

Capitalist wiles aside, Soviet traders operate from a highly advantageous position. "Ironically, the very centralization that makes the Soviet economy inefficient at home increases [Soviet] clout abroad." For example, a retired U.S. grain trader who has dealt with the Soviets points out that "no more than half a dozen people buy all the grain for Russia."[42] In the commodities trade, in particular, the USSR can be virtually unassailable. As *The Wall Street Journal* points out, "the Soviets . . . are the largest players in commodities ranging from palladium to wheat," and they "have the closest thing to inside information in the commodity trade. . . . They alone know what they will do."[43]

In their quest for Western technology, the Soviets have displayed equal shrewdness. They have played off potential suppliers against each other with unmatched zeal and have shamelessly exploited the naivete of many American officials and the disarray in U.S. government agencies responsible for stemming the hemorrhage of technology to the Soviet bloc. Soviet foreign trade agencies have built up "a vast network of influence" to grease the wheels of East-West trade "even when security needs in the West demand policy adjustments."[44]

It is difficult to avoid the conclusion that East-West trade, particularly the sale to the USSR of turnkey projects and sophisticated equipment and technology, has produced opposite effects from what proponents of detente envisaged. Far from enmeshing the Soviet Union in a Kissingerian "web of constructive relationships" that might "leaven the autarkic tendencies of the Soviet system" and foster its integration into the international economy, Western exports have reinforced both autarky and totalitarianism. First of all, as previously noted, Western imports supply the "missing dynamic" in the totalitarian system, enabling the Communist economy to postpone internal reform.

Secondly, by providing "turnkey" plants and training Soviet personnel in their operation, the West has contributed to economic self-sufficiency in the USSR. Thirdly, by helping the USSR to overcome its economic inefficiency and sluggish growth, Western equipment and technology enable it to improve the consumer sector (however slightly) while still sinking the bulk of its investments into the military. The Kremlin obtains both guns and butter. Thus, Western inputs help stave off discontent among the Soviet population that eventually could lead to political unrest. Dr. Igor S. Glagolyev, a senior researcher in the Soviet Academy of Sciences who was granted political asylum in the United States in 1976, declared that "Soviet society would be confronted with intolerable strains without all the assistance [they] have received from Western countries."[45] While the infusion of Western products and technology has postponed the day—possibly *ad infinitum*—when Moscow must undertake major reallocations of its resources from the military to the civilian economy, the massive imports of U.S. grain enable the Soviets to maintain collectivized agriculture—a hallmark of the totalitarian system.

In addition to bolstering Soviet political control at home, the pattern of East-West trade has helped the Kremlin to maintain its domination of Eastern Europe. For one thing, the influx of Western goods and technology into the Soviet bloc helps improve living standards there, thus keeping the populations quiescent and stabilizing the local Communist regimes—all to the benefit of the Soviet Union. For another thing, the West has refrained from demanding a political payoff in the form of a longer Soviet leash on the satellites in exchange for more trade. Western exports to the Soviets of oil and gas drilling technology are especially counterproductive to the purported U.S. goal of fostering liberalization within the Soviet bloc. By boosting output with the help of foreign equipment, the Soviets can more easily supply energy to the East Europeans (with resulting political leverage) and still produce enough to sell in Western markets for the hard currency needed to invest in military-related production.

The Soviets have displayed increasing skill and ability in copying Western processes and finished products that eventually could flood European and Third-World markets and pose a stiff competitive challenge for Western producers. The mistaken assumption on the part of Western exporters that Soviet domestic needs would easily absorb the products of Western-built enterprises could cost them dearly. On a global scale, if the Soviet Union succeeds in unlocking Siberia's treasure house of energy and raw material resources during the coming decade with the assistance of Western (and Japanese) capital and technology, it will become a world power in more than just a military sense.

The arguments outlined above do not argue for a radical cutback in East-West trade, but only for what many Western officials have called commercial prudence. Virtually every product has dual—or multiple—uses. As Khrushchev once said, buttons can hold up a soldier's trousers. There also can be drawbacks to exporting certain goods, even though they have no military or strategic applications. A Polish dissident, for example, lamented that being arrested with handcuffs manufactured in the West is extremely disconcerting. However, "dual-use" technology in the sense that it has an important strategic military application should neither be exported as part of general East-West commercial transactions nor be utilized as a bargaining chip in trade negotiations. As for the desirability of conducting and even expanding nonstrategic trade with the USSR and the Soviet bloc, we should proceed with the caveat that it is one thing to trade with the Soviets and quite another thing to subsidize their economy.

The USSR will strive to increase substantially its borrowing from capitalist governments and banks in order to finance the imports of equipment and knowhow it needs to pursue Gorbachev's economic modernization program—not to mention the grain it requires to help feed the Soviet workers and the armed forces. Certainly, the Soviet economy is not the proverbial "basket case," and the country's creditworthiness is high by virtue of the variety and wealth of its natural resources.[46] Nevertheless, Moscow's economic and financial prospects are far from rosy, and Washington's possibilities for wresting political concessions in exchange for trade benefits probably are better now than they have been in some time.

On the agricultural front, it is still too early to predict the effects of the Chernobyl nuclear power plant disaster on food supplies in the Ukraine. This region, once the breadbasket of Russia, has grown enough agricultural produce in recent years to feed the local population and some other parts of European Russia. If a substantial portion of the land proves to be radioactive, large-scale food imports could be essential on a long-term basis.

Washington has been remiss in failing to use its agricultural bounty as leverage to pry concessions from Moscow. There are two major reasons for this phenomenon. First, a strong moral imperative leads many U.S. officials to shrink from using food as a weapon—or from waging "economic warfare" in any form. In the wake of Chernobyl, one can sense a fear that the United States would be accused of preying upon a human tragedy to play politics—despite the fact that American doctors played a major role in performing bone marrow transplants on victims of the accident. More importantly, however, the political clout of the American farmer constitutes a brake on any attempt by the government to curb grain sales to the Soviet Union.

As indicated above, the Reagan Administration moved to loosen some restrictions on non-strategic trade with the USSR, even while clamping down on the illicit transfer of technology. Since virtually every item of technology can be adapted for dual (civilian and military) use, the problem of differentiating nonstrategic from strategic trade is enormous. As with arms control, verification also is a problem. Many Soviet factories have both civilian and military production lines; and, short of on-site inspection on a regular basis, there is no way to determine how imported technology and equipment is utilized.

Another impediment in U.S. efforts to link trade with Soviet foreign policy behavior lies in the attitude of the West European allies. The Europeans remain committed to carrying on a robust trade with the Soviet bloc. Jobs and the health of many West European industrial enterprises still are closely tied to Eastern trade, and West Berlin relies on the USSR for virtually its entire supply of natural gas. Thus, the Soviets exercise both economic and psychological leverage over the European NATO allies. In particular, the Europeans worry that if they "provoke" the USSR, it could turn off the gas spigots or perpetrate a new Berlin crisis. Moreover, "our allies seem to perceive commerce with the Russians as a sign of healthy relations, as a portent of less tension to come."[47]

*The Economist* has stated that "East-West trade has turned out to be less of a constraint on Soviet adventurism abroad (as the theorists of linkage) expected) than on the West's willingness to block that adventurism."[48] Concern for the cohesiveness of NATO notwithstanding, Washington must not let its allies take the lead automatically on the East-West trade issue. The United States possesses unique leverage vis-a-vis the USSR: it is the largest and most desirable source of grain; it retains a monopoly of technology and knowhow in certain specialities, such as advanced oil recovery techniques, or at least a vast qualitative edge over other potential suppliers to the Soviets; and, with minor exceptions, it does not rely on customers in the Soviet bloc to alleviate unemployment or spur industrial production. U.S. leverage should be applied in order to raise the cost for Moscow, both literally and figuratively, of maintaining the totalitarian political system at home and the Soivet empire abroad. When he was President Reagan's senior Soviet affairs adviser, Richard Pipes stated quite correctly that "no responsible persons can have any illusions that it is in the power of the West to alter the Soviet system or to 'bring the Soviet economy to its knees.' What one can and ought to strive for is compelling the Soviet regime to bear the consequences of its own priorities."[49]

In addition, there is a moral and ideological dimension to this issue that generally is overlooked. By behaving precisely according to their caricature in Soviet propaganda, Western capitalists contribute to the Kremlin's efforts to portray them before the world as the greedy and corrupt leaders of a bourgeois class that consistently places profit above principle and politics above conscience. Insofar as Washington pursues business as usual with Moscow, despite such atrocities as the KAL shootdown and the rape of Afghanistan—not to mention the perpetuation of the Gulag Archipelago—it also gives credence to the Soviet stereotype of the U.S. government as the tool of the rapacious capitalists and the multinational corporations.

Presidential leadership is essential in formulating and implementing policies on East-West trade. It is essential first of all in order to provide coordination between the public and private sector in confronting the Soviet government monopoly over foreign trade. It also is necessary to mitigate the harmful effects of interagency squabbling among the Commerce, State, Defense, Justice and other departments that play a role in trade with the Soviet bloc. Finally, it is needed to provide continuity and to display firmness in the face of the vicissitudes of Congressional and public opinion. This is not to say that the President must run roughshod over conflicting opinions or, in the case of the Reagan and incoming Bush Administration, alienate big business and farmers—two key Republican constituencies. Nevertheless, the White House must give precedence to the national interest and emphasize that what is good for business is not always good for America. And in agriculture, it surely ought to be possible to devise programs for alleviating the farmers' financial plight without resorting to a policy that often has the doubly negative effect of subsidizing the Soviet Union and penalizing the American consumer.

As for the argument that trade promotes peace, innumerable studies have demonstrated that some of the bitterest wars in history—notably the two World Wars—were fought by opponents that carried on a thriving commercial relationship prior to the outbreak of hostilities. By the same token, the relative absence of trade need not promote or even reflect antagonisms that could lead to war. In the Soviet-American case, the economies simply are not symbiotic, and the United States established many of its trading patterns when Tsarist Russia and then the Soviet Union were relatively autarkic.

In contrast to America, the USSR is still self-sufficient to a great extent. Grain appears to be a major exception to the pattern, but the loss of grain imports probably would not prevent the Soviets from feeding their population. The loss would fall most heavily on livestock, with a consequent reduction of meat in the Soviet diet and on the capacity for storing grain for use in wartime. There is little evidence that a drop in the availability of meat would spark food riots of the type that convulsed Poland twice in the last decade. Moreover, the Soviets have displayed a remarkable ability to rally the poppulation around the flag of the motherland in times of crisis and to blame difficulties on foreign scapegoats.

Can the Soviet Union opt out of foreign trade altogether, retreating into virtual autarky and severing one of the links that the detente-minded West sought to bind into a Kissingerian "web of relationships"? History is on the side of those who would reply in the affirmative. Russia has aspired to be a great military power—not a commercial one. Ever since the era of Peter the Great, Russia has embarked on periodic buying and borrowing sprees in the West, only to retreat when its needs were satiated or international circumstances became unfavorable. The most recent spree occurred during the 1970's, when detente made the political climate congenial and when recession in the West, especially in Europe, enhanced the capitalists' desire to do business with the Soviet bloc. President Carter's sanctions in the wake of the Soviet invasion of Afghanistan and President Reagan's embargoes in the aftermath of the Soviet-inspired imposition of martial law in Poland put a damper on East-West trade, but the Soviets responded by stepping up their campaign to acquire Western equipment and technology through both legal and illegal channels.

Evidence indicates that if the Kremlin needs or wants an item badly enough, sooner or later it probably will succeed in obtaining it. Moreover, with every infusion of Western technology and knowhow, the Soviets themselves become more adept at producing sophisticated items. They also narrow progressively the technology gap, so that the importation of Western products and expertise becomes less urgent—although a continuing flow of spare parts and technical assistance for existing imports is essential.

It is noteworthy that in a speech to the 25th Communist Party Congress in February 1976, Premier Alexei Kosygin suggested the creation of an export sector of the Soviet economy. He envisioned it as a privileged sector, akin to defense, which would receive special treat-

ment in the provision of funds and managerial talent and would produce goods of higher quality than was the case in the rest of the
economy. Kosygin proposed the construction of enterprises geared
solely for the export of products to the West. The proposal seems
never to have gotten off the ground. A semi-autonomous export sector
would have had to obtain manpower and funding from managers and
bureaucrats in other segments of the economy, thus jeopardizing their
ability to meet planned production targets. It also would have had to
brave the wrath and jealousy of powerful officials in the defense sector. In addition, since the Soviet economic structure is so heavily com-
partmented, the Western technology acquired by the export sector
probably would have been unavailable to the overall civilian economy,
which must produce enough basic necessities to ensure minimal consumer satisfaction—and thus political quiescence. Economic issues
aside, the political side effects of a separate export sector were potentially momentous enough to give Soviet leaders pause:

> . . . by its very nature, an export sector would be linked to the economic
> and political world beyond the Soviet Union's closely guarded borders.
> The increased numbers of executives and managers who would be as-
> signed to it would of necessity spend long stretches of time living and
> working in the West, just as a carefully selected few do now. They would
> wheel and deal with Western businessmen. . . . socialize with them . . .
> dress like them, talk like them, and inevitably some would start to think
> like them. The possibility of ideological infection from prolonged contact
> with the Free World has always terrorized Soviet leaders . . . and in the
> end, they may be unwilling to risk the political hazards of trade. [50]

Thus, if they were faced to choose, the Soviets would be likely to
opt for autarky over trade-cum-fraternization.

Autarky is relative, however. As Marshall Goldman has pointed
out, "foreign trade still accounts for a small proportion of the total
gross national product of the USSR. Nevertheless, it is a key proportion in terms of earning the hard currency needed to pay for the technology that the Soviet Union apparently realizes it must have . . . to
become a true industrial nation."[51] In addition, as Carl Gershman
writes, "the one change that can be detected in the pattern of Soviet
trade relations with the West involves the absorption of Western technology, which no longer occurs at fitful intervals . . . but appears . . .
to have become an uninterrupted process."[52]

Unless a revolution of rising expectations deluges the Soviet population, the USSR could exist comfortably for some time with a mini-

mum of East-West trade. It can afford to wait out the West, in the anticipation that various constituencies in the democratic societies will press their governments to promote commerce with the Soviets. On the other hand, Gorbachev's regime does not appear content to await passively an expansion of commercial ties with the West. In his speech at the 27th Communist Party Congress, the General Secretary outlined plans for capital investments to the tune of some $270 billion to modernize and re-equip production lines during the 1986-90 Five-Year Plan.[53] Plans on this scale will require a significant amount of Soviet borrowing in the West.

The United States, for its part, can be expected to continue "selling the rope." Why? Perhaps it is simply "a blind faith in the virtues of East-West trade."[54] Perhaps American businessmen are mesmerized by the vision of a boundless Soviet market—much as they have been attracted to China. Lenin predicted correctly that

> . . . the capitalists of the whole world and their governments, in their rush to conquer the Soviet market, will close their eyes [to various Soviet diplomatic subterfuges] and will thereby be turned into blind deaf mutes. They will furnish credits which will serve us for the support of the Communist Party in their countries and, by supplying us material and technical equipment which we lack, will restore our military industry necessary for our future attacks against our suppliers. To put it in other words, they will work on the preparation of their own suicide.[55]

Marshall Goldman attested to the accuracy of Lenin's forecast when he wrote in 1975 that "otherwise cautious executives all but trample over one another in their effort to establish a foothold on this new [Soviet] frontier."[56]

The special humanitarian and political factors that motivate the United States to sell grain to the Soviet Union already have been discussed: using food as a weapon is morally repulsive to democratic societies, and American farmers are victims of their own success, in that huge surpluses depress prices. With regard to nonagricultural trade, numerous other motivational factors apply. First of all, Calvin Coolidge's credo that "the business of America is business" remains very much alive. Secondly, pure capitalist and corporate greed plays a role:

> There are always leaders of commerce who have the morals of the marketplace and whose political convictions are as flexible as the stock mar-

ket tape. Regarding the Soviet Union, they lack even the redeeming realism of the young lady from Kent.
Who said that she knew what it meant
When men took her to dine,
Gave her cocktails and wine;
She knew what it meant—but she went. [57]

Thirdly, the Soviets are generally regarded as reliable customers; trade has been interrupted more often by U.S.-imposed sanctions and embargoes than by Soviet reneging on contracts.

Still another factor is that many American businessmen have developed a vested interest in trade with the USSR—either because it is the last best hope for companies that are in a precarious financial condition or because a long history of commercial transactions has bred familiarity. A poll taken for *Fortune* magazine as far back as 1945 indicated that business leaders were the "most friendly" toward the Soviet Union of any U.S. interest group. Dwayne Andreas of the US-USSR Trade and Economic Council opined that "we have good relations, all the businessmen, with the Russians. They would rather talk with us anytime than [with] one of these diplomats, because we treat them decently; we don't go off and call them names."[58]

Yet another argument cited by advocates of increased trade with the East is that such trade consistently produces a surplus that can be used to offset partially the large deficits that the United States accumulates in commercial transactions with Japan and other important trading partners. Moreover, to the extent that trade with the Soviets helps provide jobs and markets for U.S. manufacturers—not to mention farmers—it can be statistically significant, especially during periods of recession.

Most of the factors listed above involve economic motivations for expanding East-West trade. There is also a broad category of political-cum-ideological arguments that trade advocates proffer. Some of these arguments posit a political payoff—in the form of less aggressive Soviet behavior—for increased trade. Others regard such a payoff as unimportant, unobtainable, or both.

Perhaps the most widely heard—if least comprehensible—expectation of a payoff resides in the notion that an influx of material goodies from the West will contribute to the growth of a consumer society in the USSR—a society that by its very nature will be peace-loving. This line of reasoning was put forth many years ago by advocates of "goulash Communism," a system that was supposed to spawn fat and therefore torpid and benevolent Communists. The other side of the argument is that rather than giving the bear more paunch, trade (especially when accompanied by generous Western credits) could give him more punch by freeing Soviet resources for the military. Indeed, during the 1970's, when detente was in full flower and the Soviet economy was booming (two facts not necessarily unrelated), Moscow's military buildup proceeded apace and intervention in the Third World reached new heights.

Other trade advocates have contended that the products of Western industry, particularly computers and electronic equipment, would entice the Kremlin to open up Soviet society and partake of the "information revolution." Although cassette players and other imported items have sped the flow of Western culture, as well as Soviet *samizdat*, throughout the country, Moscow has forbidden the sale of personal computers to unauthorized users and can be expected to tighten up ideological orthodoxy in direct proportion to the freer flow of goods and information from the West.

Those in the United States and elsewhere who call for an expansion of East-West trade irrespective of any specific quid pro quo embody a pseudo-pragmatic outlook that views U.S.-Soviet trade as desirable in itself. Averell Harriman once declared:

> It is unthinkable to me that our two great nations cannot work together in trade. I believe . . . that trade should not be linked with any other questions. Trade is not a gift from the United States to the Soviet Union. It is an outrage that for all these years we cannot have normal trade relations with the second greatest nation in the world. [59]

Robert D. Schmidt, Executive Vice President of Control Data Corp. and a member of the American Committee on East-West Accord, wrote in a foreward to a Committee publication,

> One reality we all should recognize is that there is no advantage in not doing business. Another is that we are not going to insure peace by trade alone. . . . But the strategic relationship is such that we must either live with the Soviets on this planet or die with them. There is no point in aggravating our relations by punitive trade policies which are politically ineffective and economically self-destructive.

A high official of Citibank inquired: "Who knows what political system works best? All we ask is if they pay their bills." Similarly, David Rockefeller, head of the Chase Manhattan Bank, remarked that Chase should not pose as a judge of foreign governments.[60] Maurice Stans, secretary of commerce in the Nixon Administration, disregarded the historical record in his enthusiasm for detente and proclaimed that countries that trade together stay together. Nixon himself has kept faith with Kissinger's theory of trade as part of the web of Soviet-American inter-relationships. In an article in *The New York Times* on 19 August 1982, the former President wrote that "the more we engage the Soviet Union in an intricate network of commercial relations, the more we increase its stake in peace." Armand Hammer asserts that

> . . . Trade is part of the dialogue between the United States and Russia, and it is crucial that we keep this dialogue going. The Soviet leadership is gradually coming to see trade, rather than confrontation with the West, as the way to improve economic conditions. If we are going to have peace, we should encourage the Soviet leadership in this direction. . . . In any event, if the United States refuses to sell the Soviet Union the products it needs, other countries will. [61]

Samuel Pisar, an international lawyer and vigorous advocate of detente, has adopted a somewhat similar view:

> Only the exchange of nonstrategic . . . goods and skills and increased contact between the two societies—industry to industry, company to company, man to man—can help draw the poison of mutual fear and distrust from Soviet-American relations. During the aborted detente of the 1970's, business managers on both sides demonstrated that they can cross ideological barriers more effectively than diplomats and politicians. [62]

The fact that the Soviets themselves have firmly rejected the so-called "convergence theory" does not seem to disturb these detentists at all.

Donald Kendall, head of Pepsico and a close confidante of President Nixon, has stated that he would "never" abandon his faith in the efficacy of commerce to mellow Moscow because

> the alternatives are God-awful. I don't want to see the world blown up. I think that regardless of how long it takes, we have to try to find a way to communicate with the Soviets, and I happen to think trade is a very good way to do that. [63]

George Will assailed Kendall's hypothesis with his usual cogency:

> Kendall's doctrine . . . implies a peculiar theory of Soviet motivation. What missile now deployed would not be deployed, what Cuban soldier

now in Africa would be at home, what nation now being molested would have gone unmolested—Afghanistan? Poland?—if trade had flourished? Is the theory that disappointment about trade caused the Kremlin to pout and have a tantrum? [64]

Finally, the argument that trade is morally and ideologically neutral is heard often by advocates of increased East-West commercial relations. However,

> . . . the fact . . . that trade is used as a way to obtain the technology needed for rapid modernization means, in the context of a command economy, that it is frequently associated with forced industrialization and the use of slave labor. The program of Westernization under Peter the Great was achieved at the cost of immense sacrifice and suffering imposed on the Russian people. Two centuries later, Stalin's first Five-Year Plan, which marked another period of intense absorption of Western technology, took an even greater toll in freedom and human life. [65]

As for the alleged ideological neutrality of the trade process, one cannot emphasize often enough that in the USSR nothing is divorced from ideology. Trade, with its concomitant transfer of technology, helps to sustain the Communist dictatorship rather than fostering reform and liberalization. This is the logical outcome when one conducts commercial relations with a regime that puts the maintenance of political control above economic development on its scale of priorities:

> The argument is . . . made . . . that the Soviet Union must liberalize its system in order to solve its economic problems, and that increased exposure to our superior economic methods will encourage Soviet leaders to take this course. This argument might be valid if the Soviet leaders were interested in nothing more than promoting economic efficiency and technological innovation. But they also have a stake in maintaining their totalitarian system, a system which is inherently inefficient and uncreative. If this fundamental contradiction were allowed to work itself out, it might conceivably lead to real reforms inside Russia, but Soviet leaders have been able to avoid the choice between reform and stagnation precisely by turning to the West for totalitarianism's "missing dynamic.". . . . The strategic as well as the moral implications of this fact have thus far been ignored. . . . [66]

Trade and economic carrots from the West notwithstanding, the Soviet Union will remain true to its history, its ideology, and its insistence that detente must be accompanied by an intensification of the international class struggle. As noted above, trade and technology transfer help free Soviet resources for military uses and for the search and exploitation of new targets of opportunity for aggrandizement. For, as Rep. Jim Courter (R.-N.J.) points out, "By now it should be clear to the Soviets that any sanctions we impose in response to their periodic crimes will be temporary measures, designed to appease public opinion."[67] Courter adds that "the supreme long-term interest that is sacrificed by the dismantling of the Afghanistan and Poland sanctions is American credibility and firmness of purpose." The United States needs these attributes in abundance if it is to restore a modicum of symmetry to the detente process. On a broader level, however, one must heed the admonition of Lawrence Brady, a former high official in the Commerce Department, that "the era of economic detente saw the Soviets undertake the largest military buildup in history—all supported by the high-technology giveaways of the United States and its allies."[68] It follows that Washington must shift the pendulum away from economic detente and toward a prudent economic containment.

# 4

# The European Allies and Detente

Since the time of the Bolshevik Revolution, a desire to exercise predominant influence over Western Europe has been the Kremlin's top foreign policy objective. The era of detente in the 1970's offered very favorable opportunities for the pursuit of this goal. West Germany became the key.

In 1969, West Germany's Social Democratic Party (SPD), in alliance with the small Free Democratic Party, won control of the Federal government for the first time in 40 years. Willy Brandt, a longtime leader of the Socialist International, became Chancellor. An architect of *Ostpolitik* ("Eastern policy"), Brandt advocated reconciliation with Eastern Europe and the Soviet Union. In the early 1970's he signed treaties with East Germany, Poland, and the USSR that essentially laid to rest the legacy of World War II and permitted political and economic detente to flower.

This series of accords gave new impetus to detente at a time when the Nixon Administration was actively seeking better Soviet-American relations. Detente in the European incarnation had its own peculiar wellsprings, however. The geopolitical, historical, economic and ideological imperatives that drove many West European capitals toward closer links with Moscow differed sharply from those that motivated Washington. The depth and variety of those imperatives accounted for European efforts to preserve the Continent as an oasis of detente long after superpower relations soured.

Having been consigned by geography to exist in the shadow of the Soviet bear, Western Europe long ago acknowledged the need to seek a modus vivendi with its huge neighbor. One need not subscribe to the "better Red than dead" axiom to recognize Europe's perceived need for some type of accommodation—as distinct from appeasement—vis-a-vis the largest and most powerful creature in the woods. Several U.S. commentators have observed that Europe's proximity to the Soviet Union fosters a hostage-type mentality akin to the so-called Stockholm syndrome, in which victims of terrorists sympathize and identify with their captors. Walter Laqueur, among others, argues, however, that such an attitude need not be preordained as a result of Europe's geography:

> . . . The fact that Cuba is less than a hundred miles from the American mainland and that its protector is far away has not notably influenced Castro's foreign policy. . . . Even Albania, not a giant among nations, has not hesitated to stand up against all its neighbors. The problem is not so much geographical as an issue of . . . steadfastness. . . . in short, the character of European political leaders and elites. Europe's weakness is largely a matter of self-perception, but for all that it is quite real. [1]

The United States, by contrast, views the Soviet Union from behind a buffer of two oceans and from the perspective of a country that has not suffered a foreign invasion since the British burned Washington in the War of 1812.

Economic and trade relations between Western Europe and the USSR, which have flourished under detente, are far more significant than those between the Americans and the Soviets—and far more balanced. A complementary pattern exists, whereby the Soviet Union exports raw materials and energy and imports manufactured goods and equipment from the West. With the important exception of grain, however, the United States has not exported sizable quantities of any commodity to the Soviet Union; imports of Soviet items have been

negligible. To some extent, the desire of several West European countries to expand their markets in Eastern Europe has given an added
impetus to detente, while the decline in U.S.-West European trade
(along with disputes over high American interest rates and related
trade and financial issues) has strained transatlantic ties. Washington's
requests for its NATO allies to increase defense spending have irri-
tated the West Europeans, whose economies are generally less than
robust, who face strong pressures for maintaining social welfare programs, and who are skeptical over the Soviet threat to boot. Moreover, Reagan's "supply-side" economics are viewed as irrelevant to
Europe's problems. Virtually all West European governments accept
the necessity for economic interventionism to help counter sluggish
growth at home and stiff competition for markets and raw materials
abroad.

On the ideological plane, West European nations are inclined to
fault Washington for placing every international problem in an East-
West context, with anti-Communist overtones that many Europeans
find inappropriate—if not downright unfashionable. The intellectual
climate in most of Western Europe has been receptive to Marxism
(although a sea-change appears to be underway in France). However,
Europe traditionally has been more comfortable than the United
States with collectivist philosophies, and the contrast has sharpened
since Ronald Reagan took office.

The advent of the Reagan Administration coincided with—and to
some extent was facilitated by—the decline in the influence of the so-
called Eastern Establishment, whose liberal internationalist foreign
policy outlook was congruent with that of the West Europeans. Reagan set the country on a more militantly nationalist course, which represented an effort to overcome the "Vietnam syndrome" but also
reflected a unilateralist, go-it-alone approach that appeared indifferent
to the concerns of the Western allies. With specific regard to Reagan's
Soviet policy, many West European officials expressed concern that
Washington had embarked on an ideological crusade against Moscow
that could jeopardize Europe's uneasy peace. It appears that the President frightened his allies in NATO more than his adversaries in the
Kremlin.

Lord Carrington, NATO's secretary general, appealed for a moderation of Reagan's "megaphone diplomacy."[2] The President's view of
the USSR as the "Evil Empire" elicited no echo in Western Europe,
which views the world from a less Manichean perspective.

As for differing U.S. and West European attitudes toward Communism, a Finnish diplomat has commented that

> . . . While Americans tend to look upon the Soviet Union as an adversary in a worldwide confrontation of ideology and power, Europeans believe they can detect behind the facade of Soviet ideology the familiar features of old Russia—a formidable and, in many ways, strange power but a neighbor they can live with. [3]

Thus, the United States and its Western allies are very much out of sync in every aspect of their attitudes and policies toward the Soviet Union:

> For Americans, Europe is increasingly depicted as a continent of pusillanimous, pacifist merchants, unwilling to sacrifice living standards for defense budgets. . . . For many Europeans, on the other hand, America has become paranoid . . . a country whose foreign policy is summed up as "the Russians are coming." The Reagan Administration's military buildup and anti-Soviet crusade, coming at a time when most Europeans believe that detente is still working on their continent and that their principal problems are economic, have led them to take their distance from us.[4]

Nevertheless, the European NATO allies are not likely to seek the protection of the wolf merely because they have disagreements with the shepherd. The strains between Washington and the European NATO capitals can be explained partly by the basic fact that the United States is a superpower with a global outlook and worldwide responsibilities, whereas the West European allies comprise a conglomerate of states with interests that are confined mostly to the regional level. France retains important economic ties and cultural influence in the Middle East and Africa, and Britain presides over the Commonwealth and occasionally embarks on military forays as far afield as the Falklands; but, by and large, the Europeans are preoccupied with political and economic interests close to home.

If Third-World and economic issues were the main points of contention between the United States and its Western allies, NATO's vitality would be assured. Unfortunately, the Alliance is at loggerheads because of conflicting views of the nature of the very Soviet threat that it was designed to combat. When the invasion of Afghanistan taught Carter his lesson about the nature of the Soviet beast, Washington trashed the remnants of detente and adopted a "hardlining" policy that dismayed West European capitals both in its substance and its suddenness. *The Manchester Guardian* wrote in mid-1980 that "at a time when the United States is entrenching itself in a position of confrontation, at least on a verbal level, it is beginning to look as if the Europeans have made detente their special preserve."[5]

The Reagan Administration came into office contending that the Soviet invasion of Afghanistan, following military interventions by Soviet or proxy forces in Ethiopia, Angola, Cambodia and elsewhere in the Third World, demonstrated Moscow's dedication to a policy of expansionism that detente had failed to curb. The West Europeans tended to downplay those issues and to argue that, at any rate, detente stands on its own merits. In the words of a West German observer, "detente is misunderstood by American conservatives as a synonym for appeasement. For Europeans, detente is a necessity. It means only a common interest in the survival of the human race."[6] Rudolf Augstein, published of the influential West German magazine *Der Spiegel*, stated that "detente is not something we can give up for anybody."[7]

Whereas Washington has viewed detente in rather abstract terms as a device for managing Soviet-American rivalry, Western Europe has formulated a much more concrete conception of detente—one that confers benefits in the form of more trade, reduced tensions in such traditional hot-spots as Berlin, and, for West Germany, contacts with family members in the East and stepped up emigration for ethnic Germans in the Soviet Union and Eastern Europe. Insofar as detente has promoted these objectives, it has been quite successful in its European context. Walter Laqueur points out that "when Soviet troops entered Afghanistan, it was said that this was an Asian problem which should be solved on a regional basis. It had nothing to do with Europe, nothing with detente." Even the Soviet-sponsored crackdown in Poland— the country on behalf of which Britain and France entered World War II—failed to ruffle the surface of detente in Western Europe:

> . . . Poland was a purely domestic problem. . . . Those who refused to help Poland in 1939 at least had a case of sorts; they were asked to "die for Danzig" (to quote the famous slogan of that year), and they had no desire to do so. But no one wants Messrs. Brandt, Kreisky and Papandreou to die for Danzig, only to stand up and be counted. [8]

In general, NATO's West European members do not regard the USSR as a 10-foot-tall giant. They believe that its powerful physique rests, to some extent, upon feet of clay—the chronically malfunctioning Soviet economy, the restive ationalities, and the embittered East

European satellites. At the same time, West European governments are acutely aware of the military realities affecting their region: U.S. acquiescence in Soviet parity on the strategic nuclear level, coupled with a continuing preponderance of Warsaw Pact conventional forces. Against this backdrop, NATO Europe believes there is no alternative to detente.

Since the United States and Western Europe differ in their analysis of the Soviet threat, they naturally diverge on the nature of their response. The United States has stationed more than 300,000 troops on West European territory as a "tripwire" to draw America into war in the event of a Soviet invasion. The troops were deployed at a time when the United States enjoyed strategic nuclear superiority over the Soviet Union and could credibly threaten to counter a Soviet invasion of Western Europe with a nuclear strike at the USSR itself. Since the Soviet Union's attainment of parity, the U.S. nuclear umbrella over Western Europe is no longer waterproof, and some U.S. critics argue that the American troops there have become virtual hostages. Few people on either side of the Atlantic believe that the United States would sacrifice New York or Chicago for Paris or Hamburg. Indeed, former Secretary of State Henry Kissinger bluntly told the allies at a NATO conference in Brussels in 1979 that they could not expect the United States to defend them with strategic nuclear weapons at the risk of exposing American cities to attack and Western civilization to destruction.

In a situation of nuclear parity between the superpowers, Washington has called with increasing urgency for a buildup of conventional forces by the NATO allies in order to raise the nuclear threshold in case of a conflict in Europe. A pledge among the NATO countries to devote annually 3 percent of gross national product (over and above inflation) to defense has been honored mostly in the breach, however. Kissinger has pointed out quite accurately that

> The alliance is thereby trapped in a precarious combination of (a) inadequate conventional forces, leading to (b) reliance on nuclear weapons in (c) a strategic environment [of superpower parity] that makes the threat of their use, and therefore their deterrent value, less and less credible, and (d) a public climate of growing nuclear pacifism that undermines what credibility remains. . . . [9]

The controversy over the neutron bomb offered the Soviet Union a golden opportunity to exploit the differences between the United

States and its NATO allies over the value of detente. The so-called neutron bomb—actually an artillery shell—was touted as eminently suitable for the European theater. It was designed to kill invading troops with a strong dose of radiation but to emit less heat and blast force than other tactical nuclear weapons, thus minimizing civilian casualties and property damage.

In 1977 President Carter decided to deploy the neutron bomb in Western Europe, largely in response to a request by West German Chancellor Helmut Schmidt. The Soviets unleashed a vicious propaganda offensive, dubbing the bomb a quintessential capitalist weapon that kills people while protecting property and suggesting that to favor the neutron bomb was to accept the risk of nuclear war. This campaign carefully overlooked the fact that the victims of the neutron bomb would be Soviet tank crews and the property to be spared would consist largely of noncombatants' homes around the battle zone. According to U.S. intelligence, the Kremlin spent more than $100 million on the campaign against the neutron bomb—a campaign portrayed by an East European Communist party official as "one of the most significant and most successful [campaigns] since World War II."[10]

Undermined by the Soviet propaganda onslaught, Schmidt insisted that another non-nuclear country on the Continent besides West Germany would have to deploy the weapon on its territory. A lack of broad West European support led Carter to cancel his deployment decision and gravely strained relations between Washington and Bonn.

Moscow's propaganda offensive against the U.S. decision to deploy Pershing 2 and ground-launched cruise missiles (GLCM's) in Western Europe was another attempt to exploit dissension in NATO's ranks but was ultimately less successful. The "Euromissiles," like the neutron bomb, represented an attempt to counter the growing Soviet military threat to NATO and enhance U.S. credibility as an ally.

The advent of the Soviet SS-20 triple-warhead mobile missile revolutionized the balance of forces in the European theater. It pitted the new missile system—along with the formidable Backfire bomber that was entering service at a rate of at least 30 per year and with the upgrading of Soviet air defenses—against a Western arsenal that consisted of obsolescent tactical nuclear devices, two squadrons of American F-111 and FB-111 aircraft based in Britain and 400 submarine-launched Poseidon warheads at the disposal of SACEUR. Except for 18 French land-based missiles (which can strike targets inside the USSR), the Soviet Union enjoyed a monopoly on intermediate-range nuclear missiles in Europe. Moreover, the Warsaw Pact's superiority in conventional forces was so great that an early resort to nuclear weapons on the part of the United States probably would be mandatory to prevent Europe's defeat in war. Would the United States be willing to risk New York for Bonn in view of the overall balance of forces? By the same token, asymmetry in theater nuclear forces created such a gap in the NATO escalation ladder that the Alliance's threat of "first use" of nuclear weapons had become increasingly less credible. The SS-20's, then, are preeminently political weapons—a fact that persistently escapes those commentators who insist on the military "irrelevance" of Euromissiles. In surveying the SS-20 deployments from a political perspective, a U.S. scholar has noted that

> It seems that the Soviet leadership . . . acted with the knowledge that a number of elements in the West would respond with indignation and determination to undertake reciprocal defensive measures, while others would be convinced that growing Soviet military superiority only made detente . . . all the more critical. . . . The Kremlin took a calculated risk, it seems, that accommodation . . . would outweigh . . . indignation. . . . In any event, the two differing responses would give the USSR possibilities for splitting Western polities. [11]

There was general agreement within NATO on the need for counter-deployments, but the West Europeans had just emerged from the bruising battle over the neutron bomb and were wary of Jimmy Carter's foreign policy flip-flops. Most of all, they were reluctant to station highly visible (and thus politically "provocative") missiles on their soil that could strike Soviet territory. Nevertheless, by mid-1979 a plan was completed for the deployment of Pershing 2's, which could strike at the USSR from West German territory, and Tomahawk ground-launched cruise missiles (GLCM's), which could reach the Soviet Union from as far away as Britain, Italy, Belgium and the Netherlands.

The Pershing 2 can travel a distance of 1,125 miles to hit targets in the western USSR up to the outskirts of Moscow (as noted in Chapter 2, its range was limited for political reasons so that it cannot hit the capital itself). A mobile, solid-fueled ballistic missile, the Pershing II carries a 200-kiloton warhead and can deliver its payload within six to eight minutes after launch, thus halving the warning time that the Soviet Union enjoyed prior to its emplacement. The Pershing II is also exceedingly accurate; it has a terminal guidance system controlled by on-board radar, which coordinates images obtained along the flight path to the target. However, as a *Washington Post* columnist pointed out, "With its one warhead, the Pershing II is a firecracker in comparison with the SS-20 dynamite sticks.[12]

The Tomahawk cruise missile travels much more slowly than the Pershing II and would take half an hour to reach most of its targets in the Soviet Union, but it is valued for its penetration ability as well as its great accuracy. It can fly less than 50 feet above the ground, evading enemy radar and closing in on its target with the help of a terrain-contour-matching system. All 572 of the new Euromissiles were assigned only to U.S. forces; no European fingers would touch the triggers. The United States agreed to shoulder the entire cost—about $5 billion—of producing and deploying the missiles.[13]

With one eye on Moscow's reaction and one eye on West Germany's vocal antinuclear movement, Schmidt pushed for the *Doppelbeschluss*—the two-track arrangement by which Euromissile deployments woud be delayed until 1983 while Washington entered negotiations with Moscow for an arms control agreement covering Western Europe. An adviser to Schmidt explained that "the Pershing was a certain stick, and with negotiations we tried to do the carrot."*[14]* On 12 December the NATO foreign ministers gave their final approval for the deployment plan.

A French observer marveled that "the Western negotiating position has deteriorated to the point that when the Soviet Union deploys weapons that threaten the whole of Europe with a disarming first strike, the simple act of trying to respond . . . is considered an outright provocation."[15] Pierre Lellouche, director of political-military studies at the Institut Francais des Relations Internationales in Paris wrote that

> It's like a guy who has a gun pointed at his head saying to his attacker, "Do you mind if I go out and buy a gun, too?" [16]

Neoconservative guru Irving Kristol most eloquently summed up the irony inherent in NATO's dual-track policy:

> The Reagan Administration never wanted to enter these negotiations, because in the past the Russians always used such occasions to gain a military advantage. The United States was dragged into the . . . negotiations by . . . the West European governments, who said they had to demonstrate to their people that their intentions were honorably peaceful before

any intermediate-range nuclear missiles could be installed to balance the Russian SS-20's. Is it not a little odd that these democratically elected governments . . . should have to prove to their people that they are not "warmongers," . . . [17]

Contrary to the impression conceived by many influential West Europeans (and fostered by Moscow), the Euromissiles were intended to "re-couple" the United States and its transatlantic allies—to provide "extended deterrence," i.e., deterrence on behalf of non-nuclear allies. Since the USSR labels as "strategic" any nuclear weapon that can strike its territory, regardless of where it is deployed, the United States was actually increasing the risk to its own homeland by deploying INF systems in the European threater that could reach the Soviet Union. Far from seeking to confine a nuclear exchange to the European continent, Washington was practically inviting Moscow to strike U.S. territory in conjunction with an attack on what the Soviets would regard as U.S. strategic systems in Europe. As

Henry Kissinger wrote,

. . . With intermediate-range American weapons in Europe, the Soviets could not threaten Europe selectively; any nuclear attack and any successful conventional attack would trigger an American counterblow from European installations. The Soviets would have to calculate even in case of conventional attack that we would use our missiles before they were overrun. Hence the Soviets would have to attack the missiles if they used even conventional weapons in Europe; that, in turn, would trigger our strategic forces. [18]

The Kremlin grasped this situation fully and threatened to attack the U.S. homeland if the Euromissiles were launched against the Soviet Union. "The Threat to Peace," a propaganda tract published by the USSR in 1981, stated:

It ought to be quite clear that . . . any preemptive strike (against Western Europe) is senseless unless it destroys or at least substantially weakens the strategic nuclear potential of the other side's retaliatory capability. . . . A first strike in Western Europe would make no sense from any point of view, for it would only expose our country to riposte by an absolutely intact U.S. strategic arsenal.

Marshal Nikolay Ogarkov, chief of the Soviet General Staff, said during a *New York Times* interview in March 1983 that if U.S. intermediate-range missiles in Europe were launched against the USSR, the

Soviets would retaliate directly against the United States, and "all-out war would ensue. [19] So much for critics' charges of "de-coupling."

Soviet-American arms control talks on intermediate-range nuclear force (INF) systems opened in Geneva on 30 November 1981. The negotiators were working against a two-year deadline imposed by NATO, which had agreed to begin deployment of the Euromissiles in December 1983 if the talks had not yielded an agreement by that date. The INF talks were the first arms control negotiations that the superpowers had conducted since the Senate's failure in 1979 to ratify the SALT II treaty. Serious difficulties plagued the negotiations from the U.S. standpoint. The perceived need to look over its shoulder at Western public opinion and to reassure NATO governments that it was indeed bargaining in good faith must have been, at best, a distraction for the U.S. delegation. Moreover, pressure from the NATO allies had obliged Washington to enter arms control talks with Moscow while the Soviets continued to wage war in Afghanistan. Having acceded to the Presidency on a platform that deplored Carter's softness toward Soviet misbehavior, Reagan found himself abandoning any semblance of linkage in his own Soviet policy. The dictum that nothing must impede efforts toward arms control thus became enshrined during the very first year of the Reagan Administration.

Lying at the heart of U.S. difficulties during the INF negotiations, however, was the dilemma of attempting to trade paper missiles for real ones. Soviet SS-20 deployments had been underway for four years when the talks began and were continuing at the rate of roughly one missile per week, according to American officials. Reagan's "zero-option" proposal hit the negotiating table with a dull thud. It also spurred a vigorous Soviet propaganda offensive charging that the President was not serious about arms control—the ultimate anathema! To complicate matters further, the INF negotiations opened against a backdrop of massive "peace" marches that engulfed most of the NATO countries.

In examining the peace movement in Western Europe in the early 1980's, one must look beyond the Euromissile issue to the basic European determination to preserve detente in the face of the "hardline" Reagan Administration. Having traditionally ignored the confrontational rhetoric that is a staple of Soviet foreign policy pronouncements, the West Europeans professed shock when Reagan fed Moscow a dose of its own medicine. Similarly, Reagan's reaffirmation of the doctrine of "flexible response," which had been a staple of NATO policy for almost two decades, created widespread dismay on a continent that had spawned a powerful antinuclear movement.

"Flexible response," postulating the use of limited nuclear options in the event of imminent defeat during a Soviet invasion of Western Europe, had been devised as a more preferable alternative than an immediate U.S.-Soviet nuclear exchange. The European NATO countries, however, began to suspect that climbing gradually up the escalation ladder was a ploy by the superpowers to protect their homelands from nuclear war and to turn Europe into their shooting gallery. Many officials and opinion molders in the NATO nations regarded the scheduled deployment of Euromissiles as a U.S. plan to "fight to the last European" while remaining safe in its transatlantic sanctuary. Such European attitudes were no less real for being irrational.

The phenomenon called Europessimism swept the Continent in the wake of NATO's two-track decision on INF modernization and of Reagan's electoral victory. In March 1981, two months after Reagan took office, national security aaffairs adviser Richard V. Allen lamaented that "outright pacifist sentiments" were resurfacing and "the contemptible better-Red-than dead slogan of a generation ago" was re-echoing in Europe.[20] While America was reaching out to reassert her global predominance and overcome the "Vietnam syndrome," Western Europe seemed to be retreating into isolationism—a brooding morbidity about its military inferiority and uncertain future in the shadow of Soviet power. "A plague on both your houses" characterized the attitude of many influential Europeans vis-a-vis the United States and the USSR—an attitude that reflected a moral symmetry equating both superpowers as obstacles to peace.

The European climate was ripe for the most ambitious Soviet "peace offensive" since the postwar Stockholm Peace Appeal. Militant pacifism was running amok, particularly in West Germany, the Netherlands and Scandinavia, fresh from campaigns against nuclear power plants and the neutron bomb. Remnants of the anti-Vietnam War movement joined the ranks. Pacifist and neutralist sentiments, once confined largely to ideological groupings on Europe's far left, now included religious, cultural, student and professional elements representing virtually all shades of the political spectrum. Their common objective appeared to be nuclear disarmament—mutual (as between East and West) if possible but unilateral if necessary. Numerous West European politicians climbed on the peace bandwagon, either out of conviction or because of a desire to identify with a popular issue.

During the 1981 peace campaign

> . . . The Soviets waged united front tactics to rally to the anti-INF banner a vast variety of religious groups, antinuclear movements, leftist factions, pacifists, environmentalists, draft resisters and other single-interest groups. . . . A standard technique of united front tactics is to form an umbrella organization for the various antinuclear groups and to fashion interlocking directorates among the constituent elements, with local Communists playing key roles. [21]

In the Netherlands, for example, the tiny Dutch Communist party ingratiated itself with the Interchurch Peace Council (IKV), Holland's premier peace lobby, which was also penetrated by a pro-Soviet group called "Christians for Socialism." Mient Jan Faber, head of the IKV, disclosed that representatives of his organization met in April 1981 in Berlin with West German counterparts to plan the series of "peace" demonstrations that erupted throughout Europe in the autumn.[22] (Faber himself was once escorted out of East Germany by police when he and a few colleagues tried to hold a peace rally there.)

In West Germany, events followed a course similar to that in the Netherlands. The German Peace Union, established as an instrument of the then-proscribed German Communist Party, became the umbrella organization for peace groups that it controlled through interlocking directorates. In December 1979, when NATO's two-track INF decision was announced, the German Peace Union and the German Communist Party met to organize resistance against the missile deployments. They worked closely with the East German affiliate of the World Peace Council, a Soviet front organization. In November 1980, the German Peace Union succeeded in assembling Protestant church leaders, pacifists, Communist front groups, and the radical environmentalist Green party into the so-called Krefeld Forum. Under the direction of Petra Kelly, the American-born leader of the Greens, the Krefeld Appeal against INF deployment in Germany was launched. It gathered a million signatures and was repeated in 1981. During this period, about 150 federal and local SPD representatives publicly urged Chancellor Schmidt "not to jeopardize the polciy of detente" by accepting the U.S. missiles on German soil.[23]

Among the highlights of peace movement activities in the autumn of 1981 were a quarter-million strong "peace march" in Bonn on 10 October that was addressed by Erhard Eppler, a member of the ruling Social Democratic Party's executive body; a "Ban the Bomb" march in the heart of London on 24 October that was sponsored by the Campaign for Nuclear Disarmament and attracted between 150,000 and 250,000 people; a demonstration in Rome on the same day that was believed to be the largest public rally there in a decade; a protest march in Brussels on 25 October which police called the biggest there since World War II, with some 100,000 demonstrators; and a 50,000-strong rally on the same day in Paris under the auspices of the Movement for Peace, an umbrella organization that included the French Communist Party, the Communist-controlled General Confederation of Labor, and about 20 other groups. The culmination of the season's "peace" campaign was a rally in Amsterdam on 21 November that attracted 300,000 participants.

On 3 November, CDU Chairman Helmut Kohl told his party's annual national convention that West Germany remained loyal to its allies but that "we belong to the German peace movement, and we want disarmament and detente."[24] In Britain, the opposition Labor Party held its annual convention in September 1981 and formally committed itself to nuclear disarmament. Citing President Reagan's reiteration of the "flexible response" policy, the pro-Soviet Scottish trade union leader Alex Kitson, chairman of the convention, told the delegates that "a limited nuclear war means a nuclear war limited to Europe."[25]

In France, by contrast, the newly elected Socialist government of President Francois Mitterrand boycotted the October peace march, although some leaders of the Socialist Party attended the rally in a private capacity. Mitterrand advocated an arms buildup to counter the growing Soviet threat, and he commented scornfully that while the East was deploying arms, the West was deploying pacifists.[26]

The 1982 Easter season witnessed a renewal of peace demonstrations. The Soviet Union also planted a forged letter in the 22 April 1982 edition of the Belgian leftist weekly *De Nieuwe*. The bogus document was dated 26 June 1979 and allegedly was sent to NATO Secretary General Joseph Luns by Gen. Alexander Haig, then NATO's supreme commander. It advocated "action of a sensitive nature" that would "jolt the faint-hearted in Europe" who opposed Euromissile deployments. The forgery evidently was designed to steer the peace movement solely in an anti-American direction, thus obscuring the fact that the missiles actually constituted *counterdeployments* to the Soviet SS-20's.

In April 1982, more than 30 West German leftwing groups convened to plan demonstrations for Ronald Reagan's visit to the Federal Republic during a NATO summit scheduled for June. According to one report, "the Communists dominated the session to such a degree that even the radical 'Greens,' who previously had collaborated closely with the Communists, were moved to protest sharply."[27] Nevertheless, the Greens were obliged to join the anti-INF rally during the President's visit, lest they become isolated in the peace movement.

On 10 June, while the summit was in session, more than 300,000 peace marchers gathered in Bonn to condemn U.S. defense policies. This rally was the largest in West Germany since its establishment as a separate nation in 1948. The communique issued at the summit reaffirmed NATO's commitment to a strong defense and to the development of "substantial and balanced East-West relations aimed at genuine detente."[28] The word "genuine" reportedly was inserted at the insistence of Ronald Reagan, who otherwise would not accept a reference to detente at all. The President told his NATO allies that he was "deeply disappointed" by the "detente of the 1970's," which had provided fertile ground for a Soviet military buildup, and that he would not support a renewal of detente if it constituted a "one-way street."[29]

Moscow's evident intention in the early 1980's was to replay the startling successful anti-neutron bomb campaign with the Euromissiles as the new target. It was not necessary for the Kremlin to control the West European peace movement in order to steer it into channels favorable to Soviet policy goals. "Europe's fear of frying," as a *New York Times* editorial dubbed it, was so palpable that Moscow had only to fan the flames of antiwar hysteria:

> . . . What is now denounced as an American scheme to plant more missiles throughout Europe was in fact the allies' preference. What is denounced as an American effort to confine a nuclear war to Europe was actually devised to guarantee that America would not escape involvement in a European war. . . . [30]

Leonid Zamyatin, head of the Soviet Communist Party's International Information Department, typified the Soviet approach when he warned Western Europe that "we are racing against an atomic castastrophe."

Moscow reiterated that the Euromissiles would create an imbalance because they could strike Soviet territory while the SS-20 could not reach America. ("One might not think that this argument would move European antimissile protesters, but apparently it does.")[31] The claim implied (incorrectly) that a balance already existed and, furthermore, that the Euromissiles were "de-coupled" from the American strategic arsenal. The fallaciousness of its arguments notwithstanding, by exploiting the kind of domestic political debate that it doesn't tolerate within its own society, the Soviet Union deepened the wedges between the United States and Western Europe on the crucial issue of maintaining European defenses.

As 1983, the "Year of the Euromissile," opened, Moscow warned that it would deploy new missile systems in Eastern Europe as well as in locations (Cuba or Nicaragua?) that would pose a threat to the United States analogous to that posed to the Soviet homeland by the Pershing II's and GLCM's. According to all indications, the USSR had intended to modernize its short-range nuclear systems regardless of Euromissile deployments. Thus, it moved to replace FROG and SCUD surface-to-surface missiles in East Germany and Czechoslovakia with SS-21's, SS-22's, and SS-23's, which were superior in both range and accuracy.

Looking back on the negotiations, a Radio Liberty analyst commented that

> The whole pattern of Soviet tactics on the Euromissile question might appropriately be termed "protection racket diplomacy," for the parallels with Mafia tactics are striking. The USSR begins by creating a profound physical threat to its neighbors' security. It follows this up by offering to protect them from that same threat, if they will make certain concessions. When the threatened neighbors probe for signs of good will or compromise, it responds by admonishing them to be "reasonable" or "realistic." When the said neighbors take steps to defend themselves, the specter of nuclear war is evoked in vague terms. The entire tactic is based on first creating fear and then seeking to exploit that fear to one-sided advantage. [32]

The Kremlin gambled that it could stop Euromissile deployments by political pressure and propaganda. Having failed in this endeavor, the Soviet Union walked out of the INF negotiations.

The Russians evidently hoped that their walkout from the Geneva arms control negotiations would spur the NATO allies to press Washington for concessions to Moscow that would permit the talks to resume. There was indeed some pressure; but Reagan, armed with his SDI, held firm. The USSR eventually had to abandon its longstanding demand that the United States must withdraw its new missiles from Europe before the Soviets would return to the negotiating table.

Gorbachev's first major foreign policy speech after coming to power in March 1985 dealt largely with the INF issue. During an interview with *Pravda* on 7 April, he announced a moratorium on the deployment of Soviet medium-range missiles in Europe. Calling upon the United States to institute a similar freeze on Euromissile deployments, he declared that the moratorium would apply both to SS-20's and to "other reply measures in Europe"—a phrase used to refer to shorter-range Soviet missiles in East Germany and Czechoslovakia. Gorbachev offered to extend the moratorium until November—the time of the scheduled vote in the Dutch parliament on acceptance of U.S. cruise missiles.

Since the Soviet Union already had deployed 414 SS-20 missiles—each with three warheads—Gorbachev's feigned restraint amounted to a risk-free propaganda stunt. The overall level of warheads on INF systems in Europe favored the Soviet bloc by a margin of nearly 10 to 1. Predictably, however, Gorbachev's "offer" muddied NATO's waters by stimulating differences among the allies over how and whether to respond. In Britain, for example, Dennis Healey, foreign policy spokesman for the opposition Labor Party, criticized Prime Minister Margaret Thatcher's rejection of the Soviet proposal and claimed that many Europeans feel "very disappointed" because "every time the Russians make a sensible proposal, there is a knee-jerk negative from Mrs. Thatcher and President Reagan."[33] In West Germany, the opposition Social Democrats called Moscow's offer "an important signal" worthy of exploration.[34] Such disarray in the Alliance was a boon per se for Gorbachev, irrespective of the negative outcome of his initiative.

In October, Gorbachev made his first foray into Western Europe since his accession to power (he had visited Britain in December 1984 at the head of a Supreme Soviet delegation). The Soviet visitor sought to win over European public opinion on arms control and to make an end run around the United States by going directly to its allies. The Soviet leader invited France and Britain to open "a direct dialogue" with the Soviet Union aimed at "a separate agreement" on the INF issue. By this time, the SS-20 force had grown to 441 launchers, of which roughly two-thirds (274) were targeted on Europe.

France and Britain rebuffed Gorbachev's overtures for a "direct dialogue" with the Soviet Union and insisted on retaining their nuclear forces for defense of their homelands. The Netherlands also swept aside Soviet blandishments; despite unrelenting pressure from the Soviet-assisted Dutch peace movement and television appearances by Soviet propaganda specialists, the parliament voted to deploy the Euromissiles.[35]

One of the few items that Reagan and Gorbachev agreed upon at the Geneva summit of November 1985 was the desirability for near-term progress on the INF issue. The Soviets, however, continued to use this issue as a wedge to divide the United States from its allies and to stimulate domestic pressures against Western goverments that harbored nuclear weapons on their territory. On 30 December 1985, for example, Gorbachev penned a letter to Ken Livingstone, a Laborite who headed the Greater London Council, London's municipal governing body. The letter was a reply to one sent by Livingstone to inform Gorbachev that London had declared itself an independent "nuclear-free zone" and sought a Soviet pledge not to use nuclear weapons against it. Gorbachev's letter observed that "the comparatively small British Isles" are being "stuffed" with nuclear weapons, the presence of which "does not consolidate anybody's security." The letter went on to say that "if Britain fully rejected nuclear weapons and dismantled foreign nuclear bases on its teritory, the USSR would guarantee that the Soviet nuclear weapons will be neither trained on British territory, nor used against it." Gorbachev wrote that any country ejecting nuclear arms or installations was eligible for such guarantees, "no matter if they are members of military alliances or not." This statement evidently was directed at France, which does not belong to NATO's integrated military command structure but maintains an independent nuclear deterrent force.

On 15 January 1986, Gorbachev unveiled the grand-daddy of all Soviet arms control proposals, and it included a sizable INF component. Gorbachev's plan called, among other things, for the removal of the Pershing II's and GLCM's, along with Soviet SS-20's targeted on Europe, while retaining SS-20's in Asia, with their potential for rapid movement into the European USSR. In addition, implementation of the plan would nip in the bud the modernization of the British and French nuclear forces and would prohibit the United States from selling Trident D-5 SLBM's to Britain.

Although they are still relatively small, the British nuclear arsenal and the French *force de frappe* are growing rapidly. By the mid-1990's, the combined total of British and French nuclear warheads will triple to more than 900.[36] Britain is equipping four submarines with 16 new Chevaline missiles apiece; each missile carries two warheads. Eventually, Britain will acquire four new submarines, each of which will carry 16 U.S.-built Trident II missiles (replacements for the aging Polaris missile force). Each Trident probably will carry eight MIRV'ed warheads (compared with the three warheads on current British SLBM's. The British also are modernizing their nuclear-capable air assets, primarily by replacing their obsolescent bombers with new Tornado fighter planes.

France is virtually unique in Western Europe in that political parties along the whole ideological spectrum support atomic weapons and nuclear power. In 1985 France doubled its inventory of SLBM's at a stroke by sending the submarine Inflexible to sea with 16 M-4 missiles, each carrying six warheads. Eventually, six submarines will carry the M-4's, which, according to the French Defense Ministry, have a range of 6,000 km (3,720 miles).[37] Older French SLBM's had only a single warhead.

The French also are modernizing their land-based nuclear forces, currently consisting of 18 single-warhead missiles. The Pluton missile, which can reach only as far as western Germany., is being replaced with the Hades, which is designed to destroy Soviet military bases in Eastern Europe. Air-to-surface nuclear missiles with the same mission recently became operational. France also is producing a neutron warhead and a mobile land-based missile similar to the proposed U.S. Midgetman. In addition, France has sophisticated Mirage IV bombers that can deliver nuclear payloads.

Although France withdrew from NATO's integrated military command in 1966, its nuclear-capable aircraft (as well as its 500,000-man army, including about 50,000 troops in West Germany) might be committed to the Alliance in case of war.[38] French military doctrine calls for the immediate use of tactical nuclear weapons in case of a Soviet invasion. If the invaders persist, France would unleash its strategic nuclear arsenal. As Evan Galbraith, a former U.S. ambassador to Paris, points out,

> France's warheads are no match in numbers with those of the Soviet Union, but they will be sufficient to destroy the Soviet Union or to bring America into the war. (The Soviets will not be able to distinguish between French and U.S. nuclear missiles launched from submarines.) [39]

Implementation of Gorbachev's three-stage proposal of 15 January would create unprecedented perils for NATO. Jeane Kirkpatrick wrote that

. . . Usually, our allies position themselves as the "peace party" and hope aloud that the United States will be more forthcoming [on arms control issues]. This time, our allies seem worried that the United States might be too forthcoming. . . . First, they have been impressed with the packaging of the latest proposal. It offers—or seems to offer—Ronald Reagan two things he badly wants: It offers negotiations without . . . the precondition that he abandon the Strategic Defense Initiative as a price for negotiating deep cuts in nuclear missiles, and it couches the offer in the language of Reagan's own "zero option," proposing a "zero option" for Europe as a "first step" to a "nuclear-free" world. [40]

Europe's fears seemed to be confirmed when Washington, evidently operating on the public relations imperative of denying Moscow a propaganda edge, came forth with a new initiative of its own. On 24 February, Reagan proposed the elimination of American Euromissiles and all Soviet intermediate-range missiles from both the European and Asian USSR.

Something strange had happened to the Pershing II's and GLCM's on their way from the drawing board to their deployment sites, however: the Western allies had learned to love them. Thus, NATO's response to Reagan's new proposal was far from enthusiastic. No sooner had Euromissile deployments proceeded in earnest than the President was suggesting their elimination.

Today, Europeans are replaying arguments presented earlier against deployment—this time to *oppose* removal of the missiles: Eliminating them would de-couple America from Europe, leave Europe hostage to other Soviet nuclear forces, and signal a lack of NATO resolve. Having paid a political price of admission to get missiles into the theater, European governments resent having to pay an additional political fee to get them out. [41]

Western Europe's concern sprang from many factors. First, the countries that accepted the missiles on their soil had endured bitter political battles that had widened domestic cleavages and distracted attention from pressing economic and social issues. Secondly, Reagan's flip-flop on the INF question was uncomfortably reminiscent of Jimmy Carter's vacillation on key defense issues affecting European security. Thirdly, the NATO countries, particularly West Germany, were acutely aware that removal of U.S. and Soviet INF systems from the European theater would leave untouched the USSR's new shorter-range missiles—SS-21's, SS-22's, and SS-23's—recently deployed in Eastern Europe. West German Defense Minister Manfred Worner complained that these new missiles could pose a threat even in the absence of nuclear warheads because the Soviets could improve their accuracy and arm them with conventional warheads to strike NATO targets. Thus, a West European defense against these missiles "must be demanded quite independently" of the American INF program, said Worner.[42]

The probability that Reagan's plan would be linked to Gorbachev's proposal for the total elimination of nuclear weapons worried the Europeans even more. There was a widespread consensus on the Continent that nuclear weapons had preserved the peace for 40 years and would continue for the foreseeable future to serve as the best deterrent to the outbreak of a conventional war, with its possibilities for escalation. A British official declared that "there are very few Europeans who could contemplate a world of no nuclear weapons—certainly without a very radical change in what is happening in the conventional balance, the chemical balance, and political relations in general."[43]

The friction that arose between Washington and its transatlantic allies over INF illuminated the ongoing dysfunction of an alliance in which one partner is infinitely more powerful than all the others combined and, moreover, lies thousands of miles away from the country that poses the chief threat to the allies. While the West Europeans welcomed nuclear arms-control negotiations between Washington and Moscow as a sign that detente endured, they became justifiably nervous when the subjects of those negotiations were weapons systems crucial to European security. The absence of European representatives at the negotiating table undoubtedly compounded the allies' anxieties. On the other hand, entering into a "direct dialogue" on nuclear issues with the Soviets, as Gorbachev suggested to Britain and France, would pit relatively weak countries against a hostile superpower and, perhaps more importantly, would legitimize the concept of "de-coupling" between the United States and Western Europe that Moscow is so eager to promote.

While the drama over the Euromissiles was still running its course, Reagan's Strategic Defense Initiative embroiled the United States and its allies in a new dispute and provided fresh grist to the Soviet propaganda mill. As was the case with INF deployments, the prospect of a ballistic missile defense shield over the United States generated concerns about a "Fortress America" that would leave its allies to fend for themselves in the face of the Soviet threat. Many influential West Europeans regarded the prospective creation of a

"Star Wars" system as a portent of American retreat into isolationism. The impending establishment of a full-fledged theater nuclear force in Western Europe generated fears there that the United States planned to fight a nuclear war with the Soviets over the dead bodies and devastated cities of its allies. Moscow, as noted above, fanned these fears energetically to deepen the "contradictions" between Washington and the other NATO capitals. Thus, on both the INF and SDI issues, the specter of "de-coupling" haunted Europe.

In his speech of 23 March 1983 that introduced SDI to the world, Reagan expressed hope that the new system ultimately would render nuclear weapons "impotent and obsolete." This was not necessarily a comforting prospect for the European allies, however. A French official typified the negative reaction when he declared that

> In order to sell the shield, the Reagan Administration was discrediting the sword. There is a tendency to say the present deterrence will not last, that we are going to a non-nuclear world. That is exactly what we cannot accept. Everybody in Europe is thinking the same way. [44]

Washington's failure to consult with its allies about the SDI program further heightened their anxieties. As Pierre Lellouche has written,

> . . . nothing can be understood about the current Alliance debate and attitudes about the SDI decision without comprehending its completely unilateral origin. . . . The announcement by . . . the guarantor and the leader of a nuclear Alliance that it had decided to modify the accepted rules of the deterrence game without informing anyone . . . in Europe was bound to raise difficult issues. [45]

Aside from the basic issue regarding the continued credibility of the U.S. guarantee to defend Europe, the SDI project placed Europe at a disadvantage technologically by stimulating the development and use of emerging technologies. Not only were European industries likely to lag behind, but the U.S. program created the possibility of a "brain drain" of European scientists who sought to participate in it. Still another European concern was that by according top priority to the SDI, the Pentagon would divert human and financial resources away from military programs that more directly benefited NATO.

If the Pentagon's funds are channeled increasingly into SDI, many European officials suspect that Washington will press the Western allies to accrue a greater portion of the burden for European defense. If the Allies balk, Congress could insist upon a phased withdrawal of

American troops from Europe. Thus, SDI has reinforced the Europeans' most deep-rooted fear—the fear of having to go it alone against the Soviet colossus. *The Wall Street Journal* summed up the multifaceted challenge that SDI posed to the allies by stating that "if Moscow, as the experts claim, opposes Star Wars because it portends stragegic change and economic challenge, so too does Europe.[46]

While Moscow exhorts the West European allies to denounce the SDI, it is moving ahead with its Warsaw Pact partners to develop a strategic defensive shield of its own. Juergen Todenhoefer, a Christian Democratic member of the Bundestag and an adviser to Chancellor Kohl on nuclear issues, revealed that during a Warsaw Pact summit on 26 April 1985, Soviet Defense Minister Sergei Sokolov handed out research contracts to bloc members for a space-based defense system. The main recipients of the contracts were said to be East Germany—which would be responsible for research in photoelectronics, technical measuring and precision engineering—and Czechoslovakia. According to the West German newspaper *Bild*, Todenhoefer's sources were "secret Soviet documents at NATO" headquarters in Belgium.[47]

Reagan's SDI, coming on the heels of the controversial INF deployment issue and a surge in the European peace movement, introduced a new note of wariness into the relationship between the United States and its NATO allies. If the Pentagon puts all its eggs in the "Star Wars" basket and seems to support denuclearization, the Western allies may become increasingly demoralized and receptive to Soviet overtures for creation of a pan-European security system excluding the United States. As Pierre Lellouche points out,

> To be sure, the goal of making nuclear weapons irrelevant has been pushed into the distant future, but it still very mujch exists. . . . The desire to disinvent the bomb is natural in a country that does not have immediate security threats at its borders and whose sole vulnerability comes from nuclear weapons falling down from the sky. One cannot help but wonder whether SDI represents an expression not only of the typically American faith in technology but also of nuclear isolationism . . . in the wider context of the evolution of U.S. strategic policy toward Europe . . . toward the "conventionalization" of NATO's defense posture . . . through "emerging technologies" (ET) and the "follow on forces attack" (FOFA) concept.
>
> Yet . . . nuclear weapons in Europe . . . are a key element of the postwar order . . . because of the U.S. presence and participation in the European equation. . . . In the long run, the American and alliance position will be on much stronger ground if and when SDI is clearly presented as reinforcing deterrence rather than undermining it. [48]

Arms control, of course, is a closely related issue on which Washington must attempt to coordinate policy more closely with the allies—to consult rather than merely inform them of pending shifts. Finally, a serious U.S. attempt to reassure the West Europeans that they will benefit from the technological achievements and spinoffs of SDI research will go a long way toward enlisting Allied cooperation on the knotty issues of trade and technology transfer vis-a-v-s the Soviet bloc.

Feeling relatively helpless to influence their powerful transatlantic partner in the sphere of military strategies and weaponry, the NATO allies have asserted themselves strongly on East-West trade and economic issues. Since the United States does not share the intense devotion of the Europeans for maintaining economic detente, this is another issue that has eroded NATO solidarity, with resultant benefit for the Kremlin.

Western Europe's eagerness to expand economic ties with the USSR reflected not only a desire to preserve detente during a period of worsening Soviet-American relations, but also a need to bolster domestic economies at a time of sluggish industrial output and high unemployment rates. Moreover, there are important historical precedents for these economic links—precedents that have no counterpart in the U.S.-Soviet relationship. In 1922, for example, more than a decade before Washington accorded diplomatic recognition to the Soviet government, Berlin and Moscow signed the Treaty of Rapallo. With this accord, Germany became the first European country to recognize the Bolshevik regime; in return, the Soviets provided the Germans with lucrative trade opportunities and permitted the Bundeswehr to train secretly on Soviet soil and acquire armaments illegally. The ensuing decades witnessed a steady buildup in Soviet-German economic ties. Although the Social Democratic Party took the lead in creating *Ostpolitik*, the Christian Democratic Union and its sister party, the Christian Social Union, have consistently favored strong trade and economic relations with the East to bring profits to the financiers and industrial magnates that form a core of their constituency. Franz Josef Strauss, the long-time head of the CSU and an outspoken foe of Communism, valued the Soviet economic connection as a boon to the enterprises in his native Bavaria (which, incidentally, relies on the Soviet Union for 90 percent of its natural gas supplies).

With the establishment of two German states after World War II, special arrangements evolved between them on the trade and economic front. In 1949 the Frankfurt Agreement on Interzonal Trade set up a "swing" credit—an interest-free credit facility for the East German State Bank at the West German Federal Bank for the purpose of financing temporary imbalances in inter-German commercial transactions. The temporary imbalances, in effect, have become permanent, for East Germany nearly always has a trade deficit vis-a-vis the Federal Republic. Inter-German trade, which carries no tariffs, functions partly as a mechanism to promote family ties across the border and to ensure smooth inter-governmental relations. This arrangement has caused disputes between West Germany and the United States, which regards East Germany as a conduit for the transfer of Western technology to the USSR.

During Jimmy Carter's Administration, U.S. policy on trade with the Soviet bloc had an adverse effect on U.S.-West European relations. In 1978, for example, Carter vetoed the sale of a Sperry Univac computer to the TASS news agency in reaction to the arrest of Soviet dissidents. The French-controlled Compagnie Internationale pour l'Informatique-Honeywell Bull stepped into the breach by selling TASS one of its computers. Washington protested sharply. After the Soviet invasion of Afghanistan in December 1979, Carter clamped an embargo on the export of technology to the USSR. The embargo scotched participation of American firms in a number of lucrative Soviet projects, and again Washington's allies availed themselves of the profits. For example, the Aluminum Company of America (ALCOA) and the Armco Steel Corporation withdrew under government pressure from an agreement to build an aluminum factory and a steel plant, respectively,in the Soviet Union. The Klockner group of West Germany and Creusot of France then signed contracts for the projects.

These contentious East-West economic issues paled before the conclusion in 1981 of an agreement for Western participation in the construction of a 3,600-mile natural gas pipeline to run from Siberia to Western Europe. This was the largest East-West commercial transaction in history. Originating at the natural gas fields—among the world's largest—on Siberia's Yamal Peninsula, north of the Arctic Circle, the pipeline would extend across the Soviet Union and Eastern Europe into West Germany, where it would link up with an existing West European pipeline network for distribution. Western countries agreed to supply money and equipment to construct the line in return for a steady flow of gas. A *Wall Street Journal* article captured the magnitude of the pipeline project when he wrote that it

. . . will require the efforts of 12 nations, dozens of companies, and more than 120,000 workers in the Soviet Union alone. It will use enough steel to build a railroad track around the world or to make half the automobiles turned out in the U.S. last year. To buy the equipment and pipe, the Soviet Union is borrowing half as much money as it did under the Lend-Lease program to help finance its massive effort in World War II. [49]

Once gas deliveries covered the costs of construction, the pipeline was expected to yield more than $8 billion annually in hard currency, replacing oil as the Soviet Union's chief earner of foreign exchange. The project's price tag was estimated at anywhere from $15 billion to $45 billion, depending on whether a second or third segment was added and on support costs.

The pipeline was expected to deliver 1.4 trillion cubic feet of gas annually to Western Europe for 25 years, beginning in 1984. West Germany, the biggest recipient, would double the percentage of its natural gas intake from Soviet sources from a current 18 percent to an estimated 35 percent when the pipeline opened. France, Italy, Austria, Belgium, the Netherlands, Sweden, Finland, Switzerland and Greece were the other projected recipients of Soviet gas. According to a study by two officials of the Chase Manhattan Bank, entitled "Soviet Gas to the West: Risk or Reward?" the USSR would supply about 35 percent of Western Europe's natural gas requirements by 1990.

The political implications of an economic project making several major U.S. allies heavily dependent on the Soviets for a vital energy source were profoundly unsettling for Washington. The Soviets had threatened cutoffs of energy supplies to Western Europe and Japan in 1980 if they supported U.S. sanctions against the USSR after the invasion of Afghanistan. Moreover, Moscow cut back gas deliveries to Europe by one third during the winter of 1980-81 for "technical" reasons (evidently a disruption in distribution caused by unusually cold weather and by a loss of Iranian gas) and would be able to exert strong political leverage on Western gas recipients. Brezhnev undoubtedly recognized this fact when he declared that an acceleration in the production and export of natural gas would be desirable for both economic and political reasons.

Ironically, in the early 1980's Western Europe didn't need more Soviet natural gas; it was more concerned with providing jobs and stimulating industries than with securing energy supplies. An official of the West German ministry of economics conceded that "we would have been able to survive very comfortably without the Soviet natural gas. The pipeline contract was dictated by pure misery—jobs were the main consideration."[50] Similarly, a top official of the Amsterdam-Rotterdam Bank in the Netherlands declared that "the whole point of the pipeline was to give work to European exporters, and the gas itself was less important." He called the Soviet pipeline "a Keynesian relic" aimed at "attracting spending to countries in a recession."[51] A U.S. commentator underscored the fact that

> The economics of the pipeline project can be understood only as neo-Keynesianism. The goal, which fit in nicely with detente's encouragement of East-West trade, was to create government spending—regardless of the fact that the money could have been better spent in creating real growth in European economies rather than in the Soviet economy. . . . [52]

Economically, the "deal of the century," as Moscow and Bonn described the pipeline project,[53] was regarded by the Reagan Administration as a massive foreign aid program for the Soviet Union. Its point of view was reflected in a *Wall Street Journal* editorial that stated: "The great pipeline debate between the U.S. and Europe isn't about natural gas at all. It's about subsidizing the Soviets in a vast capital project they couldn't otherwise afford."[54] Sen. Jake Garn (R.-Utah) wrote that

> The pipeline project . . . will provide the Soviet Union with a much-needed boost in foreign-exchange earnings, help the Soviets maintain their control over Eastern Europe, bail the Soviets out of serious energy and economic difficulties, expose West European banks to a heightened risk of financial ruin, and grant Moscow large-scale economic and political influence over West European affairs. . . . [55]

The Reagan Administration contended, furthermore, that the Soviets could use their export earnings from natural gas (and the spinoffs from pipeline technology) to strengthen their military machine.

Ironically, Ruhrgas, the West German utility leading the gas buyers' consortium, is partly owned by American oil companies—Exxon (15%), Mobil (7.4%), and Texaco (3.5%). While clearly relishing the spectacle of discord between Washington and West European capitals over the pipeline project, Moscow hastened to guard itself against the possibility that U.S. pressure would force cancellation of Western participation in the program. Once burned, twice shy, Moscow was determined to prevent a repetition of the damage and inconvenience caused by American trade sanctions imposed after the invasion of Afghanistan.

During the second half of 1981, as the crisis in Poland deepened and plans for the imposition of martial law were finalized, the Soviet Union hastened to secure the necessary Western contracts for pipeline construction.[56] According to one report, the final contract was signed on 14 December 1981, the day after the Polish regime declared martial law.[57] Moreover, the Soviet Union attempted to insulate the pipeline project from political pressures by signing agreements with Western firms down to the subcontractor level for the necessary materials and components.

West German enterprises reaped the largest share of pipeline-related contracts, to the tune of more than $2 billion. France obtained nearly $2 billion in contracts for the Soviet pipeline—a boon that came when more than 2 million French citizens were unemployed. The sum of pipeline-related contracts for Italy totaled approximately $1 billion. Britain, a country rich in natural gas, joined nevertheless in supplying equipment for the Soviet pipeline.

Disputing U.S. contentions that they were subsidizing the pipeline, the Western allies argued that they would be paying bargain rates for gas and receiving up to 20 percent above market prices for the steel and equipment they provided to the Russians. In fact, Italy seemed to be the only country to obtain an attractive price (about $4 per thousand cubic feet of gas over a 20-year period), and only because the Soviets faced stiff competition from Algeria, which has a pieline under the Mediterranean to Italy. West Germany and France, the main end-users for the Soviet gas, agreed to a starting price of $4.75 to $5 per million BTU's, rising to at least $5.70 by 1984.

Similarly, there was much room for skepticism regarding the European contention that high prices for the materials and equipment supplied to the USSR justified Western participation in the pipeline project:

> The Soviet Union was a monopsonist, the sole "buyer" of pipe and equipment from Europe and the sole supplier of gas to several competing buyers. . . . The Soviets played off the European bidders against each other on each aspect of the project by announcing the best offers, then inviting more competition. Axel Lebahn, until recently the Moscow representative of Deutsche Bank AG, which led the German consortium that provided the largest share of the pipeline's financing, recently reported that Western exporters of equipment were forced to cut their prices by as

much as 60% because of their weak position as independent bargainers against the USSR . . . [58]

Moreover, as *The Wall Street Journal* editorialized,

The initial credits [for the project] have carried interest well below European market rates. Any way you figure it, the foregone interest by European banks adds up to a lot of money, far more than seems likely to be recovered with higher price tags on pipe and compressors. . . . The fact that no one is revealing these price tags gives good cause for such suspicions. . . . [59]

Although many details of the credit arrangements remained murky (due,in part, to the obvious reluctance of West European governments to divulge their unfavorable position), the main outlines were clear. In West Germany, a three-way arrangement evolved during 1982. Banks set up loans to German companies that had contracted for the supply of materials and equipment for the pipeline. The loans, totaling between $1.1 and $1.6 billion, were at market rates and were insured by the government. The companies, in turn, lent money to the Soviet Union at 7.8% interest—well below the market rate of 10-11%—to purchase their goods. The Soviets were to pay 20% above the market price for the equipment, thus making the effective interest rate about 11.2%. In the aftermath of a meeting with Soviet officials in July 1982, a Deutsche Bank spokesman claimed that the banking consortium would "eventually get market rates," but he declined to elaborate.[60]

In contrast to the West Germans, the French provided a direct loan to the Soviet government. A consortium of French banks, led by Credit Lyonnais, offered $850 million in credits, payable over a ten-year period, at 7.8% interest. Credit insurance was provided. A follow-up agreement for $140 million in credits at market rates was signed by the USSR and French banks without French government guarantees. The Italian government provided credits to the USSR to cover the lion's share of the contracts granted to Italian firms for pipeline work. The interest rate was 8.25%, the developed countries' consensus rate at the time the agreement was signed. Using the same rate, a British bank extended a $348-million credit line to the Soviets that was guaranteed by the British government.[61] In sum,

The Soviets have been playing a brilliant game in Western Europe. By holding out the lure of juicy contracts and seemingly low-priced gas, they have played one European country off against another and wangled nearly 100% financing at below-market rates for their credit-starved economy. Western European politicians, eager to stave off recession by whatever means possible and protect their own jobs, played along with Moscow, pretending that detente hadn't gone up in flames as a result of Afghanistan and Poland. [62]

On 29 December 1981, in response to the Soviet-mandated imposition of martial law in Poland, President Reagan embargoed U.S. technology exports and the sale of oil and gas equipment to the Soviet Union, thus confirming Moscow's worst fear that sanctions would jeopardize the pipeline project. The Caterpillar Tractor Co., which had contracted to supply 200 pipelaying machines valued at about $80 million, was the chief U.S. victim of the President's decision. Of the West European suppliers for the pipeline project, West German government officials and industrialists most strongly rejected the notion that Moscow was responsible for the martial law crackdown in Warsaw. An editorial in the *Frankfurter Rundschau*, the West German newspaper most closely linked with the Social Democratic Party, complained that not only was Washington trying to "send the Germans to the battlefield" (an apparent reference to the INF dispute) but, with its sanctions, was expecting them "to buy American coal rather than Russian natural gas."[63]

Washington beseeched its allies not to "undercut" the U.S. sanctions. However, many Europeans interpreted the "no-undercut" policy as applicable only to direct Soviet-American deals in which U.S. companies acted as main contractors—not as subcontractors.[64] Far from heeding West European pleas to lift the sanctions, Reagan extended them on 18 June 1982 to overseas subsidiaries and licensees of U.S. companies. Declaring that Moscow and Warsaw had done nothing to alleviate repression in Poland or soften martial law, the President said he would penalize foreign companies that exported to the USSR pipeline equipment embodying technology licensed from American industries.

The rotor shafts and blades that were to drive the turbines for the pipeline's compressor stations proved to be the Achilles heel of Russia's embargo-proof scheme. General Electric was prohibited from providing these items.

Washington's European allies assailed the embargo not only because of their financial stakes in the pipeline project, but also because Reagan (under pressure from the farm lobby) had lifted the grain embargo imposed by Jimmy Carter after the Soviet invasion of Afghanistan. The Administration's counter-arguments that the United States sold grain to the Soviets for cash while Western Europe subsidized the export of pipeline equipment rang hollow in European capitals. As *The Washington Times* editorialized,"We ask [the Europeans] to understand the difference between our grain-for-cash and their gear-on-credit. This is an accurate but somewhat fine distinction to ask them to accept under the circumstances."[65]

In Britain, the Thatcher government, heretofore one of Reagan's staunchest allies, ordered John Brown Engineering Ltd. to defy the U.S. sanctions and deliver to the Russians the turbines it had produced with General Electric-supplied rotors. The French government also ordered enterprises to honor contracts with the Soviet Union involving embargoed items. French Foreign Minister Claude Cheysson declared that the pipeline issue was pushing the United States [and Western Europe] toward "a progressive divorce."[66]

The furor against sanctions reached its highest level in West Germany, where "Osthandel" (literally, "East-trade") is a sacred cow. Describing the atmosphere in the Federal Republic in the aftermath of Reagan's ban on the transfer of oil and gas technology to the USSR, an American journalist wrote:

> . . . Industrial leaders . . . insist that sanctions are pointless, a line that ironically dovetails with that of the left wing of Chancellor Schmidt's Social Democratic Party. The West German public has also been told that about 200,000 jobs are dependent on Osthandel, not to mention the lives of a few major companies such as AEG-Telefunken [West Germany's second largest electrcial and electronics industrial group]. . . .

> There is an additional twist in West Germany's reluctance to impose sanctions. West German banks not only hold about a quarter of Poland's debts to the West; those banks, in the absence of a significant stock market in the country, provide most of the essential financing for West German industry. This has created a circle of interwoven interests among ailing companies needing trade with the East and loans at home, banks that must prop up local companies while seeking to avoid a Polish default . . . as well as a government whose decade-long credo has been detente. [67]

A number of U.S. officials and institutions evidently opposed Reagan's sanctions on the grounds that they were damaging relations with the European allies as well as the Soviet Union. Confronted with pressure from several quarters, the President announced the end of the embargo in November. "As a face-saving gesture," wrote Anderson, "it was announced that the European allies would join in a tough general agreement on trade with the Soviets."[68] Such an agreement was not forthcoming, because the allies regarded trade and economic ties with the USSR as a basic ingredient of detente, because even anti-Communist leaders like Mitterrand didn't believe in the desirability or efficacy of using trade as a weapon, because the Europeans generally doubted that economic pressure would modify Soviet behavior in the international arena, and because economic and commercial transactions with the Soviet bloc boosted industrial output and employment in Western Europe. The general cooling of European ardor for the pipeline project resulted not from political considerations but from the energy glut and the attendant drop in oil and gas prices. Over the longer term, there is every reason to believe that the Western allies will seek cooperative ventures in the energy field with the Soviet Union, both because of their continuing devotion to detente and because of a desire to reduce their dependence on oil from the turbulent Middle East.

At the height of the pipeline controversy, Senator Garn noted the political and psychological factors that underlay— and overrode—the purely economic motivations for European participation in the project:

> The fact is that the West Europeans face a reality quite different from ours. They are physically much closer to the growing military muscle of the Soviet Union. . . . Coupled with this growing fear of Soviet strength is increasing doubt over U.S. military strength and U.S. willingnes to use that strength in defense of Western Europe. . . . Thus . . . "faith" in Soviet energy reliability is actually born of fear and intimidation. That is why alternatives to the Soviet energy package, regardless of how attractive, have gotten a cold reception in Europe. . . . [69]

The pipeline project symbolized Western Europe's commitment to what Senator Garn called "a separate detente with the Russians." Simmilarly, Irving Kristol wrote that

> For our NATO allies, the pipeline is desirable precisely because it will enhance Soviet economic growth—and thereby, they hope, diminish the Soviet appeasing for foreign expansion. It is the spirit of detente in its most appeasing form that this pipeline represents, not merely a new source of gas, such new sources being available everywhere. [70]

In Kristol's judgment, the pipeline issue "reveals a deep fault within the NATO alliance. . . . The foreign policy of Western Europe is in an appeasement mode vis-a-vis the Soviet Union; the U.S. under Ronald Reagan is in a more confrontational mode."

The outcome of the pipeline controversy was a Reagan victory of sorts. The U.S. sanctions forced a delay in construction and obliged the Soviets to divert pumping equipment from their domestic gaslines. The pipeline opened on schedule in the first week of January 1984, but only a minimal amount of gas flowed, thus depriving the Kremlin of revenues that a larger volume would generate at marginal additional cost. On 12 January a *Wall Street Journal* editorial opined that

> Getting accurate information on this pipeline project has been a problem from the first. . . . Our latest report is that only one of the 41 compressors is now built, and that one is only in the testing stages; that is, the Soviets have been unable to complete the installations affected by the Reagan sanctions. . . . [It appears] that Euroconsumers have been taken, providing below-market credit terms in exchange for above-market gas prices. . . .

Other factors entered the picture as the world inflation rate fell and the Organization of Petroleum Exportng Countries (OPEC) lost its stranglehold on the international oil market. The Soviet Union had planned for these contingencies by inserting a floor-price clause in its contracts. In addition, a "take-or-pay" clause committed Western buyers to pay for 80% of the contracted volume of gas at the stated price.[71] Both France and West Germany reportedly sought to renegotiate their contracts, but the Soviets held them to the original terms on price and volume.[72]

An interesting footnote to the pipeline controversy occurred in November 1984, when the Soviet Union declared that it would withhold fuel shipments to Britain until the Thatcher government settled the bitter coal strike there on terms favorable to Arthur Scargill's mineworkers' union. Scargill himself emerged from a meeting at the Soviet Embassy in London to announce that the Russians had contributed more than half a million dollars to the union's strike kitty. "We are fighting a class war," he explained. As *The Wall Street Journal* remarked, "the Scargill exercise makes it clear that oil and gas are not simple trade commodities for the Russians, but an implement for waging the 'class war.'"[73]

So long as the Soviet gas pipeline operates below capacity because of low demand and apparent technical difficulties, opportunities for the Kremlin to use its energy leverage for coercion or blackmail will be small. Even under present conditions, however, West Berlin, parts of West Germany, Austria, Turkey and even France and Italy rely to an uncomfortable extent on Soviet gas supplies. The overall situation could change abruptly if oil and gas prices rise, if the Soviets complete the new pipeline (alone or with the aid of imported components), if they complete a second strand and link it with the existing line, and if a combination of these things occurs before a massive new Norwegian gas project comes to fruition.

The Norwegian deal involves development of the Troll and Sleipner natural gas fields in the North Sea and construction of more than 800 miles of pipeline to Belgium, France, and West Germany. In June 1986 a consortium of West European firms announced the signing of a contract binding them to purchase $64 billion worth of Norwegian gas over a 27-year period running from 1993 to 2020. Norway ultimately could supply about 30% of Europe's natural gas requirements, thus cutting deeply into Soviet export prospects.[74]

Aside from the Soviet gas pipeline, the question of the Soviet bloc's growing debt to Western banks became an irritant among the NATO allies during the 1980's. Pressure from some Reagan Administration officials to declare Poland in default, thus putting into question the creditworthiness of the entire Soviet bloc—including the USSR itself—brought the controversy to a head. The Western allies received some support, however, from Secretary of State Haig and other U.S. officials, who argued that declaring Poland in default would have the most severe impact on West German banks and thus would weaken Chancellor Schmidt, who already was under siege from his party's left wing.[75] Poland's debts were ultimately rescheduled.

The Versailles summit of June 1982 witnessed open animosity among the NATO allies. Reagan had to settle for a vaguely worded declaration committing the Seven (including Japan) to "limit" credits to the Soviet bloc through "a prudent and diversified economic approach."[76] In addition, the President failed to obtain a consensus that would have required Allied governments to charge a commercial interest rate of 12.25% on loans to the USSR and the Soviet bloc, thus withholding subsidized loans at a time when most commercial banks had begun to limit such loans.

On the issue of exporting strategic or "dual-use" items to the USSR and Eastern Europe, the Versailles participants came closer to a consensus. The declaration pledged the seven countries to "work together to improve the international system for controlling exports of strategic goods" to the bloc and to make "national arrangements for the enforcement of security controls."[77] Shortly before the Versailles summit, Lawrence J. Brady, Assistant Secretary of Commerce for Trade Administration, declared that the leakage of technology to the USSR and Eastern Europe "is massive, not only from the United States but more so from the rest of the Free World."

The allies increasingly came to acknowledge the severity of the problem. France, which had provided competitive financing and "counter-trade" deals to ease the Soviet Union's debt burden and hard-currency difficulties, made a quick turnaround when the Kremlin exploited this generosity. In 1983, Paris expelled 47 Soviet officials for conducting a massive campaign of espionage and pilfering of technology. The expulsions resulted from information passed to French intelligence by a KGB agent in Paris. The agent, code-named "Farewell," provided thousands of documents detailing Soviet scientific and technological espionage in France.[78] Then, in 1984, the West German government received a Soviet "wish list" of Western technology that reportedly was the size of a thick telephone book. The list, as published by Bonn, contained 27 sections devoted to items from satellite tracking systems to agricultural equipment that the Soviets sought to acquire by means fair or foul.[79] Largely as a result of these revelations, the European allies expanded substantially the catalogue of items forbidden for export to the Soviet bloc.

Soviet treachery notwithstanding, the West European allies were convinced of the need for continuing detente. Sir Oliver Wright, the British ambassador to the United States, reflected the prevailing sentiment when he commented that "for Europe, detente worked well: there was peace in the most dangerous and most important part of the world."[80] The very fact that a Soviet-American summit took place in 1985—irrespective of its outcome—dramatically altered Reagan's image in the eyes of European public opinion. Evans & Novak exclaimed a week after the summit that " . . . a mood of post-Geneva exhiliaration and admiration for Ronald Reagan is running at riptide throughout Western Europe. Only months ago, the President was excoriated here [in West Germany] as a latter-day Attila the Hun."[81]

Europe's devotion to detente—and to arms control as its anchor—explains the unanimously negative reaction from the Allies when Reagan announced on 27 May 1986 that he no longer would consider himself bound to adhere to SALT II. Secretary of State Shultz formally conveyed Reagan's decision to the Allies at a meeting of the 16 NATO foreign ministers in Halifax, Nova Scotia, on 29 May. According to one source, "if there had been a vote" at Halifax, "it would have been 15 to 1 against the United States."[82] Several of the European leaders evidently feared that a resurgence of the peace movement in the wake of Reagan's decision could result in joint anti-government protests by the peace activists and groups protesting high unemployment and economic hardship.

The European NATO partners continued to regard SALT II, with all its imperfections, as the most potent symbol of superpower "restraint." Furthermore, they avowed that fresh arms control measures were needed in order to keep the arms control "process" alive. As Britain's Thatcher put it,

> I am very anxious that there should be another summit between President Reagan and Mr. Gorbachev, and I recognize that one has to be a success for both of them, and therefore it must produce some specific advance in arms control agreements. That means we have all got to work jolly hard at Geneva to get that advance. [83]

As pressures mounted on Washington from its NATO partners to be more forthcoming on arms control to facilitate a new summit, Moscow unleashed a propaganda offensive portraying the United States as NATO's bully. Gorbachev dramatized his allegations of U.S. pressure on the West Europeans by stating that

> . . . In Greek mythology, there is the legend about the abduction of the goddess Europa [a Phoenician princess who was kidnapped by the Greek god Zeus in the guise of a white bull and carried off to Crete]. Now, as a geographic concept, Europe remains in place, but the impression is created that the independent policy of some West European countries has been abducted and taken across the ocean. [84]

Moscow's "remedy" for the malady that its propaganda apparatus has helped to perpetuate is the creation of a pan-European collective security system, excluding the United States, its nuclear weapons, and its 300,000-plus "tripwire" forces. "Come home, Europe!" cries the USSR, to paraphrase a Vietnam-era slogan. Steps along the path to a "pax Sovietica," as envisaged by Moscow, would include the establishment of nuclear-free zones in various parts of Europe (excluding the USSR, of course), the dissolution of NATO and the Warsaw Pact (leaving the Soviet Union, unlike the United States, in possession of bilateral defense treaties with each of its allies), and a collective security system (actually a misnomer, since the USSR would be stronger militarily than all of the system's members combined).

The concept of nuclear-free zones in Europe can be traced back at least as far as 1958, when Poland formally introduced the Rapacki Plan, calling for a ban on the production or deployment of nuclear weapons in Poland, Czechoslovakia, and the two Germanies. Named for Polish Foreign Minister Adam Rapacki and almost certainly inspired by the Soviet Union, the plan evidently was designed to forestall the introduction of nuclear arms into West Germany and to ensure Soviet predominance in the heart of Europe by virtue of conventional superiority. Various European statesmen have subscribed to the concept of nuclear-free zones in Europe. Former Swedish Prime Minister and peace activist Olof Palme was a major advocate of such a zone for Scandinavia. Gerhard Eppler, a prominent member of the left wing of West Germany's Social Democratic Party, has suggested the establishment of a central European nuclear-free zone along the lines of the Rapacki Plan. Other schemes for freeing the Continent of nuclear weapons have proven less attractive to the Kremlin. For example, when the European Campaign for Nuclear Disarmament (END), a British organization, called for "a nuclear-free Europe from Poland to Portugal," a Soviet spokesman complained that "this strangely geographically truncated Europe conceals [a] harebrained scheme to split the Socialist countries of Europe from the Soviet Union."[85]

Aside from nuclear-free zones, Moscow's European diplomacy has also promoted schemes for a nonaggression treaty between NATO and the Warsaw Pact and for "no-first-use" of nuclear weapons. Beyond ridding Europe of nuclear weapons, the USSR aims to "decouple" Western Europe's defense from that of the United States. Punching enough holes in the U.S. nuclear umbrella to discredit its usefulness would be one method of attaining this goal. With their steady military buildup in both nuclear and conventional caategories, the Soviets have moved toward a blitzkrieg capability that would virtually devastate Western Europe before NATO could credibly respond. As noted above, however, Moscow would much prefer to capture Europe without firing a shot by denuclearizing NATO and then eroding its cohesiveness to the point of collapse.

The Soviets also have called for the dissolution of both NATO and the Warsaw Pact. The Soviet Union's proximity to Eastern Europe and its retention of bilateral defense agreements with each Warsaw Pact member would ensure Soviet control even in the absence of a formal alliance. On the Western side, by contrast,the NATO members probably would scatter in their 16 different directions (perhaps fashioning "Little Entente"-style arrangements along the way), while the United States would retreat behind its ocean buffer (and possibly its "Star Wars" shield), leaving Europe in a "Finlandized" position at best.

Soviet political schemes for the demise of NATO are by no means incapable of realization. Fostering and exploiting "contradictions" between America and its NATO allies has been a staple of Soviet foreign policy for decades. The removal of the U.S. nuclear guarantee to Western Europe would cripple the Alliance militarily, even if its political structure remained intact. Already, the automaticity of the guarantee is in doubt in the minds of many Europeans, who, moreover, have been lulled by Moscow's propaganda into underestimating the Soviet threat to their security. As one commentator noted,

> . . . President Reagan came into office believing that the quarrels with Europe were essentially Jimmy Carter's fault and could be patched up with a strong measure of leadership and more military spending. Alas, the belief was misplaced. The problem was not that there were holes in the American nuclear umbrella, but that Europe no longer felt the rain. [86]

Two decades ago, Charles de Gaulle pulled France out of NATO's integrated military command and advocated the creation of a "Europe from the Atlantic to the Urals"—a concept that the Kremlin found congenial. In 1980, a year before he became president of France, Francois Mitterrand wrote that "nothing disposes me to postulate the necessity of the Atlantic alliance, and I would be satisfied with a situation that would make it defunct."[87] Egon Bahr, a leading antinuclear spokesman for West Germany's Social Democratic Party, is on record as avowing that

> As long as the Atlantic alliance is the measure of all things for Western Europe, Moscow will hold on to what it has with all its strength. Eastern Europe cannot emancipate itself from the Soviet Union without Western Europe emancipating itself from the United States. [88]

One of the USSR's most cherished foreign policy objectives is to create a European collective security system with itself as guarantor. Moscow sought the convening of a European security conference without U.S. participation, but the NATO allies objected. Their devotion to detente notwithstanding, they understood fully the implications of a Soviet-style collective security system in Europe:

> The Soviet Union would attain military and political superiority vis-a-vis all other combined European states once the United States left Europe, which would be inevitable under a collective security arrangement. . . . In Europe, the creation of a collective security system as a substitute to the present state of bloc confrontation can have only one practical consequence—the extension of Soviet supremacy to Western Europe and the concomitant termination of the U.S. presence in Europe. . . . [89]

In August 1975, 35 nations gathered at Helsinki for the Conference on Security and Cooperation in Europe. "Basket 1" of the conference's Final Act, the most momentous portion from Moscow's standpoint, stipulated that European frontiers were inviolable. Some Western officials stated that this stricture meant only that force could not be employed to alter borders. Peaceful change—e.g., German reunification—was deemed to be permissible. The salient point, however, was that the signatories at Helsinki placed their imprimatur on Soviet control of Eastern Europe. The Final Act also called, inter alia, for the signatories to refrain from interference in each other's domestic affairs. This pronouncement came at a time when the Soviets and their agents in the Portuguese Communist Party were busily subverting the Portuguese revolution in order to detach the country from NATO and transform it into a "people's democracy."

From Moscow's perspective, the Helsinki conference sanctified Europe's role as an oasis of detente at a time when superpower relations were cooling rapidly. Soviet officials began to speak of "differentiated detente" and "divisible detente," with the implication that U.S.-Soviet frictions need not ruffle the smooth surface of Soviet relations with Western Europe. Even when Moscow began to deploy SS-20 missiles, the Soviets exhorted the NATO countries to extend political detente into military detente. Arnaud de Borchgrave, then a senior editor of *Newsweek*, captured the essence of "military detente" when he wrote that "Moscow and its allies are striving to achieve such manifest [military] superiority that Europe's decisionmakers will gradually acquire conditioned reflexes of appeasement whenever political demands are made."[90]

A German scholar has portrayed how the emerging climate of detente in Europe aroused hopes among non-Communist intellectuals, especially in West Germany and Scandinavia, that genuine peace was at hand:

. . . The propinquity of the Soviet empire, which assured an awareness of its repressive nature, now began to provide incentives for ignoring the repressive characacter of the Soviet regime. The more relaxed relationship and the benefits derived from the emerging modus vivendi were seen as a great relief by the Northwest European Left. The frightening prospect of an East-West confrontation in Europe finally seemed avoidable. Detente was widely viewed as a security guarantee which must not be jeopardized by any other issue. An anti-confrontationist attitude emerged: any conflict with the Soviet Union is perceived as a possibly dangerous confrontation, and peace—the avoidance of conflict—becomes an end in itself.

. . . The proponents of an anti-confrontationist policy felt that security could be achieved only together with the other side, not against it. . . . To people such as . . . Olof Palme . . . Willy Brandt, or . . . Egon Bahr, the postulate of a Western deterrence maintained vis-a-vis the USSR was highly confrontationist and therefore counter to the imperative of cooperative security.

From this it followed that common security could not be equated with any variant of NATO's strategic wisdom but had to be an alternative to it. The implication of this view was that the present dualism of the alliances on both sides—and hence the existence of the North Atlantic pact—had to be replaced by another security system that jointly provided for the security of both Western and Eastern countries. The idea was that a system of collective security should be created in Europe.[91]

On 1 June 1979, on the eve of the SALT II summit in Moscow, Brezhnev declared that "Europe, which . . . set the beginning of the process of political detente, can and must become an example of realization of detente in the military field." According to Radio Moscow, "the SALT II agreement could become a stimulus to this" realization.[92] Meanwhile, the May 1979 issue of the Soviet journal *International Affairs* ran an article stating that

The policy of detente does not simply cast doubt on the very existence of military blocs but poses a reasonable prospect for their liquidation. . . . The NATO ringleaders understand that detente . . . spreading to new spheres of the interrelations of states, will show . . . that military-political alliances in our time cannot serve as the basis for the creation of a reliable system of international security. . . . In conditions of detente, contradictions are sharply increased in the ranks of existing imperialist blocs, above all NATO, which is going through a permanent crisis. [93]

A half year later, the USSR invaded Afghanistan, shattering Jimmy Carter's illusions about the nature of the Soviet beast and leading him to discard detente. The President argued unsuccessfully with West European governments that detente was indivisible and that a firm, united stance might convince the Soviets to withdraw from Afghanistan. He urged the NATO allies to follow his lead in imposing trade sanctions on the Soviet Union, boycotting the 1980 Olympics in Moscow, and generally minimizing high-level contacts with the aggressor. However, a West German newspaper cautioned against overreaction to Afghanistan, arguing that "battles lost in Kabul cannot be won in Berlin."[94] Chancellor Schmidt asserted that "we will not permit ten years of detente and defense policy to be destroyed" because of the Soviet rape of Afghanistan.[95] French President Valery Giscard d'Estaing, who became the first Western leader to meet Brezhnev (in Warsaw in May 1980) after Afghanistan, declared that "the balance of power in Europe is a separate problem" from Afghanistan, which belonged in the realm of Soviet-American "bloc politics." And the French magazine *Le Nouvel Observateur* queried, "Why should Germans die for Kabul when they are not sure Americans are willing to die for Berlin?"[96]

Moreover, Europe put its money where its mouth was. The European Economic Community reversed an initial decision to withhold butter from the Soviet Union and began to sell it at a cheap rate. On 17 March 1980 the Kremlin announced its first major contract award since U.S. sanctions were imposed; it was a $118-million deal with the French for offshore oil-drilling rigs for use in the Caspian Sea.[97] West Germany signed a long-term economic and trade agreement with the Soviets, encompassing, inter alia, cooperation in energy and industrial production. The West Germans reportedly went so far as to suggest a "division of labor"among Western countries in their responses to Afghanistan; according to an American official, this suggestion meant that "we do the fighting, and they do the trading."[98] A number of U.S. allies, disregarding pledges not to take over cancelled American contracts, competed openly to fill gaps created by Washington's ban on export licenses for high-technology items. As one commentator noted,

It was popular during the last decade to argue that political differences between the United States and Europe did not affect the utility of the alliance. What does it matter, it was asked, if Americans and Europeans hold different views on Vietnam, Palestine, the Persian Gulf, trade, oil, the dollar and nuclear proliferation, so long as they hold the same view about the Soviet Union? Afghanistan has demonstrated that the European and American differences today concern the very centerpiece of the NATO structure: the Soviet Union and the Soviet threat to Western Europe. Afghanistan has given birth in Europe to the idea that "detente is divisible." [99]

Predictably, Moscow proved adept at exploiting the "contradictions" between the United States and the European allies that already had emerged with the neutron bomb and INF issues and were sharpened by the post-Afghanistan sanctions debate. The newspaper *Sovetskaya Rossiya* opined that "the rifts . . . between the United States and Western Europe deepen because a vast majority of West Europeans have become convinced of the advantages of international detente. . . . Economic relations with the Socialist countries are exceedingly beneficial."[100] Moscow hinted that it could withhold lucrative economic contracts from European countries that succumbed to American pressure over Poland.

The election of Ronald Reagan also disturbed the West Europeans—conservatives as well as Socialists. Any expectations they might have had that he would follow in the pro-detente footsteps of fellow conservative Republican Richard Nixon were smashed with Reagan's "Evil Empire" speech. Moreover, many European officials suspected that the new President and the sun-belt Republicans in his entourage were "Asia-firsters." A West European ambassador confided to an American journalist that " . . . I was talking to a Texan, and he told me that Europe was 'just an obsession of the New York establishment.'"[101]

The Soviet natural gas pipeline, the Kremlin-mandated clampdown on Poland's Solidarity trade union movement, and the introduction of Reagan's SDI became additional bones of contention between Washington and West European capitals. The Kremlin exploited them masterfully. Soviet propaganda called U.S. policy on Poland an attempt to sabotage detente and thus endanger the security and prosperity of its Western allies. *Sovetskaya Rossiya* stated that "Washington's violent fury" over Poland was a smokescreen for "completely subordinating the junior partners in the North Atlantic bloc" to the United States.[102] *Pravda* regarded SDI as "an attempt to ensure the permanent technological superiority of the West over the Socialist countries, and . . . over the United States' own allies as well."[103]

When the USSR launched a missile against a South Korean jetliner in September 1983, leading to the deaths of its 269 passengers (including conservative American congressman Larry McDonald), the Europeans briefly joined Washington in condemning Soviet barbarity. Moscow's walkout from arms control negotiations two months later, however, buried the KAL tragedy and re-ignited latent European fears of nuclear war. By early 1984, Reagan was under heavy pressure from the West Europeans to moderate his stance vis-a-vis the USSR. He made a conciliatory speech on 16 January of that year, continued to affirm his interest in arms control, and generally presented a positive image, particularly when matched against a succession of sickly and stodgy Soviet leaders—Brezhnev, Andropov, and Chernenko.

With Gorbachev's accession to power in March 1985, the "Great Communicator ' encountered unexpected competition in the public relations sphere. Moreover, the new General Secretary displayed a determination to woo America's Euroepan allies, even while expressing a desire for a superpower summit. He had already tested the Western waters in December 1984, when he led a Supreme Soviet delegation to Britain. Prime Minister Thatcher (the "Iron Lady" of British politics) invited him to lunch at her country residence, Chequers, on that occasion and later declared that "I like Mr. Gorbachev. We can do business together."[104] The British media referred to Gorbachev's meeting with Thatcher as "the summit of smiles." The highest-ranking Politburo member to visit London since Prime Minister Alexei Kosygin traveled there in 1967, Gorbachev spent considerable time making overtures to British engineering and chemical enterprises, most of which had expressed displeasure with President Reagan's trade and economic sanctions against the Soviet Union. Gorbachev has since indicated the importance he attaches to Britain—where a Labor Party election victory could lead to unilateral nuclear disarmament—by appointing Leonid Zamyatin as the new Soviet ambassador. Zamyatin was head of the International Information Department, a body established by the Communist party's Central Committee in 1978 to coordinate Soviet propaganda and disinformation in Western Europe.

France was the first Western country that Gorbachev visited after becoming General Secretary. He evidently hoped to place Franco-Soviet relations on an even keel after a period of ups and downs during Mitterrand's regime. Moscow had enjoyed excellent relations with Paris during the tenure of Mitterrand's conservative predecessor, Giscard d'Estaing. Soviet press coverage of the 1981 French election campaign lauded Giscard while taking aim at Mitterrand's "Atlanticist" foreign policy views. The French Communist Party lent Mitterrand crucial suport in the runoff election and demanded a role in his government. Four Communist ministers were duly appointed. On 16 May 1981, six days after the historic victory of the Socialist Party, *Le Monde* carried an article from the Soviet press agency *Novosti* that reaffirmed traditional Franco-Soviet friendship and called cooperation between the two countries "the barometer of detente in Europe." However, Mitterrand remained firm in defense of Euromissile deployments. In an address to the West German parliament on 21 January 1983, he cautioned that Europe "must not be deprived of a means to answer the nuclear weapons specifically directed against her."[105] An American correspondent noted:

> It is illustrative of the softness of West German opinion on the missiles— and the government's own uncertain voice—that the most ringing defense of nuclear deterrence came . . . from France's Socialist president. [106]

During the summer of 1984, the French Communists quit the coalition government, and Mitterrand evidently perceived less need to pursue a strong anti-Soviet foreign policy to counterbalance his working relationship with the Communist Party at home. He moved toward a more Gaullist-style posture of flouting the United States and courting the USSR. However, Mitterrand did not visit Moscow until June 1984—three years after his election as president—and, while there, he embarrassed his hosts by publicly raising the issue of Andrei Sakharov, the dissident physicist, human rights activist, and Nobel Peace Prize winner who had been consigned to internal exile.

Gorbachev traveled to Paris in October 1985, in a trip noteworthy for its public relations aspects. The 54-year-old "baby" of the Soviet Politburo, Gorbachev portrayed himself as the representative of a new generation of officials who would breathe fresh life into the Soviet system. Gorbachev was accompanied by his wife, Raisa, who, by Soviet standards, represented sartorial splendor and who posed graciously with French couturiers. Mrs. Gorbachev made news simply by appearing in a public forum; the very existence of Chernenko's wife, by contrast, was a well guarded secret until she showed up at his funeral. Western media promptly dubbed the Gorbachevs the "Gucci comrades."

Much as Gorbachev valued cordial relations with Britain and France, West Germany remained the focus of his efforts to drive wedges in the Atlantic Alliance and to revalidate detente. There were several peculiarities with regard to West Germany that rendered it vulnerable to Soviet carrot-and-stick approaches. First of all, its geographic position is unique among the Western allies:

> Sharing a one-thousand-mile border with the Warsaw Pact countries, West Germany would bear the brunt of any attack mounted by the East.

*Ostpolitik* (detente, German-style) was enshrined by the new co-alition government under Willy Brandt that took office in 1969. The so-called Eastern treaties with the USSR and the Soviet bloc were signed in the early 1970's, paving the way for closer diplomatic and economic cooperation. The special elections of 1972 were fought and won on the issue of the Eastern treaties. Willy Brandt was forced to resign as chancellor in 1973, when one of his closest aides was discovered to be an East Germany spy, but this episode did not derail *Ostpolitik*.

During the Nixon Administration, West Germany's *Ostpolitik* ran along a parallel track with America's policy of detente. Bonn, along with other Allied capitals, welcomed the SALT I treaty and expressed support for follow-on arms control measures. When U.S.-Soviet relations began to sour in the mid-1970's, West Germany continued to proclaim its devotion to detente. Chancellor Schmidt was in the forefront of West European leaders hailing SALT II, which was signed in June 1979. Commentator Josef Joffe noted at the time that

> . . . SALT remains the last slender threat in the fraying fabric of global detente. . . . If the thread should snap as a result of Senate rejection [of SALT II], European detente will inevitably unravel along with the painstakingly . . . constructed network of agreements which goes by the name of *Ostpolitik*. The Bonn government has praised SALT II so compulsively not because it is wildly enthusiastic about the substance of the agreement, but because it is obsessed with the political consequences of its rejection. . . . [109]

With the Soviet invasion of Afghanistan and Jimmy Carter's decision to withdraw SALT II from Senate consideration to avoid a humiliating political defeat, plans were set afoot in West Germany (and elsewhere in Europe) to pursue a "separate detente" with the Soviet Union. Schmidt visited Moscow in June 1980. At a Kremlin banquet in his honor, Brezhnev stated that "I would be less than sincere if I said that our views coincide in everything. But we're unanimous, perhaps, in the main thing, namely in the belief that no harm should be done to the policy of detente."[110] For Bonn, this policy of detente was not designed to express displeasure with Washington but rather to preserve a relationship with the East that was deemed both desirable and politically necessary. Joffe pointed out that

> . . . As a superpower which, apart from a link of mutual deterrence, shares few ties of interdependence with the Soviet Union and Eastern

Europe, the United States can live with the ups as well as with the downs of East-West relations. There is little trade and even less interaction. The relationship between West Germany and the countries of the Warsaw Pact is quite different. Far more vulnerable than the United States, West Germany has more tangible stakes in the detente game. [111]

By 1980 West Germany had become the primary Western trading partner of every Soviet-bloc nation, including the USSR itself. A Soviet commentator wrote at the time that "it is no accident that in the present complex situation, we see in the FRG a whole collection of the most prominent representatives of the business world who are among the most steadfast opponents of a return to the Cold War."[112] In January 1982, while Schmidt was on an official visit to the United States, *Newsweek* reported that

> In a country that once considered work a birthright, last month's unemployment rate rose to 6.4 percent, the highest since the postwar reconstruction. The 1.7 million jobless workers have exerted enormous political pressure on Schmidt, threatening his delicate balance of support from both business and labor. Seeking economic growth where he can find it, Schmidt has opened West Germany's doors wide to trade with the East bloc. . . . More than 700 West German firms have entered into production agreements with the Soviet bloc, and an estimated 450,000 West German jobs depend directly on trade with the East. . . . [113]

In the course of pursuing *Ostpolitik*, Schmidt began to fancy himself as an interlocutor, or broker, between the superpowers. *The New York Times* editorialized that

> . . . The dream of German reunification, family ties with East Germany and a lucrative trade all depend on detente. And the Social Democratic sponsors of this "Ostpolitik" have acquired a powerful partisan stake in its success. [114]

The SPD's left wing would have been a powerful brake on any attempt by Schmidt to veer away from detente. Influential figures in the CDU—still West Germany's largest political party—increasingly began to advocate a softer line toward the Soviet bloc. A *Washington Post* correspondent on the scene in the autumn of 1981 reported that

> Behind their call is certainly no new-found love for the Soviets, but rather a tough political judgment that the CDU must portray itself as a dynamic, rather than reactionary, successor to the government of Chancellor Helmut Schmidt. Implicit in this tack is an acknowledgement that West Germany's commitment to detente, fostered during the past dozen years

of Social Democratic rule in Bonn, is irreversible and could not be refuted or ignored by a future conservative government here.[115]

Even while the CDU was inching closer to the SPD on the detente issue, the SPD itself underwent an internal split. Chancellor Schmidt's decision to permit the deployment of Euromissiles on West German soil aroused anti-American and anti-NATO sentiments that were latent among many segments of the West German population—especially, but not exclusively, on the left. The Soviets, predictably, raked the embers of fear and anger about the missiles. On 16 September 1981, for example, the Soviet ambassador to East Germany, Pyotr Abrasimov, declared:

> We must not forget that if American medium-range missiles are deployed in Western Europe, they will not only be aimed at the GDR and other Socialist countries, but also in effect at West Berlin and at the Quadripartite Agreement. . . . [116]

Abrasimov intimated that deployment of the Euromissiles could cause the reopening of the Berlin question.

The ascendant left wing of the SPD played an active role in the West German "peace" movement's protests against Euromissile deployments. Erhard Eppler, a member of the SPD's executive body, told the INF rally in Bonn in 1981 that "the peace movement shows that the old nations of Europe are more than just chessmen on the board of the world powers, *both* world powers."[117] Willy Brandt, who retained his post as chairman of the SDP after his forced resignation from the chancellorship, parlayed his reputation as the architect of *Ostpolitik* into symbolic leadership of the peace movement and the radical left in general. In Brandt's opinion, the proper response to Soviet aggression and threats "is more detente, not less."[118] Egon Bahr has scorned the United States as "the former occupation power,"[119] and Erhard Eppler has warned that West Germany must not become a U.S. "nuclear colony." With colleagues espousing such views, it was up to Chancellor Schmidt to admonish a 1981 meeting of the SDP to "stop behaving as if the Americans were your enemies and the Soviets your friends!"[120]

The crackdown on the Solidarity trade union movement in neighboring Poland did nothing to deflect West Germany's commitment to *Ostpolitik*. On the contrary, it inspired fear in Bonn that Moscow would seal the cracks in the Iron Curtain and freeze the political climate in Europe. When Gen. Wojciech Jaruzelski's regime imposed martial law on 13 December 1981, at the Kremlin's behest, Chancellor Schmidt was in East Germany hobnobbing with Communist Party chief Erich Honecker. He announced that Honecker "is just as shocked as I am that this was *necessary*."[121] He evidently concurred with Honecker's (and Brezhnev's) claim that the Polish events were an internal matter, for upon his return home the Chancellor stated that the Kremlin would never "damage the [detente] of the last ten years with one stroke of the pen."[122] A letter on the Polish events that Brezhnev sent to Schmidt reportedly was "most obliging in tone" and reinforced Bonn's inclination "to regard the Soviet role in Poland, short of *flagrante delicto* evidence, as one of noninvolvement."[123]

A few weeks later, Schmidt was in Washington for a summit with Reagan. He dismissed the President's contention that the Soviet Union had ordered martial law in Poland by proclaiming that Brezhnev is "no terrorist."[124] Meanwhile, back in West Germany,

> . . . pro-Solidarity demonstrations . . . attracted only a fraction of the tens of thousands who commonly join anti-nuke marches. . . . West Germany's powerful trade union federation refused to call out its members to protest the arrest of Solidarity members in Poland. . . . The federation's Bavarian chapter called a symbolic work stoppage, but the 100,000 workers who participated stepped off the job for only five minutes—less than the duration of a coffee break. [125]

When Reagan and Schmidt met in Bonn in June 1982, the Chancellor reiterated that his country was tenaciously attached to detente and that the peace movement wielded enormous political clout. As if to add credence to Schmidt's remarks, Reagan received a letter (via U.S. Ambassador Arthur Burns) from 59 Social Democratic members of the Bundestag. The signatories, constituting 25 percent of the party's 236 parliamentary deputies, wrote that "we cannot abandon and do not wish to abandon detente policy, nor do we wish to keep quiet about the success achieved so far." The letter warned that West Germans "cannot accept and do not wish to accept someone dictating to us the forms of solidarity with the oppressed people in Poland and the USSR."[126]

In October 1982 the SPD lost power in Bonn when the small Free Democratic Party deserted it to form a coalition with the Christian Democrats. Schmidt was replaced as SPD chief by Hans-Jochen Vogel, and Kohl became chancellor of a CDU-Free Democratic coalition government. In Moscow, Yuri Andropov became General Secretary of the Soviet Communist party upon the death of Brezhnev in November.

Moscow had reason to hope that if the SPD made a comeback in elections scheduled for 6 March 1983, it would cancel the deployments. The Euromissile issue was of such cardinal importance for the Soviets that they risked blatant interference in the West German election campaign to bring the "peace" candidate to power. Vogel, who was close to the SPD's left wing "peace" activists, stated that, if elected, he would deploy the U.S. missiles only under extraordinary circumstances. Kohl, for his part, reportedly told President Reagan that he would honor West Germany's commitment to deploy the weapons even if other would-be host countries reneged.[127] Vogel may have overplayed his hand by publicly labeling Kohl the "Raketenkanzler," or "rocket chancellor." At any rate, the Euromissiles quickly emerged as the central issue of the electoral contest. Vogel sent Ronald Reagan a letter urging him to display greater flexibility in arms talks with the Soviets.[128]

Andropov invited Vogel to Moscow in January and treated him like a head of government. The men talked for two hours—the longest meeting Andropov had ever held with a foreign leader—and also held a separate conversation with only an interpreter in attendance. The INF issue evidently topped the agenda. Vogel subsequently exulted that the new General Secretary was "fully and completely conscious of his responsibility for the fate of mankind."[129]

Hardly had Vogel returned home when Soviet Foreign Minister Gromyko journeyed to Bonn, where he reportedly hinted at further concessions on arms control. As a *Washington Post* correspondent observed, "the extraordinary thing about the visit was that Gromyko could be in West Germany in the middle of an election campaign without arousing controversy and that the visit itself came at the initiative of the incumbent Christian Democratic government . . . presumably because the Kohl government wanted to demonstrate that it was capable of continuing a dialogue with Moscow and thus acquire some political capital."[130] At a press conference in the West German capital on 18 January, Andropov declared that he had pointedly asked Kohl whether he would continue to adhere to the policy of detente, and "the Chancellor answered in the affirmative."[131] Gromyko also enjoined West Germany "to display its own self, to be guided by its own interests" in foreign policy "and not to yield to foreign [read: U.S.] influences if they do not meet these interests—the interests of maintaining good relations with the Soviet Union." Gromyko's statement was remarkable not only because it criticized West Germany's closest ally from a platform in Bonn but also because the term "self" conjured up the specter of German nationalism—with all its negative connotations from the Hitlerite past. In abetting the growth of nationalism in West Germany—even of the leftwing, anti-American variety—the Soviets mounted a tiger that they could not ride safely.

Commenting on the Kremlin's campaign diplomacy, *The Wall Street Journal* editorialized that

> It is, of course, true that Mr. Vogel visited Washington as well as Moscow, and that Vice President Bush, as well as Foreign Minister Gromyko, visited Bonn. But at election time somehow there should be a difference between the power with armies threatening West Germany and the power with armies protecting it. And if Mr. Andropov or Mr. Gromyko were serious about offering [arms control] concessions, he would be offering them to our negotiators in Geneva rather than to the opposition leader in Germany. [132]

As the day for the West German vote drew near, Bonn's tolerance for Soviet meddling wore thin. On 25 February, government spokesman Juergen Sudhoff denounced "the massive and unprecedented manner in which the Soviet Union is interfering in the election campaign and internal politics of the Federal Republic of Germany."[133] The attack came in response to an "interview" that Gromyko gave to *Pravda* on the previous day. The foreign minister exhorted West Europeans to "show signs of political maturity" by refusing to accept "the role of uninvolved observers or popularizers of the American position" in the missile negotiations. He urged them, instead, to "speak up clearly for a just solution" of the INF problem based on Andropov's proposals.[134] Soviet embassy staffers in Bonn distributed the interview widely in German translation. In addition to Gromyko's remarks, the Soviet Union beamed a German-language radio broadcast into the Federal Republic that predicted social unrest if Kohl won the election. Moreover, the Soviet news agency *Novosti* warned that Kohl's commitment to deploy U.S. missiles would lead West Germany to "the nuclear gallows."

The concerted and blunt Soviet propaganda offensive drew negative responses from across the entire West German political spectrum. Even Egon Bahr, a leading advocate of nuclear disarmament, rejected Soviet charges that Washington alone bore the blame for the missile impasse. "After all," said Bahr, "it is the fault of the Soviet Union that there was no security for Europe without the United States."[135]

In the end, it is difficult to avoid the conclusion that the Soviets contributed heavily to Kohl's victory—though economic issues certainly played an important role. Columnist Morton Kondracke observed correctly that "Mr. Andropov blew the election. He encouraged Mr. Vogel to move so far toward Moscow on Euromissile policy that the SPD lost credibility with voters."[136] A *Wall Street Journal* editorial on the outcome of the election pointed out that "the West German electorate has delivered a stinging rebuke to Yuri Andropov for his brazen efforts to manipulate the voting. The Social Democrats have been severely and justifiably punished for their flirtation with the extreme left."[137] The SPD took 38.2 percent of the vote—its lowest percentage since 1961.

The margin of the CDU's victory was impressive, but, under the country's proportional representation system, the razor-thin success of the Greens prevented the Christian Democrats from winning an absolute majority in the parliament.[138] More importantly, the return of the Christian Democrats to power did not presage an immediate downturn in Soviet-West German relations. Kohl journeyed to Moscow as the first conservative West German Chancellor to visit the Soviet capital since Konrad Adenauer in 1955. The Italian newspaper *La Stampa* opined that

> . . . every Bonn government, whether Christian Democratic or Social
> Democratic, has to find a way of establishing a relationship of preferential
> dialogue with the Kremlin. The more the German voters fear Russian
> expansionism, the more they ask their government to avert it by means of
> such a relationship. Bonn will always be the first to open and the last to
> close the dialogue with Moscow. . . . [139]

The Soviet-German summit participants did not mince words. For example, Premier Nikolai Tikhonov warned that deployment of the Pershing 2 and cruise missiles "would mean that for the first time in postwar history a military threat again stems from German soil to the Soviet people."[140] This remark apparently was aimed at whipping up antiwar hysteria in the USSR and Europe alike.

As the date for Euromissile deployments neared, the USSR proffered a mixture of carrots and sticks to West Germany, with heavy emphasis on the sticks. On 1 September, *Pravda* accused West Germany of adopting "pan-German views" aimed at the reunification of the country and "the liquidation of the Socialist German Democratic Republic." A few weeks later, in a letter sent by Andropov to a group of SPD representatives in the Bundestag, the Soviet Union and West Germany were depicted as the progenitors of detente; the letter declared that "the people of our countries . . . cannot look indifferently on how attempts are being made in the name of interests alien to Europe" [read: U.S. interests] to destroy its fruits.[141] In the wake of the Bundestag's vote on 22 November for final approval of the Euromissile deployments, TASS proclaimed that "the Rubicon has been crossed." The Kremlin also intensified its propaganda offensive, charging the government in Bonn with being soft on Nazism, devoted to rearmament in conjunction with France and other European powers, and supportive of "revanchism" (reestablishment of Hitler's Third Reich through the recovery of lands and ethnic German minorities lost during World War II).

Moscow's propaganda blitzkrieg against Bonn peaked on 10 July 1984 with the dispatch of a "memorandum" involving the 1945 Potsdam Agreement that set up the political framework for post-Nazi Germany pending a peace treaty (no such treaty has ever been signed). "It should be recalled," said the memo, that "devolving on [West Germany] as one of the legal heirs to the former Reich is the commitment established by the Potsdam Agreements that no threat to neighboring states or the world at large should ever come from German soil. This commitment must be observed undeviatingly." However, a Soviet spokesman warned that the USSR would act "either together with others, or , if necessary, unilaterally" to uphold Potsdam and other postwar accords.

It is worth noting that the U.N. Charter provides a legal justification for "enforcement action" if peace is threatened, as Moscow claimed was the case when the Euromissiles were deployed in Germany. Such enforcement action, according to Article 53 of the Charter, requires the authorization of the U.N. Security Council (on which the United States, among others, enjoys veto power), "with the exception of measures against any enemy state." The term "enemy state" is defined as "any state which during the Second World War has been an enemy of any signatory of the present Charter." Reinforcing this principle, Article 107 stipulates that "nothing in the present Charter shall invalidate or preclude action" against an enemy state "by the Governments having responsibility for such action." The Soviet government clearly falls within this category.

The freeze in Soviet-West German relations that followed the onset of Euromissile deployments led East German Communist chief Honecker to cancel a visit to Bonn in 1984, under pressure from the Soviet Union. A year later, Gorbachev received Johannes Rau in Moscow. A fast-rising star in the opposition Social Democratic firmament, Rau had supported Schmidt's Euromissile policy but also maintained close personal ties with the SPD's left wing. In addition, Rau's position as minister-president (the elected state governor) or North Rhine-Westphalia made him extremely sensitive to the importance of trade with the Soviet bloc. His state houses the Ruhr industrial complex, where output was lagging and unemployment rising. Rau already was being touted as a future SPD candidate for chancellor. TASS reported that Gorbachev and Rau "noted with satisfaction the fruitfulness of contacts" between the Soviet Communist party and the SPD "and expressed themselves in favor of further deepening . . . these contacts."

Shortly after Rau's return to Bonn, a major spy scandal clouded Soviet-West German relations. Not until the summer of 1986 did a semblance of normality return to the ties between the countries. Foreign Minister Hans-Dietrich Genscher visited Moscow in July of that year. He and Gorbachev stressed the importance of upholding SALT II (which Reagan had recently disavowed) and evidently agreed to disagree on the Euromissile issue. Soviet Foreign Minister Shevardnadze expressed hope that the USSR and the Federal Republic would cooperate "like partners in a dialogue."[142] Gorbachev implied that the dialogue should persist irrespective of the United States when he emphasized "the mutual responsibility" of the Soviet Union and West Germany "for building a 'European home.'"[143]

"Europe for the Europeans," or variations on that theme, has become a staple of Soviet propaganda under Gorbachev's regime. It is an integral part of his campaign for a "divisible [from America] detente." Even before he became General Secretary, Gorbachev was associated with attempts to drive wedges between the United States and Western Europe. During his visit to London in December 1984, he told the British Parliament that Europe is "our common home," not "a theater of military action." His address to selected members of the French National Assembly in October 1985 emphasized "the Continent's common destiny." A month later, *Pravda* ran an editorial entitled "Europe Is Our Common Home" as part of a Soviet media blitz using the leitmotif of a unique link between the Soviet Union and Western Europe.

The unspoken question remains, "What kind of Europe?" A polarized Continent symbolized most starkly by a divided Germany, each half dependent upon a superpower guarantor for its ultimate security? Or a pan-European collective, marked by the absence of security ties to the United States, the hovering presence of the Soviet military colossus (with the reflexive political accommodation that every European nation would exercise), and a neutralized, possibly demilitarized, and reunified Germany?

Ultimately, the debate over the future of Europe and of NATO revolves around Germany. However,

> What makes debate particularly difficult in West Germany is the fact that the country's foreign policy of the past 20 years has been built on a set of assumptions which have turned out to be fallacious. Originally, the premise behind *Ostpolitik* was that improved relations with the East would increase leverage with the Communist governments and gradually would lead to a loosening of controls. This has not happened. Instead, it seemed to work the other way. West Germany itself became dependent on the jobs thereby created and on the human contacts, to such an extent that today no politician with a wish to survive would dare challenge the policy's basic tenets.

> With *Ostpolitik*, a specific set of beliefs has developed that prevent a realistic appraisal of the world situation. Where 20 years ago the Soviet Union was universally recognized as the chief cause of tension in Europe, the tendency has increasingly been to downplay the ideological differences and to see the USSR as just another superpower, cautious and sensible . . .

Moreover, as a British commentator has observed, "so many Germans have become so used to the vocabulary and the psychology of detente and arms control that they are now less resistant to Russian militarism. . . ."[144] Against this backdrop, the following observation by a West German foreign policy specialist is especially pertinent:

> It is important to remember that *Ostpolitik* continues to depend on the leverage provided by the United States. . . . For all its impressive economic strength, West Germany is still a political middle-weight and no match for a superpower like the Soviet Union. The Alliance is the ultimate guarantee of West Germany's political independence, and without the larger insurance provided by the West, a solitary German "reinsurance policy" a la Bismarck would merely compress rather than widen Bonn's margin of maneuver. [145]

Meanwhile, the hopes—or illusions—aroused by *Ostpolitik* remain a major factor in West German politics, and reunification seems as far away as ever:

. . . the Russians turned to exploit the cracks in NATO. And they dangled a choice before West Germans, between perpetual danger in NATO and a safe neutrality leading to some kind of reunion with East Germany. . . . [However], it is preposterous to think the Russians would soon relax their grip on East Germany if West Germany turned neutral. Even if disarmed, a rejoined Germany would become a powerful magnet drawing the rest of Eastern Europe out of the Soviet orbit. No conceivable damage to NATO could compensate the Kremlin for such a menace. But German nationalism has been known to feast on such dreams. [146]

Rising leftwing nationalism in West Germany is a phenomenon with which the Soviet Union and the United States alike will have to contend. While both seem to regard it as preferable to the ultrarightwing variety, its spread into East Germany could be very dangerous for the stability of the Soviet bloc and thus for the peace of Europe as a whole. Even if it remains largely confined to the Western part of Germany, it will prove a major disincentive in any Soviet calculation of the consequences of German reunification.

There is, in fact, no foreseeable scenario that would allow for the release of East Germany—Moscow's most prosperous and reliable satellite—from the USSR's vise. Even if West Germany agreed to withdraw from NATO in exchange for reunification, the Soviets would be unlikely to acquiesce, for they can visualize the collapse of the Atlantic Alliance somewhere down the road as a result of its own internal "contradictions." Moreover, German reunification would be "far more dangerous [to the Soviets] than half a dozen smoothly functioning NATO's stacked one upon the other."[147]

The German question aside, Moscow might well harbor ambivalent feelings about the desirability of NATO's possible demise. According to Adam B. Ulam, director of the Russian Research Center at Harvard University,

The ideal arrangement from the Soviet point of view is for the United States and Western Europe to be bound together in a less than happy marriage in which both partners continuously squabble rather than deciding on a trial separation, which might eventually result in a reinvigorated, politically united, more powerful Western Europe. [148]

More broadly, the Soviets confront a dilemma in dealing with NATO Europe. When U.S.-West European relations are cozy, there is only a very narrow Euro-wedge for the Kremlin to exploit. When relations are embittered, Moscow cannot use Western Europe as a pressure point against Washington. Its importance in this capacity was typified in a recent remark by Aleksandr Bovin, a prominent Soviet foreign policy commentator. "We would like to utilize Western Europe's potential to make good, via the transatlantic channel, the obvious shortage of common sense in the incumbent U.S. Administration," he said.

Irrespective of the future of NATO as an institution, both the West Europeans and the Soviets are determined that detente must prevail. Tory columnist Peregrine Worthstone wrote in the London *Sunday Telegraph* that "a separate relationship with the Soviet Union and a less close one with the U.S. are no longer options that only leftists can be expected to espouse."[149] The truth of this proposition attests to the enormous success that Soviet propaganda has registered across the length and breadth of the political spectrum in Western Europe. The key to its success has been the manipulation of the concept of detente to lull Western suspicions of the growing Soviet military threat:

> By the 1970's, the West Europeans had begun to change their relationships to both superpowers . . . making the Cold War seem a remnant of the past. To the degree that detente "took" in Europe, the alliance became less important. The Europeans never pushed things to the breaking point with Washington, for it was nice having the United States back there just in case. That was the problem. America had become a contingency plan for Europe. The Europeans took Washington for granted. Everybody knew the United States would be there . . . "when the chips are down." The problem was that, with detente, the Europeans believed the chips never would be down. . . . [150]

Joseph M.A. H. Luns, NATO's Secretary General, has noted that

> There is a certain irony . . . which may not be entirely surprising, that the much-quoted detente is now contributing in a not inconsiderable way to a negative influence on the internal cohesion and solidarity of the alliance partners. I might even say that this was one of Moscow's goals when it helped to initiate detente. . . . [151]

The INF treaty exacerbated many of the problems that NATO has encountered in defining its relationship with the Soviet Union. Completed at the end of 1987 for the Washington summit and ratified by the U.S. Senate on the eve of the Moscow summit in May 1988, the treaty embodies the "double zero" option. Both intermediate-range and short-range ground-based nuclear missiles (those in the 300-3,400-mile range) are banned by the treaty. These systems include, principally, the SS-20 on the Soviet side and the Pershing 2 and ground-launched cruise missiles on the NATO side.

The Reagan Administration extolled the accord as a vindication of its decision to emplace "Euromissiles" as counters to the SS-20's, and it portrayed the treaty as returning Europe to the status quo ante SS-20 deployments. However, a great deal of water has passed under the bridge since Reagan unveiled the "zero option" in 1981. First of all, the European NATO governments that had agreed reluctantly to emplace the U.S. missiles on their territory and endured bitter political struggles to win popular acceptance for their decision were left hanging on a limb when the treaty obviated the need for deployment. Once again, as in the neutron bomb episode, Washington failed to follow through on a strategic issue and seemed to ignore the political and psychological, as well as the military, consequences of its lapse. More-over, Moscow realized—even if Washington did not—that the political "de-coupling" inherent in the treaty far outweighed any strictly military advantage that the Soviets might accrue by retaining the SS-20 force. Already, West Germany, the chief bulwark of NATO on the Continent, is demanding "triple zero"—the elimination of battlefield nuclear systems. For the Bonn government, limited nuclear war de-notes a war limited to German soil ("the shorter the missiles, the deader the Germans").

If West Germany rebuffs U.S. exhortations to modernize the Lance nuclear missiles and nuclear artillery systems on its soil or to take other steps bolstering a tactical nuclear capability, NATO's strat-egy of flexible response probably would be degraded beyond repair. Western Europe indeed would become safe for conventional war—but, even more so, for Soviet nuclear blackmail. Europe's passion for detente would shade by necessity into reflexive accommodation to So-viet demands. Neither U.S. nuclear-capable aircraft (faced with the need to penetrate Soviet air defenses) nor submarine-launched ballistic missiles (which are less accurate than the Pershing 2 and lack the phys-ical presence provided by the Euromissiles) can substitute for the INF systems about to be withdrawn. If NATO loses its capacity for nuclear deterrence in Europe, it can only be a matter of time until the 300,000-man "tripwire" of U.S. troops on the Continent will be summoned home by Congress.

It is a measure of the success of Soviet "peace" and anti-nuclear propaganda and of the institutionalization of detente in Western Eu-rope that the INF treaty drew an enthusiastic response despite its serious flaws. The principal anomaly in the pact is that the SS-20, the chief weapon slated for elimination, has never been seen by any of the Western arms control negotiators. The Soviets reluctantly and belatedly supplied a photograth of the missile inside its cannister. The cannister itself is the same one used by the SS-25 missile, which is not banned by the treaty. Thus, the Soviets could conceal SS-20's inside these containers, beyond the view of either technical or human inspection. Even more disconcerting was the familiar sight of Western intelligence agencies and defense specialists arguing among themselves about how many SS-20's the Soviet Union actually possesses. The numbers ranged from less than 700 to more than 1,200.

Other flaws in the INF pact include a prohibition on conventionally as well as nuclear-armed GLCM's (on the ground that the two varieties are indistinguishable to outside observers) and a proscription on "futuristic" missiles, armed with microwave or particle beam devices rather than explosive warheads. Precluding the deployment of such "new-age"missiles (an issue that, according to Caspar Weinberger and other officials, was not even raised in the course of the negotiations) forecloses U.S. utilization of exotic technologies that it is far ahead of the Soviets in developing. The ban also could crimp seriously the Strategic Defense Initiative. All of these drawbacks in the INF treaty stand above and beyond the issues of verification and compliance that the United States never has addressed adequately in its advancement of the arms control "process."

The weaknesses of the treaty result from a combination of hasty and careless negotiating and of wishful thinking. Once Moscow agreed to the "zero option," many U.S. officials and non-governmental arms control advocates suggested that failure to complete the INF pact would create intolerable strains not only for NATO, but also for Mikhail Gorbachev, who allegedly regards progress in arms control as a necessary concomitant to *perestroika* (restructuring of the Soviet economy).

The European NATO allies stand ready to assist *perestroika* through increasing trade and credits as well as "restraint" in modernizing Western defenses. In the spring of 1988, for example, West Germany furnished the Soviet Union an "untied" loan of $2 billion.The allies will not allow themselves to be outdone by the United States, which since the appointment of East-West trade enthusiast William Verity as Secretary of Commerce has displayed unseemly haste in seeking trade deals with the Soviets. In April 1988, Verity led some 40

Reagan Administration officials to Moscow for the tenth meeting of the U.S.-USSR Joint Commercial Commission. At the same time, more than 500 American businessmen journeyed to the Soviet capital for the annual meeting of the "non-governmental" U.S.-USSR Trade and Economic Council. The group members sought lucrative trade deals and seemed receptive to Soviet-style joint ventures. With detente leaping forward on every front and attempts to link arms control and trade to Soviet human rights performance all but abandoned (Reagan's rhetoric at the 1988 Moscow summit notwithstanding), the West European allies have eagerly welcomed Washington aboard the bandwagon.

Meanwhile, the Soviet threat to Western Europe has not diminished at all. What has diminished is Western Europe's perception of the threat's existence. One reason for the altered perception is Gorbachev's subtle and sophisticated propaganda approach—a far cry from accusations of German "revanchism" and specters of a "nuclear Pompeii." Gorbachev has mastered fully the art of intimidation that the Soviets directed at Western Europe long before he came into office. As depicted in a *Wall Street Journal* editorial,

> Intimidation is a core element in [the Soviets'] strategy. . . . They say to Europeans: We alone can protect you—by not attacking you. The Americans can never offer you that kind of security. They can't even protect El Salvador. The more powerful and dangerous the Soviet Union can be made to look and the more bumbling and indecisive the Americans, the more credible that threat-promise becomes. . . . The trick is to keep the West Europeans apprehensive without making them so panicky they run the other way. [152]

Gorbachev tells the Europeans that the solution to their security dilemma is a born-again detente. He portrays Europe as the cradle of detente and exhorts the Western allies to safeguard detente in the face of alleged American efforts to destroy it. "In achieving a radical turn toward the policy of peace," Gorbachev has intoned, "Europe would have a special mission. That mission is erecting a new edifice of detente." The Soviet leader portrays his country as a core member of a common European civilization, which he purports to uphold against the incursions of the "cowboy culture" prevailing in Ronald Reagan's America. *The Washington Post* has editorialized quite correctly that "the Kremlin's European policy is aimed precisely at inscribing a separate European agenda and at characterizing the United States as irrelevant, if not hostile, to it."[153]

Gorbachev, of course, is not playing his "Eurocard" to the neglect of the rest of his hand. Relations with the United States probably still top the Kremlin's foreign policy priorities. However, the new Soviet leader clearly believes that Europe has a major role to play in the "rebirth," the "consolidation," and the "revival" of detente—formulations that crop up persistently in Soviet statements and writings—until the Administration in Washington takes up the slack. According to some knowledgeable observers, however, Washington—even under the "hardline" Reaganites—is playing into Soviet hands. As Evan Galbraith, former U.S. ambassador to France, has cautioned, the USSR remains committed to achieving predominance in Europe:

> Given U.S. nuclear arms and the North Atlantic Treaty Organization's conventional forces, an outright Soviet invasion is unlikely. War remains an option for the Soviets, but it carries a high degree of risk and probably is not necessary. The Soviets can win without it. Instead, they have chosen psychological warfare with a two-pronged thrust: intimidate and terrorize the Europeans into an accommodation by exploiting their fear of a nuclear holocaust, and promote detente and self-deception by dissimulation and appeals for peace. . . .

> Meanwhile, the U.S. makes matters worse by promoting detente. Cultural exchanges, bank loans, increased trade, "differentiating" between the Soviets and their satellites—all of these U.S. actions cause the Europeans to think wishfully that the Soviets are indeed reasonable. Detente is not only a delusion, it is a danger. The U.S. abets the Soviet effort to delude the allies and thus moves them toward the accommodation the Soviets seek. [154]

# 5

# Human Rights: The Unstable Element of Detente

If the term "human rights" is taken to mean the inalienable rights that individuals possess by the grant of God and the Bill of Rights, it has no application in the Soviet context. In the USSR, Communist propaganda notwithstanding, rights are determined by class, and collective rights take precedence over individual ones. Even the ruling class—the *nomenklatura*—perceives itself less as a group of individuals than as a vanguard force whose power and legitimacy are enshrined in Marxist-Leninist doctrine.

The three pillars of Tsarist Russia—the autocracy, the Russian Orthodox Church (strictly subordinate to the throne), and the army (likewise subordinate) have their counterparts in the Soviet Union, where the "official" church and the armed forces take orders from the Communist Party. The major difference is that the dictatorship has become totalitarian, extending its tentacles into every area of its subjects' lives and craving not only political domination but also thought control. The line between political dissent and treason is a thin one, and the accusation of "anti-Sovietism" covers a broad range of alleged sins. In a book containing a selection of his speeches and writings, Yuri Andropov declares that "defenders of human rights" are seeking the rights to slander Soviet reality, violate the social order, and undermine the roots of the Communist system.[1]

Although the USSR claims to be part of European civilization, it rejects the norms and values of the Judeo-Christian ethic and is more in tune with the Byzantine tradition of the East. It is also worth emphasizing that despite their espousal of Marxist-Leninist internationalism, the Soviets are intensely nationalistic and xenophobic. It is said that familiarity breeds contempt. In Moscow's case, there is a contempt for familiarity, which smacks of fraternization. Thus, the Soviets pick and choose carefully the commodities and expertise they need from the West—all the while attempting to seal off the country's population from foreign influences and the ideological contamination they bring.

Detente, as originally envisioned by Richard Nixon and Henry Kissinger, did not entail efforts to encourage or coerce the USSR to respect human rights. To the contrary, a report on "The Meaning of Detente" that was put out by Kissinger's State Department in 1974 stated that "attempts to make increased freedom within the Soviet Union a rigid precondition for improved relations (would) risk obtaining . . . neither improved relations nor an increased regard in the Soviet Union for human rights."[2] Gerald Ford, whom Kissinger also served as Secretary of State, declined to invite Alexander Solzhenitsyn to the White House. Solzhenitsyn, the chronicler of the Gulag and himself its most famous survivor, had been forced to emigrate in 1974. Whatever efforts Washington chose to make on behalf of Soviet dissidents during Kissinger's tenure were conducted through "quiet diplomacy" to avoid public embarrassment to the Kremlin.

Congress had an entirely different mindset about the relationship between human rights and detente. In the aftermath of the Nixon-Brezhnev summit in Moscow in May 1972, the Soviets looked forward to a major expansion in trade that would bring them badly needed Western industrial equipment and technology. A comprehensive trade pact was signed in October, including provisions for most-favored-nation (MFN) tariff treatment and Export-Import Bank credits for the USSR. Soviet arms deliveries and diplomatic support to the Arabs during the 1973 Yom Kippur War, coupled with the continuing repression of Soviet dissidents and restrictions on emigration, led Congress to attach the Jackson-Vanik Amendment to the Trade Reform Act of 1974. This legislation made the granting of MFN tariff privileges and Export-Import Bank loans to the Soviet bloc conditional upon freer emigration.

Faced with Congressional restrictions, Moscow disavowed the comprehensive trade agreement, which had been envisaged as a major component of detente at work. The greatest monument to detente, however, was erected in the summer of 1975, with the convening of the 35-nation Conference on Security and Cooperation in Europe (CSCE). The Kremlin had been pressing for nearly two decades for a conference on European security that would ratify the postwar division of the Continent, thus confirming Soviet domination of the East. The conclave, which took place in Helsinki, issued a Final Act on 1 August that was signed by the representatives of every European nation except Albania and by the United States and Canada. The document comprised three "baskets" of issues. "Basket One", by far the most momentous, dealt with security issues. It proclaimed the inviolability of Europe's frontiers, thus satisfying Moscow's demands for the recognition of its wartime conquests. In this sense, the Helsinki accord, which was a non-binding declaration of mutual intent, served the Soviet Union as an ersatz peace treaty for World War II.

"Basket Two" dealt with East-West cooperation in economic, scientific, technical and environmental matters. Finally, "Basket Three" enjoined the signatories at Helsinki to promote a freer flow of information and wider human contacts across East-West boundaries, with special attention to the reunification of families, more freedom of movement for journalists, and greater access to foreign publications and broadcasts. The Final Act stipulates that "the participating States will respect human rights and fundamental freedoms, including the freedom of thought, conscience, religion, or belief. . . . " The Helsinki accord also states that "everyone has a right to leave any country, including his own." Moreover, it affirms the signatories' commitment to the Universal Declaration of Human Rights, which was adopted by the U.N. General Assembly on 10 December 1948.[3] The Kremlin's attitude toward "Basket Three" was typified by the remark of a Communist Party official that "we signed the Helsinki accords, but morally we are against them."[4]

Many Western observers opined that it was well worth conceding "Basket One" to the Soviets—since no Western nation had any intention of forcibly altering European frontiers anyway—in exchange for "Basket Three." Marshall Shulman (later the Soviet affairs adviser to Secretary of State Cyrus Vance) told his students at Columbia University that Moscow would rue the day it signed "Basket Three." Most U.S. liberals, evidently projecting their own respect for international agreements onto the Soviet Union, speculated that Moscow would have to think twice before persecuting human rights activists and other dissidents. They seemed to have forgotten that, aside from the non-binding nature of the Helsinki accords, the Soviets violated the SALT I arms control pact with impunity[5] and thus were unlikely to observe a human rights declaration if it didn't suit their purposes.

Indeed, from the Kremlin's perspective, the transgsression lies not with those who infringe the terms of an international agreement, but with those who draw attention to the infringement. Thus, when "Helsinki Watch groups" sprouted up to monitor the Soviet Union's compliance with the Final Act, the stage was set for confrontation.

Moscow celebrated the Helsinki accords as a great victory, and news media throughout the USSR and the Soviet bloc gave extensive coverage to the CSCE documents. *Pravda* printed the accords in full. Rejoicing seemed justified. As a Western correspondent in Helsinki observed, "the West accepted the postwar division of Europe, thereby implicitly endorsing Soviet ideology's claim that the triumph of Communist governments is an historical inevitability. In return, the USSR made unenforceable promises to facilitate human contacts, which proved meaningless."[6]

While the Communist regimes were focusing on the security provisions of "Basket One," however, the various strands of the dissident movement were studying the language on human rights that was incorporated into the accords (and printed verbatim in the newspapers). Helsinki gave the Soviet dissident movement a new lease on life. It had been virtually paralyzed by massive arrests during the early 1970's, by lack of publicity in the West (where only a few prominent individuals, notably Solzhenitsyn and Sakharov, received notice), and by inability to coordinate the various strands at home. The Jewish emigration movement, the human rights activists, the religious believers, and the disaffected national minority movements all had their special priorities and agendas. The language of the Helsinki accords, affirming the right to freedom of worship, national self-expression, and emigration, made the Final Act a rallying point for the disparate Soviet groups. All of them regarded pressure on the Kremlin to observe the Helsinki document as essential to their survival.

On 12 May 1976, the Public Group to Promote Observance of the Helsinki Accords in the USSR was established in Moscow. Its founders included professor of physics Yuri Orlov, a Corresponding Member of the Armenian Academy of Sciences and a founding member of the Moscow branch of Amnesty International, who became the group's chief spokesman; pediatrician Yelena Bonner, Andrei Sakharov's wife; mathematician and Jewish activist Anatoly Shcharansky; and former General Petr Grigorenko. Similar organizations emerged in the Ukraine, Lithuania, Lativa, Georgia, and Armenia; the original association thus changed its name to Moscow Group for Furthering Implementation of the Helsinki Agreements in the USSR. During the course of its existence, the group issued about 200 documents detailing Soviet government abuses of the human rights provisions of the Helsinki accords. In response to an appeal by the Moscow group, a Helsinki Watch Committee was formed in the United States with the participation of numerous influential political officials and public figures.

Moscow's East European satellites, like the Soviet Union itself, witnessed the emergence of various groups dedicated to human rights. The best known was Charter 77 in Czechoslovakia. Its manifesto, charging the Soviet puppet regime in Prague with violations of human rights, appeared in Western newspapers on 6 and 7 January 1977. The re-emergence of public dissent in Czechoslovakia after a nearly decade-long silence in the wake of the Soviet invasion coincided with the election of President Jimmy Carter and his advocacy of human rights worldwide.

Carter's commitment to human rights as a cornerstone of American foreign policy was strikingly evident during his Presidential campaign, although he focused more on right-wing authoritarian regimes than on Communist totalitarian ones, to use Jeane Kirkpatrick's now-famous distinction. After he became President-elect, Carter sent a telegram of support to Vladimir Slepak, a leader of the Jewish emigration movement and member of the Helsinki Group in Moscow. On 23 December, Secretary-of-State-designate Cyrus Vance met with Andrei Amalrik, a popular Soviet writer who had been expelled from the USSR. Carter's inaugural address contained statements to the effect that the human rights campaign represented a U.S. ideological offensive. Within a week after the Carter Administration took office, the

President wrote to Sakharov to express concern for his fate and support for the Helsinki monitoring groups in the Soviet Union, while the State Department issued a statement of concern about the fate of the signatories of the Charter 77 manifesto in Czechoslovakia. On 1 March 1977, Carter welcomed Vladimir Bukovsky, a leading exiled dissident, to the White Hose—a gesture that contrasted vividly with President Ford's refusal to receive Solzhenitsyn.

Carter's concern with human rights was institutionalized with the upgrading in 1977 of the State Department's Office of Human Rights and Humanitarian Affairs into a Bureau. In the Soviet Union, by contrast, the KGB acquired increased resources and prestige to handle the outgrowths of detente: organized dissidence and an expansion of contacts between Soviet citizens and Westerners. Under Andropov's stewardship, the KGB made incarceration of dissidents in psychiatric hospitals a standard practice.[7]

Brezhnev delivered a speech in Tula on 18 January 1977 (two days before Carter's inauguration) in which he stated, inter alia, that it woud be "futile" to attempt "to teach us to live according to rules that are incompatible with Socialist democracy." These rules evidently referred to the moral underpinnings of Carter's human-rights crusade. "Detente," intoned Brezhnev, "means a certain trust and ability to take into consideration each other's legitimate interests." From the Kremlin's perspective, free expression of human rights would undermine the very legitimacy of the regime.

On 12 February 1977, *Pravda* ran an editorial entitled "What is Hidden Behind the Noise About Human Rights?" The newspaper depicted U.S. human-rights policy as a "smokescreen" behind which "enemies of detente" waged a "propaganda campaign" against the USSR and its allies with the aim of interfering in their domestic affairs. *Pravda* became even more strident in the wake of Carter's meeting in Washington with Bukovsky, who had spent a dozen years in Soviet prisons and labor camps for exposing the USSR's misuse of psychiatry for political purposes. On 2 March 1977, a *Pravda* lampoon entitled "Guess Who's Coming to Dinner?" portrayed a racist Southern family regaling a Soviet dissident. The master of the house was depicted as a member of the Ku Klux Klan who expressed relief that the mystery guest was not black.

During an interview with *U.S. News and World Report* that was published on 14 March, Georgiy Arbatov, Director of the Institute on the USA and Canada, took a direct jab at Carter's human-rights policies:

> Q. Many Americans find it hard to understand why the Soviet Union insists on supporting Communist political aims around the globe but regards Carter's support of Soviet dissidents as interference in your internal affairs.

> A. Nobody here expects President Carter not to speak about his own values. . . . We've said several times that ideological controversy will remain in a time of detente, and this presumes we can both express our views. What does cause apprehension here is [that] in the future it might occur to somebody to challenge our electoral and political system. It's this kind of activity we find incompatible with detente.

> Q. What about the Helsinki Accords? Doesn't the West have the right to examine the Soviet Union's human-rights record?

> A. The Helsinki Agreement is not a menu from which you can pick out one chosen item; you have to take it as a whole. And one of its most important provisions concerns noninterference in the internal affairs of another country. . . .

> I don't think Americans would be very favorably inclined toward us if our correspondents in the United States cooperated with the Symbionese Liberation Army [SLA] or the Weathermen. Would Daniel Ellsberg have been cleared in court if he had had contact with Soviet representatives in the U.S.? If we established close ties with the American Indians who fought at Wounded Knee, with whom we sympathize deeply, wouldn't this be regarded as interference in your internal affairs?

> There's a border line which has to be judged by the political wisdom of any statesman—where expression of support for certain ideas ends and overt interference begins. The vital rule of detente is not to trespass over this border line.

Arbatov's ease in equating terrorist organizations—the SLA and the Weathermen—with Soviet human-rights advocates spoke volumes about Moscow's attitude toward dissent.

The Kremlin matched its rhetoric with deeds. It zeroed in on the Helsinki monitoring groups, which had become a special object of Carter's affections. The plan for stepped-up repression was outlined during a high-level briefing for Soviet editors. According to information that was leaked to the dissident *Chronicle of Current Events*, the briefing official declared:

> The editors of newspapers and journals receive numerous demands from Soviet people that, at last, firmness be shown and the dissidents silenced.

It has been decided to imprison the 50 most active dissidents and deal severely with their associates. It is time to show strength and not pay attention to the West.

With regard to emigration, the official reportedly said:

The Soviet Union showed its good will by signing the Helsinki Agreement. We know that in reality no reunification of families is taking place. Young people are using emigration for selfish purposes. Let those who challenge authority go, rather, and build the Baikal-Amur Railway line. [8]

The arrests of the Helsinki monitors began on 3 February 1977 with Aleksandr Ginzburg, a 41-year-old poet and Jewish activist in the Moscow Group. A Soviet press campaign accused him of debauchery and currency speculation. Yuri Orlov, the overall head of the Helsinki Watch movement, and some Georgian members of the movement also were detained. On 4 March an article in the Soviet government newspaper *Izvestia* accused prominent dissidents, including Shcharansky, of links with U.S. intelligence. On 14 March the KGB aarrested Shcharansky. It probably regarded him as more dangerous than most other dissidents because he belonged to two different movements—the human-rights monitors and the Jewish activists. He also was a computer scientist with wide professional contacts and a fluent English speaker who conversed regularly with Western journalists. The authorities had rejected his application to emigrate to Israel on grounds that his work in an oil and gas research institute had given him access to state secrets. His wife, Avital, who had departed for Israel a day after their wedding in 1974, publicly challenged the Soviet authorities to let him join her as they had promised.

On 4 October 1977, while the Kremlin was preparing kangaroo trials against Shcharansky, Ginzburg and Orlov, the first follow-up meeting to the Helsinki conference opened in Belgrade, Yugoslavia. The Helsinki Final Act contained provisions for a series of review conferences to assess the participants' compliance with the 1975 accords. However, the proceedings at Belgrade were perfunctory. The Soviet delegation stonewalled Western attempts to probe Moscow's adherence to the "Helsinki process"—a "process" that already was proving to be as devoid of substance as its arms control equivalent. Some members of the Carter Administration seemed empathetic to Moscow's concerns, despite the President's obsession with human rights. For example, Marshall Shulman, Secretary of State Vance's Soviet affairs adviser, told a Congressional subcommittee that the United States admittedly had sought to undermine Soviet authority by exploiting human rights issues.[9]

In mid-1978, the trials and sentencing of members of the Helsinki monitoring groups began. Orlov, nominated by the Norwegian Parliament for the Nobel Peace Prize, was sentenced in May to seven years in a strict-regime camp, to be followed by five years in internal exile. This was the maximum penalty under Article 70 of the criminal code of the Russian Soviet Federated Socialist Republic (RSFSR), dealing with "anti-Soviet agitation and propaganda."

During a Moscow show trial on 13 July that captured worldwide attention, 30-year-old Shcharansky was charged with high treason for allegedly working on behalf of the CIA and was sentenced to three years in prison and ten in a strict-regime labor camp. The CIA charge was a slap in the face of Jimmy Carter, who had personally denied that Shcharansky had any spy connections. The Shcharansky verdict followed by one day a sentence against Ginzburg of eight years in special-regime camps and three years in internal exile. Ginzburg was a major figure in the Russian Social Fund, which Solzhenitsyn had established before his involuntary exile to the West in 1974. It distributed the royalties from his publications and other monies to the families of Soviet political prisoners. Ginzburg later recounted that one of his interrogators said: "Don't think we'll forgive you the billions the Soviet Union lost because you caused the trade agreement with the United States to fall through."[10]

By the time the Reagan Administration came into office, a tight lid had been clamped on virtually all forms of Soviet dissent. Reagan was less inclined than his predecessor to embark on a crusade on behalf of human rights worldwide, but he was determined to keep a spotlight focused on abuses in the Soviet bloc. One of the Administration's opening salvoes occurred in March, two months after Reagan's inauguration, when the U.N. Commission on Human Rights held its annual meeting in Geneva. Richard Schifter, the U.S. delegate, publicly accused the USSR of behaving like the Nazis in suppressing political and religious freedom. He likened the Soviet Union's practice of consigning human right activists to internal exile with South Africa's use of "banning." Schifter declared that "the message from our people is that we must not accept a double standard in international affairs, one standard for the Soviet bloc and its friends, and another for all other countries."[11]

A mixed bag of arrests, trials, forced emigration and other forms of coercion decimated the Helsinki network to the extent that, on 8 September 1982, the Moscow Group was obliged to announce its dissolution. A concerned commentator wrote that "the Soviets . . . have taken the Helsinki contract and torn it to shreds. They were tested on this by their brave monitors, and they mugged the monitors. . . . "[12]

If the fate of Soviet peace activists generated concern in the West, that of Soviet Jewry inspired genuine alarm. Jewish emigration dropped precipitously from a record high of 51,320 in 1979, to 21,471 in 1980, to 9,400 in 1981, to 2,688 in 1982, and to 1,315 in 1983. In 1984 it bottomed out at 896, the lowest figure since the emigration movement began in the aftermath of the 1967 Arab-Israeli War. Insofar as the level of Jewish emigration has been a barometer of Soviet-American relations, its sharp drop reflected the demise of detente. The fact that the majority of Jewish emigrants settled in the United States rather than, as previously, in Israel also proved to be a sore point with Moscow. Those settling in Israel could be passed off as religious fanatics, but those choosing the United States offered living proof that the capitalist West is more attractive than the Communist paradise.[13]

At a time when Soviet Jews, Catholics, and various Protestant sects were under the greatest organized assault since Stalin's death, the Kremlin scored a major propaganda victory by hosting the American evangelist Billy Graham. He arrived in Moscow to participate in the World Conference of Religious Representatives for the Protection of the Sacred Gift of Life Against Nuclear Catastrophe. The conference was sponsored by the Russian Orthodox Church and opened on 10 May 1982. Graham turned aside appeals by high Reagan Administration officials to boycott the conference lest the Kremlin use his presence for propaganda purposes. He delivered a 30-minute sermon on disarmament and Christian rebirth at the Moscow Church of Evangelical Christian Baptists, the capital's only Baptist church, on the eve of the conclave.[14] Graham's sermon contained no mention of human or religious rights.

During the disarmament conference, which was designed to foster opposition to nuclear weapons at a time when the United States was preparing to deploy intermediate-range missiles in Western Europe, Graham evidently made every effort to avoid offending his Soviet hosts. The man who used to revile Communists as devil-worshippers apparently was hoping for a future invitation to the Soviet Union for a full-scale preaching tour. An aide told reporters privately that the evangelist "wants to develop this relationship" [with the Soviet authorities].[15]

While the Kremlin was welcoming prominent Western visitors and hosting international conclaves devoted to peace, the KGB was embarking on a no-holds-barred campaign to destroy the remnants of the Soviet unofficial peace movement, the Jewish emigration movement, and groups demanding religious freedom. The anti-dissident crusade extended even further beyond the familiar categories of Jewish activists, religious believers, and "peaceniks." A KGB official reportedly told a dissident in Moscow early in 1983 that "we have entered a new phase. A big campaign is underway in Moscow. We are purging the capital of harmful elements—criminals, drug addicts, queers, and dissidents."[16]

While the USSR's violations of human rights and clampdown against dissidents were in full swing, another follow-up session to the Helsinki conference took place. Unlike the 1977-78 Belgrade review session, the Madrid conference, which opened in November 1980, made some advances—at least on paper. However, it was painfully evident that the Soviet Union still refused to accept the validity of human rights as a subject for East-West discussion.

Moscow strongly resisted Western attempts at Madrid to transform the Final Document into a human rights charter that could effectively support political change in the Soviet bloc. Soviet bulllying proved effective, and many of the human-rights provisions that the West had promoted for nearly three years at Madrid were diluted or omitted altogether in the Final Document.

Chief U.S. delegate Max Kampelman stated at the conclusion of the Madrid conference that

> . . . . The United States is fully aware . . . that the Helsinki Final Act cannot attain its objectives when certain states, particularly the USSR, continue to violate its provisions. There are no enforcement mechanisms. . . . The Madrid meeting has been, therefore, the appropriate forum at which to insert political and moral pressure into the process. . . . The message [to the Soviets] was clear: "Conform to the promises made in 1975 if you wish to be recognized as a responsible member of the international community." [17]

Kampelman emphasized that "it is important that we keep raisng standards for responsible international behavior." The trouble with Kampelman's message was that the USSR has higher priorities than to be a member in good standing of the international order. Such a message might well be heeded by a status-quo power but not by one that defines itself in terms of a revolutionary ideology with internationalist pretensions. It is quite clear that Moscow views with contempt Kampelman's notion of the Helsinki and Madrid documents as a written code of behavior by which all signatories must abide. The Soviets dance to the beat of a different drum. Under these circumstances, it is difficult to quarrel with *The Wall Street Journal*'s contention that "the real value of the 'Helsinki process' may ultimately lie in the willingness of the West to abandon it."[18]

As the 1985 summit between Reagan and Gorbachev approached, Sakharov was in the sixth month of a hunger strike initiated by the Kremlin's refusal to let Yelena Bonner travel abroad for medical treatment. His wish was finally granted, although she had to promise, in exchange for a three-month exit visa, to refrain from interviews with the Western media.

Human rights issues were clearly a sideshow at the summit. Secretary of State Shultz declared that the two leaders held "extensive discussions" about human rights, but he provided no specifics. The summit communique said simply that Reagan and Gorbachev "agreed on the importance of resolving humanitarian cases in the spirit of cooperation."[19] Evidently, the President raised the question of human rights in one of his private sessions wiwth the Soviet leader. Reagan insisted that Soviet violations of human-rights accords constituted an important obstacle to improved East-West relations, but he reportedly declared his intention of relying on "quiet diplomacy" and foregoing opportunities to score propaganda points to promote Soviet compliance.[20] Gorbachev, during an impromptu meeting with the Rev. Jesse Jackson, denied all knowledge of a human rights problem. Pressed on the specific issue of Jewish emigration, he told Jackson that "the problem, or so-called problem, of Jews in the Soviet Union does not exist."[21]

Nevertheless, in the aftermath of the Reagan-Gorbachev tete-a-tete, Moscow made good on a pre-summit promise by informing nine Soviet spouses or relatives of American citizens that they would be permitted to emigrate. The first of this group to arrive on U.S. soil was Helle Frejus, an Estonian who had not seen her American husband in four years and had to leave her two daughters behind in the Soviet Union. She came to America on 29 December 1985. Among those who followed was Irina McClellan, wife of Woodford McClellan, a professor of history at the University of Virginia. The couple had been separated for 11 years. The emigration of a few selected Soviet citizens, however, by no means signaled a greater willingness by the USSR to abide by the agreements it had signed at Helsinki and Madrid to promote the reunification of families. Moscow was even less inclined to increase Jewish emigration, although a few exceptions were forthcoming. Altogether, only 1,139 Jews were allowed to leave the USSR in 1985, and the number of trials and arrests of Jewish activists in the country increased.

Representatives of the 35 signatories of the Helsinki Accords gathered in Bern, Switzerland, on 15 April 1986 for still another follow-up conference. They departed six weeks later, on 27 May, with virtually nothing to show for their efforts. In the aftermath of the Bern conference, rumors in the Soviet Union suggested that Gorbachev would be willing to guarantee higher levels of Jewish emigration as part of a package deal leading to establishment of Soviet-Israeli diplomatic relations, which Moscow severed in the wake of the 1967 Arab-Israeli War. The rumors took on added substance in August, when the Kremlin suddenly recalled that it owned church property in the Holy Land and proposed an exchange of views with Israel on consular issues. Soviet and Israeli representatives held a meeting in Helsinki on 18 August, but the Soviets announced the next day that no further discussions would be held because the Israelis had raised political questions, including the status of Soviet Jewry.[22]

On 6 November, 1986, coinciding with the start of a Helsinki review conference in Vienna, Moscow publicized new regulations on emigration that Soviet authorities portrayed as liberalizing but in reality were more restrictive than in the past. Emigration on grounds of reunification of families was now interpreted very narrowly—covering only husbands, wives, children, and siblings. Moreover, the authorities could deny the right of emigration not only for reasons of "state security" but also "in the interest of insuring the protection of social order, health, or the morals of the population."[23] The Soviets also proposed a meeting in Moscow on the subject of humanitarian affairs. Foreign Minister Shevardnadze, who made the proposal, stated that such a conclave should discuss not only human rights as understood in the West but also such issues as unemployment, homelessness and inadequate social welfare in Western countries. The reaction of the West was reflected in the comment of an Austrian newspaper that the Moscow meeting would be akin to "a debate in the fox den about raising chickens."[24]

In December 1986 the Soviet regime installed a telephone in Sakharov's apartment in Gorki for the first time in his seven years of internal exile. The first caller was Gorbachev, who told Russia's most famous dissident that his internal exile was over and his privileges as a member of the Soviet Academy of Sciences were reinstated. Gorbachev probably can rely upon Sakharov to speak out in favor of arms control and against SDI; but the physicist also is likely to remind the world publicly, as he did before his exile, that "as long as a country has no civil liberty, no freedom of information, and no independent press, then there exists no effective body of public opinion to control the conduct of the government. . . . Such a situation . . . is a menace to international security."[25]

Some other Soviet human-rights figures, not as world renowned as Sakharov but equally long-suffering, were released during 1986 and 1987. They included the Christian poet Irina Ratushinskaya and the Jewish refusenik Iosif Begun. A bit of the old flavor returned to Moscow, however, when KGB agents roughed up demonstrators demanding Begun's release. Inna Meiman, wife of a leader of the Helsinki monitoring group in Moscow, was belatedly given permission to emigrate. She and her husband, Naum, had applied desperately for an emigration visa for several years in hopes of obtaining medical treatment in the West for Mrs. Meiman's spinal cancer. Alas, she came to the West only to die; the long wait had caused her disease to advance to the incurable stage. The Soviet regime denied her husband permission to travel abroad to attend her funeral.

There was also talk of allowing 10,000 Jews out of the USSR—a considerable improvement over recent performance but a far cry from the half-million Jews who are believed to be awaiting an opportunity to emigrate. As Morris B. Abram, chairman of the National Conference on Soviet Jewry, remarked:

> We must not be deceived that the dove has come from Noah's Ark with a green twig in his beak, because the Soviets have the capacity of releasing people in driblets and then creating new prisoners. They receive much publicity from the release of one person and then imprison others who receive no publicity. In this way, they throw dust in our eyes. [26]

For every dissident or group of dissidents that is released, the KGB (which, by all accounts, has accumulated authority and prestige unparalleled since Stalin's time) will replenish its stock of human bargaining chips. In 1987 the Kremlin allowed 8,000 Jews to emigrate—a tenfold increase over the previous year but less than 20 percent of the 1979 high.

Whereas the Kremlin adamantly rejected Henry Kissinger's theory of linkage, it has proposed some linkage of its own. For example, when Undersecretary of Commerce Lionel Olmer led a trade delegation to Moscow early in 1985, Soviet State Bank director Vladimir Alkhimov avowed that "if good relations were restored with the United States (read: if MFN and cheap trade credits were forthcoming), 50,000 Jewish emigres annually would be 'no problem.'"[27] According to Melvyn Krauss, an economist and senior fellow at the Hoover Institution, "the basic parameters of the Gorbachev strategy have been established: to catch the West's attention, send out a 'loss leader' like Shcharansky, then make a deal for increased Soviet emigration in exchange for Western economic concessions."[28]

Even if the United States were inclined to meet the Soviets more than halfway on trade, Congress would first have to repeal the Jackson-Vanik Amendment. Congress displays few signs of moving in this direction, and it is difficult to foresee what benefits, if any, a repeal would confer. Jackson-Vanik is a convenient scapegoat for those in the Kremlin who want to prevent the embarrassing spectacle of wholesale emigration; but other scapegoats are available. In the meantime, it is worth noting a 1983 remark by Morris B. Abram:

> The Jackson-Vanik Amendment was one response to the impetus which Soviet anti-Semitism added to the desire of Soviet Jews to be repatriated to Israel, despite the great personal risks involved. After its enactment, Jewish emigration from the Soviet Union rose from less than 1,000 a year to more than 51,000 in 1979. Exit permits have now been reduced to a mere trickle, but U.S. policy is no more responsible for this Soviet human-rights violation than it is for endemic Soviet anti-Semitism. [29]

As noted in the title of ths chapter, human rights is the unstable element of detente—"most unstable" might be a more appropriate formulation. Arms control, economic cooperation, trade and technology transfer, and other "hard" issues can be measured with some degree of accuracy through the manufacture and deployment of weapons systems, the signing of quantitative agreements, and the exchange of knowhow and raw data. Human rights, by contrast, is a "soft" issue. Progress in this sphere is much less susceptible to accurate measurement than is progress in other detente-related categories. Nor should human rights advances be reduced to a numbers game. Divergent U.S. and Soviet approaches to human rights represent, above all, a clash of fundamental values. The United States must promote its own values with more aggressive self-confidence than it has displayed in the past. Such a course of action, in addition to its political and moral benefits, can exert a highly positive effect in the arena of international public opinion to which we attach so much importance.

George Will has pointed out quite correctly that "U.S. officials often raise [the issue of human rights] in an apologetic manner, explaining to the Soviets that human-rights violations are a political problem for any U.S. administration. They say America is a 'nation of immigrants' and ratification of agreements and detente generally will be difficult without some Soviet gestures. This approach blames the U.S. public for the awkwardness U.S. officials feel when forced to deal with the essential truths about the Soviet regime."[30] At the same time, Washington goes out of its way to assuage Moscow's anger when embarrassing incidents occur on the human-rights front. The incredible mishandling of the recent attempted defection of a Soviet seaman is a case in point. The hapless sailor risked his life swimming ashore from his ship and slashed his wrists to signal his determination to avoid return to the USSR. The U.S. government's decision to send the man home to an almost certain death sentence had a threefold negative effect: it represented a cave-in to Soviet bluster; it betrayed the human rights of a Soviet citizen at a time when the Reagan Administration was attempting to reinforce linkage between human rights and the rest of the detente menu; and it made a mockery of U.S. traditions of political asylum and individual self-determination.

In short, the United States must proudly display its own values and norms of human behavior without entertaining any illusions that the USSR will subscribe to them in the foreseeable future. A Western correspondent has observed that, at least partly as a result of detente, "Soviet society as a whole is irreversibly, if not overwhelmingly, more open to foreign influence than in decades past."[31] Or, to put it another way, the Iron Curtain has not been raised, but it is more porous. However, "seemingly unchanged—indeed, through much of Russian history—is the fact that active dissent is the province of a relative few. While many Soviets seem increasingly aware of the outside world and increasingly vocal among themselves in criticizing Soviet failings [there is a] tendency to keep such thoughts within bounds. The rule: Thinking, talking, joking against the Soviet system is one thing; going public is another."[32]

The Soviet regime is determined to keep dissent within bounds while working relentlessly to place the onus for disrupting detente squarely on Western shoulders. Human-rights gestures are likely to remain no more than gestures; a new era of free self-expression in the Soviet Union is nowhere on the horizon, and large-scale emigration is too dangerous for the Kremlin to contemplate. We must shun the illusion that the release of a few prominent Soviet dissidents is a major concession to the West.

Moscow has never attached any intrinsic value to human rights but occasionally has proved willing to use dissidents as bargaining chips to achieve tangible benefits—arms control concessions, trade, credits, and Western technology. Many Western observers expressed hope that the "Helsinki process" would move human rights to the front burner of Soviet concerns. These observers overlooked the fact that on the Kremlin's scale of priorities, political ranks far above arms control agreements, trade pacts, or the other paraphernalia of detente. To the extent that the exercise of individual rights jeopardizes the sanctity of the Communist system, rights must be proscribed.

In injecting the issue of human rights into the linkage of the detente process, the West has attempted to graft an accoutrement onto the Soviet body politic that finds no roots either in Russian history or in Communist ideology. Human-rights injunctions represent a foreign intrusion that cannot be absorbed. Rejection has been the inevitable upshot. A major improvement in the human-rights situation in the USSR would entail more than the kind of "mellowing" that many Western proponents of detente anticipate. It would entail even more than a gradual liberalization in the sense of internal reforms. It would necessitate the dismantlement of the totalitarian regime, which is propped up by its vast apparatus of repression, and a systemic change in the direction of political pluralism. By demanding that Moscow must respect human rights in the form of individual liberties and the free expression of ideas, political or otherwise, the West is asking the Soviet ruling class—the *nomenklatura*—to commit political suicide.

The Kremlin regards Western pressure on human rights as an insidious campaign to undermine the power and the very legitimacy of the Communist system. The Soviets appeared both puzzled and disturbed by Jimmy Carter's messianic crusade on human rights, although it was directed more frequently at rightwing dictatorships in Central and Latin America than at the Soviet bloc. The continuing emphasis on humgn-rights issues under the Reagan Administration, although less strident, has kept the USSR on guard. At times, Moscow has yielded; in 1979, for example, it permitted more than 50,000 Jews to emigrate, in hopes of winning U.S. Senate ratification of SALT II, and in 1986 Gorbachev let Sakharov's wife obtain medical treatment in the West as part of his "charm offensive" to win propaganda points abroad. However, for every Western "victory" on the human-rights front, there are innumerable setbacks. For instance, Shcharansky was released from the Gulag and permitted to emigrate; but the Kremlin insisted that he must be traded for Soviet spies, thus reinforcing the allegation that he himself had committed espionage. Moreover, for every dissident permitted to emigrate, hundreds and even thousands are left stranded. Thus, tactical successes, such as the Shcharansky case, tend only to underline the intractable nature of the human-rights issue.

As the detente process evolves along its cyclical course, one becomes aware of a recurring phenomenon. When superpower tensions are high, the Kremlin battens down the hatches and rallies its subjects around the flag of the Soviet motherland, using such devices as the fanning of antiwar hysteria and appeals to the xenophobic instincts of the Russian people. When there is a relaxation of tensions, i.e., detente, the guardians of Soviet orthodoxy increse their ideological vigilance, lest a freer flow of people and information between East and West contaminate the Soviet poplation with "rotten bourgeois liberalism." Thus, an automatic Catch-22 element is built into detente where human rights are concerned.

On several occasions, the Soviet Union has permitted the emigration of dissidents or preserved them from almost certain death because the West raised an outcry on their behalf. This fact suggests that Western pressure indeed can achieve results. Some caveats must be cited, however. First of all, only a handful of Soviet dissidents have gained an international reputation that gives them name recognition in the West. Secondly, some of the most prominent dissidents, notably Solzhenitsyn, have been exiled against their will. They retain a love for Mother Russia despite their antipathy toward Communism and may lose their creative impulse when separated from their homeland. Finally, some of these dissidents evidently are sent abroad because the Soviet authorities regard them as troublemakers who might acquire a following at home. Thus, their emigration, far from presaging a relaxation of human-rights restrictions, is intended to tighten the reins over potential dissidents left behind.

The reader should not infer from the above observations that Western agitation for human rights in the USSR is misplaced or improper. On the contrary, the glare of international publicity (in contrast to "quiet diplomacy") regarding Soviet human-rights violations shines some much-needed light into the bear's cave. The West should expend less effort worrying about whether to "embarrass" or "provoke" the Soviets and more effort trying to capitalize on the few successes it has achieved. In this regard, Ronald Reagan's failure to invite Yelena Bonner to the White House contrasted poorly with French President Mitterrand's willingness to welcome her at the Elysee.

As compared with arms control, human-rights violations in the Soviet Union are relatively easy to pinpoint and verify. The West need not rely upon "national technical means," for it has at hand some splendid—and sobering—testimonials from former inmates of the "prison of nations," as Dostoevsky called Russia. Further dissemination of these testimonials, along with more persistent efforts to secure the freedom of other Soviet human-rights victims and prisoners of conscience, will help to discredit the notion of moral symmetry that too often is applied to the two superpowers.

Finally, Western attempts to link Soviet respect for human rights with the other strands of Kissinger's web of detente have been instructive in gaining insight into Soviet behavior. The contempt that Moscow has shown toward the West is a natural extension of the scorn that it heaps upon its own citizens. It is part and parcel of a policy of coercion and intimidation designed to play its opponents off against each other, keep them weak and divided, and avert a challenge to Soviet totalitarianism. Squabbles between the United States and its Western allies and among various U.S. government agencies and interest groups over what carrots to offer the Kremlin serve only to bolster its contempt.

Professor Stanley Hoffman of Harvard University has written that "we need not be ashamed to place detente above the immediate promotion of human rights in the Soviet Union . . . [because] there is a human right to peace, which detente enhances."[33] Ronald Reagan came closer to the truth, however, when he stated after his Geneva summit with Gorbachev that "we discussed human rights. We Americans believe that history teaches no clearer lesson than that countries which respect the rights of their citizens tend, inevitably, to respect the rights of their neighbors. Human rights, therefore, *is* a peace issue."[34] One might also reply to Professor Hoffmann and like-minded commentators that there is a human right to inner peace, which derives from exercising the dictates of one's conscience without fear of persecution.

Washington does not demand that Soviet citizens subscribe to Western values. It understands and respects the fact that Soviet dissidents espouse sentiments ranging across the ideological spectrum from ultraright-wing Russian nationalism and religious obscurantism through Western-style democratic liberalism to Eurocommunism and radical Socialism. The West should simply insist on the right of peaceful self-expression for Soviet dissidents—a right that is enshrined in a number of international agreements signed by Moscow. This does not seem too high a price to extract for the fruits of detente, most of which continue to flow along a one-way street toward the East.

# 6

# The Uses and Misuses of Detente: A Guide for U.S. Negotiators and Policymakers

During the height of detente in 1973, a *Washington Star* reporter wrote that

> . . . in the world of cliches, it is always comforting to have a reliable, steady favorite like "detente." It meets all the requirements: It is French, and therefore impossible for Americans to pronounce with any degree of certainty; it is short enough to fit in a one-column headline . . . yet full-bodied enough to add solidity and a sense of importance to a four-column head-cum-kicker; its meaning is only hazily grasped by its users; and, perhaps most important of all, it means nothing whatever to the reader.

William Safire's definition of detente as "an improvement in relations between nations, warmer than accommodation, cooler than rapprochement"[1] best describes the concept of detente as portrayed in this study.

The Soviets eschew the word "detente" altogether, preferring "peaceful coexistence" or the Russian word *razryadka*, which they define as "the state of international relations resulting from the observance of the principles of peaceful coexistence." At first, Moscow perceived "peaceful coexistence" as a formula for easing the pressure on the young Bolshevik state from "capitalist encirclement." Soviet Russia portrayed itself as a lonely island in a sea of hostile "imperialist" powers. On 30 November 1920, *Pravda* published a statement by Lenin that said: "As long as capitalism and Socialism exist, we cannot live in peace; in the end, one or the other will triumph. A funeral dirge will be sung over the Soviet republic or over world capitalism."

In an address to the Polish Communist Party, Nikita Khrushchev declared:

> . . . We must realize that we cannot coexist eternally [or] for a long time. One of us must go to the grave. We do not want to go to the grave. They do not want to go to the grave. So what can be done? We must push them to their grave.

Shortly after the 1973 superpower summit, *Pravda* reiterated that "peaceful coexistence doesn't mean the end of the struggle of the two world social systems. The struggle between the proletariat and the bourgeoisie, between world revolution and imperialism, will be waged up to the complete and final victory of Communism on a world scale."[2] On 27 November 1985, *Pravda* stated that use of the term "detente" has "caused a certain confusion in the minds of American philistines. Americans do not properly understand it and sometimes even associate it subconsciously with the word *entente* (understanding) or even *entente cordiale* (meeting of minds) . . ." The Soviet journal *Za Rubezhom* echoed the same view by pointing out that peaceful coexistence does not imply an effort toward "preservation of the status quo," because such a world would be "as petrified and lifeless as a lunar landscape, a world without social cataclysms and storms, where imperialism could continue unhindered its tyranny in the areas remaining in its sphere of influence."

Thus, the fundamental Leninist precept of "Kto kogo?"—literally, "Who, whom?"—still defines Moscow's attitude toward the capitalist West. As Fedor Burlatskiy, a well known political commentator with close ties to Gorbachev, put it, "We have to think about the future. . . . Either we will be able to ride on it, to rule it, or other peoples and states will begin to pass us and to push us around. . . ."[3] No Soviet leader ever has claimed that detente is more than an interlude in the epochal struggle between Communism and capitalism. However, the Soviets have moved the inevitable denouement far into the future and have sought to maximize their chances of achieving victory without resorting to war. Undoubtedly they appreciate the wisdom expounded by the ancient Chinese strategist Sun-Tsu: "To subdue one's enemy without fighting is the acme of skill."

In order to seek the fruits of war without waging an armed struggle, the USSR launched a massive nuclear buildup to neutralize American strategic superiority and deter a nuclear war that would destroy Communist as well as capitalist civilization. It also developed a formidable across-the-board conventional war machine for use as a political instrument of intimidation and coercion as well as a strictly military force. Moreover, the Kremlin created and refined a whole array of measures—*spetsnaz* operations, "fraternal assistance" to Communist parties worldwide, the establishment and sustenance of international front groups, aid to "national liberation movements," subversion, espionage, and disinformation—to promote a shift in the "correlation of forces" in favor of the Socialist camp and paralyze the West's will and capacity to respond. Concurrent with and transcending all these strategies is detente itself—the Soviet pursuit of relaxation of East-West tensions for the purpose of deflecting Western attention from the above-mentioned measures while simultaneously rendering those measures more effective.

Soviet foreign policy is distinguished by its dualistic nature. Institutionally, the dualism was embodied during Lenin's time in the existence side by side of the People's Commissariat for Foreign Affairs, which operated on a government-to-government level, and the Comintern (Third International), which conducted party-to-party relations with Communist movements around the globe. Today, the Ministry of Foreign Affairs and the International Department of the Communist Party's Central Committee perform roughly the same respective functions.

The Soviet Union fosters relaxation of tensions in order to secure tangible benefits from the very capitalist governments it targets for eventual extinction. Thus, for example, the Soviets proclaimed their peaceful intentions in order to coax arms-control concessions from the West, induce the bourgeoisie to "sell the rope" in the form of trade concessions and credits, obtain subsidized U.S. grain to help feed the Soviet army and the captive cities of Afghanistan, and connive for West European financing for a natural gas pipeline that could be used to block the flow of vital energy to Western populations and industries in a crisis. Moscow exhibits a perverse brilliance in exploiting the passion of U.S. and West European public opinion for peace while acquiring—often at bargain prices or by outright theft—the products and technological knowhow of the advanced capitalist societies.

Under Brezhnev, Moscow's pursuit of relaxation of tension assumed an air of semi-permanence that it had lacked in the past; to some extent, detente became an institutionalized feature of the Soviet foreign policy landscape. At the 24th CPSU Congress in 1971, Brezhnev introduced his "Peace Program," which aimed at relaxing international tensions and slowing down U.S. military programs while the Soviets strengthened their position vis-a-vis the West. Brezhnev, the product of Russian peasant culture and orthodox Marxist-Leninist education, met his most eager partner in detente in the person of Richard Nixon, a rightwing Republican with close ties to Big Business and a political reputation built on going for the Communist jugular. Each half of this improbable partnership harbored his own motivations for alleviating superpower tensions.

Major General Jan Sejna, who served as first secretary of the Communist Party in Czechoslovakia's Defense Ministry until his defection in 1968, recounted his attendance at a secret meeting on 22 February of that year at which the Soviet and East European Communist leaders discussed "peaceful coexistence" at length. According to Sejna's book *We Will Bury You,* East German Communist boss Walter Ulbricht criticized the Kremlin's emphasis on peaceful coexistence on the grounds that it was undermining the ideological cohesion of the Soviet bloc. Brezhnev replied that the Soviets needed 10 or 15 years to catch up with the West in such critical areas as computers, electronics, antisubmarine warfare techniques, and agricultural productivity before it could afford the risk of an East-West confrontation. By proffering peaceful coexistence, Brezhnev argued, the USSR could persuade the advanced capitalist countries to allow a steady flow of trade, credits, and technology Eastward. Bolstered economically and militarily by Western largesse, the USSR would be poised to exert heavy pressure against its adversaries—for example, by cutting them off during a crisis from Middle Eastern oil sources. It is eerie to recall that as early as 1973 (five years after the Prague meeting) Moscow felt emboldened to encourage Arab use of the oil weapon against the United States as punishment for supporting Israel in the Yom Kippur War. That same year, Brezhnev asserted during a congress of the Czech Communist Party that

> . . . we Communists have got to string along with the capitalists for awhile. We need their credits, their agriculture, their technology. But we're going to continue massive military programs and by the middle of the '80s we'll be in a position to return to a much more aggressive foreign policy designed to gain the upper hand in our relationship with the West.

Nixon had his own strong motives for fostering detente. First, he was eager to solicit Moscow's help in bringing about a negotiated (and face-saving) solution of the Vietnam War. Secondly, Nixon wished to make his mark in history by effectuating a rapprochement with both Communist giants—the USSR and China. He sought to exploit the Sino-Soviet dispute to give both of the antagonists a stake in detente with the United States. Finally, the President seemed eager to implement the Kissingerian theory of "linkage"—i.e., the spinning of a web of interdependence between America and Russia—to moderate Soviet hostility toward the West and usher in a "generation of peace."

Professor John Lewis Gaddis has pointed out that

> Nixon and Kissinger . . . embraced detente as a means of updating and reinvigorating containment . . . a way to make containment function more efficiently, but through a method at once more ingenious and less risky than the old "massive retaliation" concept. . . . The Nixon Administration sought to engage the Soviet Union . . . in a direct effort to reduce tensions through diplomacy. These negotiations proceeded, not on the basis that all differences with the Russians could be resolved, but rather on the expectation that they could be managed. . . . [4]

The Nixon-Kissinger policy, however, was rooted in U.S. weakness and in Kissinger's belief that the country lacked either the military muscle or the political will to compete vigorously with the USSR. The two major architects of detente recognized that Vietnam had destroyed the domestic base of support for a containment policy vis-a-vis the USSR. Thus, as Norman Podhoretz wrote in his book *The Present Danger*,

> . . . Nixon, who had once denounced containment as "cowardly" and would in the past have been expected to abandon it, if at all, in favor of a more aggressive stance, moved instead in the other direction—toward withdrawal, retrenchment, disengagement. . . .

To be sure, the new policy did not call itself by any such unattractive name as "strategic retreat." It was called "Detente" and it was heralded as the beginning of a new era in the relations between the United States and the Soviet Union.

Hardly had detente been fully launched when Watergate intervened. Moscow was dubious that such a "trivial" incident could derail American foreign policy and entertained some suspicion that Watergate was a plot by Nixon's enemies to destroy his rapprochement with the Soviets. Although dismayed by Nixon's resignation, the Kremlin presumably was reassured by the accession of Gerald Ford, a Republican with much the same constituency as his predecessor—a constituency that included business enterprises seeking more East-West trade. Moreover, Ford's retention of Kissinger as Secretary of State provided continuity in the Soviet-American relationship.

Nevertheless, Soviet-American relations slid quickly downhill. The USSR, incensed by the Jackson-Vanik Amendment to the 1974 Trade Reform Act, rejected the comprehensive trade agreement that had been worked out in the aftermath of the 1972 Moscow summit. Jewish emigration, which peaked at more than 51,000 in 1973, declined in each subsequent year. Massive Soviet arming of the Arabs for their 1973 war against Israel and of the North Vietnamese for their final offensive against South Vietnam in 1975, as well as Soviet-Cuban intervention in Angola, destroyed whatever hopes the United States had harbored for superpower cooperation on regional conflicts. Ford met with Brezhnev at Vladivostok in 1974 to build a framework for SALT II, but the momentum of arms control already was decreasing.

Part of the problem lay in Washington's inability to test adequately the concept of linkage. Kissinger strove to apply positive and negative reinforcement to moderate Soviet behavior, but this process presupposed some centralized control over the linkage process. The "Imperial Presidency" was a vehicle tailor-made for steering Kissinger-style detente; but the rapid decline of the executive branch's control over foreign policy in the wake of Watergate, Nixon's resignation, and the vigorous assertion of Congressional prerogatives wrought havoc with foreign-policy decisionmaking. Thus, aside from Jackson-Vanik, Congress balked at funding the weapons programs that the Nixon Administration had planned as a concomitant of its arms control policies.

It was not long before Nixon's and Kissinger's critics began to complain about the "overselling of detente." It was denounced as a sellout, a giveaway, and a "one-way street." One critic asserted that pursuing detente was "like going to a wife-swapping party and coming home alone."[5] Another proclaimed that "detente is dead. The second Cold War has begun."[6] *Pravda* denounced those in the United States who alleged that the Soviets were obtaining unilateral advantages through detente. "Some people with weak nerves [are] losing self-control, are even speaking in extremes," said *Pravda*.[7]

As the 1976 electoral campaign got underway, Ford banished the word "detente" from his political vocabulary, replacing it with "peace through strength." This slogan also became the byword of the newly created Committee on the Present Danger, founded by veteran arms control negotiator Paul Nitze and others to alert the American people to the growing Soviet military threat. Meanwhile, Ronald Reagan launched his campaign for the Republican presidential nomination by telling a New Hampshire audience that

> . . . Detente has become a one-way street. The Soviet Union is using detente to further its aim for world conquest and we're leaning over backward to obey detente on our side. I think it's time for us to straighten up and eyeball them and say, "Hey, fellas, let's get this back on the track where it's something for something, not all one way." And that could begin with the situation in Angola right now, saying to the Russians: "Out!" [8]

Reagan's electoral victory initially may have had a salutary impact on the Soviets, especially if they regarded him as another Nixon-style practitioner of *Realpolitik*. However, his first presidential news conference, on 29 January 1981, certainly must have dampened their optimism. On that occasion, Reagan proclaimed that the Soviets are bent on "the promotion of world revolution and a one-world Socialist or Communist state." He added that "the only morality they recognize is what will further their cause, meaning that they reserve unto themselves the right to commit any crime, to lie, to cheat in order to attain that."

Secretary of State Haig proclaimed that "this Administration will stress linkage as a fundamental fact of East-West relations."[9] However, one of Reagan's first foreign policy acts as President was to abandon the restrictions on grain exports to the USSR that Carter had imposed after the invasion of Afghanistan. Reagan portrayed the lifting of the sanction as fulfillment of a campaign promise to American farmers, but it contrasted vividly with his outspoken criticism of Soviet behavior.[10]

Brezhnev presumably welcomed indications that Reagan, unlike Carter, viewed the superpower relationship as the central issue of U.S. foreign policy; the Soviets also were eager to exploit differences between Washington and some of the other NATO capitals over the Euromissile issue. Radio Moscow called Brezhnev's "peace offensive " in Western Europe a program for saving detente."[11] Meanwhile, "scholar" and propagandist Georgiy Arbatov—newly ensconced as a full member of the Central Committee—published a *Pravda* article entitled "A Difficult Choice." It contended that the United States no longer possessed the power to deal with the Soviet Union "in old ways" and that the right wing would be obliged to make "quite an abrupt turn—a difficult and even agonizing turn."[12]

In the aftermath of the assassination attempt against Reagan in March 1981, the President reflected at length on Soviet-American relations and the broader issue of peace. Sen.Paul Laxalt (R.-Nev.), one of the President's closest political allies and friends, recalls a visit to the hospital, where he found Reagan preoccupied with economic issues. "Ron, as important as it is, I don't think the Good Lord has spared you just to save the economy," Laxalt remembers saying. "You have a higher destiny—one day to work out a meaningful agreement with the Soviets."[13] Nancy Reagan also reportedly began imploring her husband to seek an accord with the USSR, particularly on arms control, to certify his devotion to peace. The President himself reminisced publicly about the detentist musings that preoccupied him after his brush with death. During the speech on 18 November 1981, at which he officially proposed the "zero option" on INF, Reagan read portions of a letter that he had written to Brezhnev during his convalescence:

"Mr. President, when we met [during the Nixon-Brezhnev summit in the United States in 1973], I asked if you were aware that the hopes . . . of millions of people throughout the world were dependent on the decisions that would be reached in those [summit] meetings. You took my hand in both of yours and assured me that you were aware of that and that you were dedicated . . . to fulfilling those hopes and dreams . . .

"When World War II ended, the United States had the only undamaged industrial power in the world . . . and we alone had the ultimate weapon—the nuclear weapon . . . If we had sought world domination, then who could have opposed us?

"But the United States . . . used our power and wealth to rebuild the war-ravaged economies of the world. . . . .May I say there is absolutely no substance to charges that the United States is guilty of imperialism or attempts to impose its will on other countries by use of force.

... "Mr. President, should we not be concerned with eliminating the obstacles which prevent our people . . . from achieving their most cherished goals?" [14]

Brezhnev, however, was intent upon preserving Moscow's strategic advantage and forestalling Reagan's ambitious plans for U.S. military modernization and Euromissile deployments. Soviet efforts to guide the West European anti-nuclear movement already have been discussed.[15] The Soviet role in the nuclear freeze movement that convulsed the United States in the early 1980's is less well known but had a discernible impact.[16]

Reagan rebuffed the nuclear freeze movement and, in March 1981, unveiled a defense-spending program with a price tag exceeding $1 trillion for the next five years. In November, however, the President announced his "zero-option" proposal for the elimination of intermediate-range missiles; and, notwithstanding Reagan's characterization of SALT II as "fatally flawed," arms control resumed its place as the centerpiece of Soviet-American relations.

In November 1982, Brezhnev died after 18 years in power. His successor, Yuri Andropov, was himself a member of the gerontocracy—and a seriously ailing one, to boot. Despite his legacy as the Soviet proconsul in Hungary when the 1956 revolution was crushed and his stewardship of the KGB and architect of its successful campaign to extirpate the dissident movement, Andropov was touted by Soviet disinformation specialists and "useful idiots" in the West as a closet liberal. Many media commentators portrayed the new General Secretary as "returning home from a day of running the Gulag, a glass of vodka in his hand, a Glenn Miller 78 on the turntable."[17] *Newsweek* proffered a headline on "Andropov's Good Vibrations."[18] *The Economist*, commenting that Andropov gave the KGB "a new urbanity and sophistication," wrote that "Mr. Andropov is a tough, but he is an intelligent tough, not just the iron-bottomed sort."[19] Vice President Bush, former director of the CIA, appeared to claim a special insight into Andropov. After heading the U.S. delegation to Brezhnev's funeral, Bush said he had conversed with Gorbachev for 40 minutes "as spook to spook."[20] Bush observed that "anyone [like Andropov] who has had access to all the [intelligence] data must objectively know that if a country goes in peace, it has absolutely nothing whatsoever to fear from the USA."[21] However, before long Andropov displayed his true colors, leading one observer to lament that the West was being subjected to "trial by Yuri." He remained intransigent on arms control, intensified the persecution of Soviet dissidents, proved unrelenting on Jewish emigration, and accelerated efforts to split the United States from its NATO allies on the INF deployment issue.

On 8 March 1983, two days after Christian Democrat Helmut Kohl, a supporter of the Euromissiles, won the West German election, Reagan delivered his now-famous "Evil Empire" speech. Speaking before the National Association of Evangelicals in Orlando, Florida, the President castigated the Soviet Union as "the focus of evil in the modern world" and said that the "evil empire" should be consigned to the "ash heap of history." He cautioned against the temptation to ignore "the aggressive impulses of an evil empire." Then, on 23 March, Reagan introduced his Strategic Defense Initiative (SDI).

By mid-1983, gloom-mongers in Russia and America alike were predicting a major confrontation between the superpowers. On 23 November, the Soviets walked out of the negotiations on intermediate-range missile forces; on 8 December, the Soviet delegation quit the START (strategic arms reduction) talks. The first Euromissiles were deployed on schedule in December. These moves shocked the American arms control community, which, along with other enthusiasts of detente, orchestrated a campaign of pressure on the President to be more conciliatory toward the Soviets. The campaign contributed to the markedly softer stance that Reagan began to adopt toward the USSR.

On 2 March 1984, Chernenko declared that "detente has struck deep roots" and called for "a drastic change in Soviet-American relations."[22] His actions belied his words, however. The Soviet Union moved to reduce East-West contacts by suspending direct-dial telephone service to the United States and Western Europe, refusing to accept pre-payment of customs duties on packages mailed from abroad (thus curtailing shipments of books, clothing, and other items to Soviet citizens), and making it a crime for a citizen to ride in a foreigner's car, let a foreigner spend the night at his house, or pass information obtained from his job to any foreigner without special permission. In May, the Soviet Union announced its withdrawal from the Olympics in Los Angeles.[23] Meanwhile, a Soviet propaganda campaign likened President Reagan's policies to those of Hitler.

The White House was not discouraged. In July, as both summit fever and election fever mounted in Washington, Reagan eased the ban on commercial fishing that Carter had imposed as part of the Afghanistan sanctions package. On 24 September, the President delivered an address to the U.N. General Assembly that came to be known as the "olive branch" speech. He emphasized that "there is no sane alternative to negotiations [with the USSR] on arms control and other issues . . . " and proposed regular Cabinet-level meetings between U.S. and Soviet officials "on the whole agenda of issues before us"; an exchange of "outlines" of five-year plans for weapons development and schedules of intended military procurement; and periodic consultaions on regional conflicts. As confidence-building measures, he also suggested an exchange of U.S. and Soviet experts to each others' nuclear test sites and an exchange of observers at military exercises. To revive the arms control negotiations that the Soviets had jettisoned, Reagan said that "we need to extend the arms control process, to build a bigger umbrella under which it can operate—a road map [for] the next 20 years or so. . . . " The only discordant note in the speech from the Soviet Union's standpoint came when Reagan declared that "the United States will continue to view human rights as the moral center of our foreign policy. We can never look at any people's freedom as a bargaining chip in world politics. . . . " [24]

Questioned after the speech about the softness of his stance, the President insisted that "I haven't changed my mind [about the Soviets]. I'm simply saying we've got to live in this world together." Secretary Shultz explained that Reagan wished to appear "constructive" and "positive" in preparation for a scheduled meeting with Gromyko and, he hinted, for the election.[25] Some commentators, however, saw more dangerous implications in Reagan's detentist musings. Patrick Buchanan typified the concern when he wrote:

> Mr. Reagan has never been naive. Yet, there he was last week at the United Nations, a virtual supplicant for detente. . . . Mr. Reagan's retainers tell us this is clever politics, Mr.Reagan is capturing the "peace issue." Yet, that U.N. speech left Mr. Reagan's supporters acutely embarrassed, enabled Mr. Mondale to chortle over "deathbed conversions," permitted the anti-Reagan press to mock his new tone, and allowed Mr. Gromyko to get away with delivering an insulting anti-American tirade to the General Assembly which even *The Washington Post* found "abusive, one-sided and unconstructive."

Interestingly, the White House announced that Reagan would confer with Henry Kissinger to discuss Gromyko's forthcoming visit.

During the 1976 Presidential campaign, Reagan had singled out Kissinger as a symbol of the unsuccessful policy of detente.

In his own address to the General Assembly on 27 September, Gromyko called Reagan's speech "nothing but an empty vessel" and declared that the Kremlin wanted "concrete deeds, not verbal assurances," regarding the improvement of superpower relations. [26] Ignoring the USSR's walkout from arms control talks, Gromyko accused Washington of wrecking the negotiations. Thus, "the Soviets took the olive branch President Reagan extended to them in his speech to the U.N. General Assembly . . . and snapped it like a twig."[27]

On the morrow of his U.N. speech, Gromyko arrived at the White House, becoming the first Soviet leader that Reagan met with during his four years in office. The President wanted to "maybe convince [Gromyko] that the United States means no harm."[28] The Kremlin's motivation for the meeting evidently was based on the belief that Reagan would win reelection and that reviving high-level contacts before rather than after Election Day was the better part of wisdom.

Gromyko's four-hour stay in the White House evidently bore no fruit. Nevertheless, detentists in the United States waxed euphoric about the Reagan-Gromyko contacts. After the two men shook hands at a diplomatic reception in New York on 23 September, *The New York Times* gushed:

> While a pianist played "It Never Entered My Mind," the President and the Foreign Minister engaged in smiling small talk as cameras zoomed in and clicked away. . . . Administration officials welcomed the sight—and, more important, the news pictures—of the meeting at the Waldorf-Astoria Hotel as evidence that the President has not, as his Democratic critics charge, dangerously alienated Soviet leaders. [29]

Patrick Buchanan, evidently reflecting conservative sentiments, complained that "the White House staff and Department of State are busy creating what Mr. Mondale calls "the new Reagan." Will someone tell me what was wrong with the old Reagan, who—before he went to the United Nations and met Mr. Gromyko—was leading in 50 states?"

Ronald Reagan, the "Great Communicator," won re-election resoundingly, but he soon met his match in Mikhail Gorbachev. The number-two man in Moscow, as he already was touted, arrived in Britain in December 1984 at the head of a Supreme Soviet delegation. "Iron Lady" Margaret Thatcher proclaimed that "I like Mr. Gorbachev. We can do business with him."[30] The American media were entranced by Gorbachev and his foray into the West. *Newsweek*, for example, rhapsodized that

> . . . In his trilby hat and gray ovrcoat, he might have been mistaken for a British gentleman on holiday. He played the part, too—stopping in at the Tower of London, browsing through the House of Lords and chatting with a bearded scholar in the . . . British Museum. . . . Throughout his visit, Gorbachev displayed a just-folks style rarely associated with the dour world of Soviet officialdom. . . . In one show of independent-mindedness, he skipped a wreath-laying ceremony at the tomb of Karl Marx and went instead on a tour of the Tower of London. . . .

Gorbachev's wife, Raisa, proved to be another public-relations asset:

> . . . She tried out several English phrases during the visit: "I like very much" and "See you later" were two favorites. She also dressed elegantly, showing up for one luncheon in a cream silk suit, pearl-drop earrings, and white boots. The British tabloids were dazzled. . . . [31]

One headline called Mrs. Gorbachev "Soviet Realism's Answer to Princess Diana."

On 11 March 1985 Gorbachev, the 54-year-old "baby" of the Politburo, succeeded Chernenko as General Secretary of the CPSU. Many in the West looked forward to a new era. *The Economist* typified the pervading optimism there when it wrote that " . . . Gorbachev . . . the first Soviet leader whose career started after Stalin, has injected a new chemistry into U.S.-Soviet relations" that could result in improved ties across the board. [32] Rep. Silvio O. Conte (R.-Mass.), a member of a Congressional delegation that held talks with the new Soviet leader, gushed that "he's a smooth guy. He'll stare you down when he talks to you, eyeball to eyeball. He's got wit. He's very dramatic. He can go from very loud to purring like a kitten." [33]

Summit fever soon resurfaced in Washington. Henry Kissinger emerged from a White House lunch with the President to warn that "this is not a personality contest. I don't think [Gorbachev] got to the top by being a choir boy." The President, nevertheless, seemed bent upon a get-acquainted session with the new General Secretary. In a column on 28 March entitled "Begging for a Summit," William Safire wrote,

> This week, Mr. Reagan fairly got down on his knees. Admitting that "there have been no signals" of acceptance, the President pleaded through reporters with the hard-to-get Russian. The date "depends on Mr. Gorbachev . . . when it could be convenient for him."

Reagan even suggested a get-together at the United Nations as an alternative to a Washington summit. "In other words," wrote Safire, "if Mr. Gorbachev won't come to Washington on a state visit, Mr. Reagan is hoping to be squeezed into the Soviet leader's busy schedule at the U.N. in New York this fall, perhaps between the Cuban and Nicaraguan leaders." Safire emphasized that "it is Mr. Gorbachev, not Mr. Reagan, who needs the legitimacy that a summit would provide. The American leader, by begging for a meeting anywhere, anytime, demeans his office and undercuts his negotiating position."[34]

The summit was finally scheduled for November. As the pre-summit period entered its home stretch, Moscow tried to pre-cook the agenda, placing arms control on the front burner, while Washington professed its desire for discussion of a medley of issues, including human rights, regional conflicts and economic relations as well as arms control. Reagan reiterated his desire to assure Gorbachev that "we mean him no harm."[35] He averred that "just like us [the Soviets have] got suspicions that they think are legitimate with regard to our intent." An "expert" in the Administration opined that Gorbachev "brings to power the same kinds of mistrust and misperception about us that a Midwestern politician would bring to the Presidency about the Russians."[36]

In a pre-summit encounter in Moscow with Gorbachev, Secretary of State Shultz and National Security Affairs Adviser McFarlane reportedly received a dressing-down:

> In one of those briefings in which the identity of the government official is never revealed, it was disclosed exactly what Gorbachev has said that sent everyone into a . . . profound depression. He said that "extremists" in the government and the "military-industrial complex" . . . were trying to stop efforts to improve U.S.-Soviet relations. . . . Gorbachev's remarks had Reagan's "adrenalin going," the senior official said, and he warned that should Gorbachev talk that way to the President himself, Reagan would be "vigorous" right back. . . . [37]

The negative vibrations from Moscow failed to discourage detentists in the United States. A White House aide declared that "given his economic priorities and the economic stringencies, we think [Gorbachev] needs a deal."[38] "Let's Make a Deal," screamed the headline on an article by veteran Kremlinologist Jerry Hough, an advocate of the hypothesis that "interest-group" politics in the USSR give a pluralistic cast to what was once a totalitarian monolith. Henry Kissinger wrote that "objective conditions in the Soviet Union" had created a "potentially malleable" situation for Reagan to exploit:

> Gorbachev requires no sentimental commitment to Western notions of peace to conclude that his country cannot simultaneously sustain fundamental reform and heightened international tensions. But for him reform poses a Hobson's choice. He can seek to improve the performance of the existing structure. . . . On the other hand, more fundamental reforms introducing incentives and markets would surely generate a Titanic domestic struggle. . . . Faced with the choice between potential stagnation and potential turmoil, Gorbachev has every incentive to seek a relaxation of international tension. [39]

The United States adopted an extremely accommodating stance toward the Soviets in a draft summit communique that Shultz submitted to Shevardnadze in October. As recounted by *The New Republic*, the Soviet Foreign Minister received the draft "seven days before most Administration officials got copies, marked SECRET. Ordinarily, such a security classification is used to keep a document out of the Soviets' hands. This time, the document had gone to them first, and the stamp was applied to keep it from leaking to noisy right-wingers and the press."[40] The report continues by stating that White House Communications Director Pat Buchanan "was appalled when he read the draft communique. It was chummier with the Soviets than anything he'd seen during the heyday of detente as a speechwriter in Richard Nixon's White House." In the end, according to a White House aide, the communique was stillborn becuse "it proved impossible to agree on arms control formulas."[41]

In a nationally televised speech on the eve of his departure for Geneva, Reagan spoke in terms reminiscent of Nixon and Kissinger. He expressed a desire "to build a foundation fo lasting peace." The President declared that "my mission, simply stated, is a a mission for peace. It is to engage the new Soviet leader in what I hope will be a dialogue for peace that endures beyond my presidency."[42]

No deals were made at the summit, much to the relief of the "hardliners" and the dismay of the detentists. The private conversations between the two leaders lasted for about five hours, but whether they could be characterized as a dialogue rather than two monologues is difficult to determine. *The Washington Post* reported that ". . . during the Geneva summit meetings, Mikhail Gorbachev depicted an American landscape—from New York buildings desecrated by swastikas to streets teeming with millions of unemployed—that was startling to his interlocutors . . . "[43] In a word, said one U.S. official, Gorbachev's views are "hidebound."

Certainly, the summit was short on substance and long on atmospherics. The media trumpeted "Reagan's celebrated walk with Gorbachev to a lakeside pool house for a fireside chat"[44]—surely the most famous stroll since the 1982 "walk in the woods" that produced an arms control initiative by that name. The President declared that the summit talks "cleared the air" and that he and Gorbachev had agreed "to keep in touch."[45] White House Chief of Staff Donald T. Regan, however, reiterated that the summit had not initiated a new era of detente. "That word has bad connotations," he explained.[46] *The Washington Post* expressed the view, echoed widely in other organs of the media, that "the most tangible accomplishment of the Geneva meeting was the agreement of Reagan and Gorbachev to hold . . . two additional summits."[47] Meanwhile, Sen. John Warner declared that speculation on which leader came out on top from the Geneva summit was "an exercise in trivial pursuit."[48]

The joint statement issued at the end of the summit characterized the meetings as "frank and useful"—euphemisms indicating a failure to agree. The two sides proclaimed their intentions to seek progress in nuclear arms reductions, control of chemical weapons, conventional-force cutbacks, confidence-building measures, environmental protection, air safety over the northern Pacific (site of the KAL shootdown), education and cultural exchanges, and the establishment of consulates in New York and Kiev.[49] Reagan's agreement to resume cultural exchanges marked the abandonment of one of the few remaining sanctions that had been imposed after the Soviet invasion of Afghanistan.

For more than five years, Reagan had resisted pressures to catapult arms control to the forefront of Soviet-American relations, but several of his aides and political handlers argued that a photo opportunity with Gorbachev at the White House would do wonders for the Republicans in the 1986 mid-term elections and that such an opportunity depended upon progress in arms control. Thus, willy-nilly, arms control reappeared at the top of the Soviet-American agenda and became the chief coin of detente and a fetish of the Reagan Administration. With pressures thus building from many directions, Reagan stumbled toward the next summit. Then, like a bolt out of the blue, the Daniloff affair temporarily blocked his path.

Nicholas Daniloff, the Moscow correspondent for *U.S. News & World Report*, was arrested on 30 August and charged with espionage.

A Soviet acquaintance had just handed him, unsolicited, an envelope containing military documents, maps and photos. Detentists in the United States hastened to speculate that the KGB had seized Daniloff to undermine U.S.-Soviet relations, or even that a "loose cannon" at the lower levels of the KGB had made the arrest without the knowledge of his superiors. This hypothesis collapsed quickly after Gorbachev rejected Reagan's personal assurances that the journalist was not a spy—thus, in effect, calling the President a liar.

Following Daniloff's release (in exchange for Soviet spy Gennadi Zakharov) came the surprise announcement that the United States and the Soviet Union would hold a "pre-summit" meeting in Reykjavik, Iceland, on 11-12 October:

> . . . the Administration, having linked cases it said would not be linked, having accepted an equation it termed unacceptable (of a spy and a journalist), and having eviscerated a principle (no trading of innocent hostages for spies) in a swap it says is not a swap, is reeling toward a summit it says is no summit. . . . [50]

Columnist Charles Krauthammer observed that "the Soviet capacity to manufacture hostges, indigenous and foreign, is unlimited. Against an endless supply of hostages, the West will need an endless supply of principles to give up in exchange. It hasn't many left."[51] Aside from the moral symmetry inherent in the Daniloff-Zakharov swap, the affair underscored the extent to which Reagan had succumbed to the arms control lobby:

> . . . the orthodox view of arms control . . . holds that all other policies toward the Soviet Union are secondary and ultimately must give way to the . . . primacy of arms control. The Daniloff affair has been a textbook example of arms-control orthodoxy. Offered the opportunity to discuss a possible arms agreement with Mikhail Gorbachev in Reykjavik, orthodoxy required the United States to accept the principle of a largely symmetrical prisoner swap and to leave some top Soviet agents in place. . . . [52]

The "snap summit" was billed as a preparatory session for the real thing. Reagan arrived in Reykjavik with a skeleton staff, while Gorbachev brought an entire retinue of experts, notably on arms control. Without any warning, the Soviet leader introduced a plan to rid the earth of nuclear weapons within ten years. It was a *deja vu* of the proposal of 15 January, but the timeframe was even more compressed. There ensued a bizarre dispute about whether Reagan had agreed to the elimination of all nuclear weapons (as Gorbachev claimed) or of ballistic missiles alone. This proved to be a moot point, however, because the Soviets tied their arms control package to cessation of SDI— a point on which the President would not yield.

In reflecting on Reykjavik, one is struck not only by the sweeping nature of the disarmament proposals and the offhand manner in which they were put forth, but also by their momentous implications for both superpowers. By agreeing in principle to Gorbachev's call for the abolition of strategic offensive weapons (50 percent in the first five years alone after the signing of an agreement), Reagan, in effect, was abandoning his policy of building up the U.S. nuclear arsenal to strengthen his negotiating position. Already, many of Reagan's programs—MX and Midgetman, for example—had been sharply scaled back or confined to the drawing board. The Soviet Union, for its part, appeared ready and willing at Reykjavik to give up its atomic weaponry, which constituted the only attribute conferring superpower status on the empire. Stripped of its nuclear capability, the USSR would rank only as the most developed of the world's developing countries and would lack the clout and prestige of even middle-level (but nuclear-armed) powers such as China, France, and the United Kingdom, not to mention such nuclear or near-nuclear nations as India, Israel, Pakistan, or South Africa. In the words of William F. Buckley, "Take away from Moscow its nuclear threat, and Gorbachev becomes another first-rank Third-World figure, somewhere between Chairman Deng [Xiao-ping] and Rajiv Gandhi."[53] Thus, Gorbachev's arms control proposals at Reykjavik and Reagan's amiable response underscored the illusory nature of the arms control "process."

Two major working groups were established at the Iceland summit—one on arms control and the other on human rights and regional conflicts. The latter group was all but forgotten in the hoopla that surrounded the disarmament schemes. Reykjavik proved once again that arms control remains the sole repository of detente. It also highlighted Reagan's apparent concern that a U.S. President's record is flawed if he fails to sign an arms control treaty with the Soviet Union.

The 1987 summit in Washington featured the intermediate-range nuclear forces (INF) pact as its centerpiece. By the time Reagan and Gorbachev exchanged instruments of ratification for the treaty in their Moscow summit of 1988, the momentum for further arms control measures appeared virtually unstoppable. American arms control enthusiasts pressed for a START treaty before the end of Reagan's term, and

Gorbachev chided the President for failing to bring about greater progress toward this objective during the summit. Those who urged a go-slow approach in Washington welcomed the upcoming Presidential election to effect a pause in the arms control "process." Now, as neo-detente struggles to make its debut in the United States and the new Administration ponders its foreign policy platforms, it is useful to set forth some guidelines to help avoid the pitfalls into which detentists often stumble.

1. *Know your adversary.*

The Soviet Union, our chief protagonist in the world, is not "just like us"—allegations of a common heritage of "Cossacks and cowboys" notwithstanding. Addressing a joint session of Congress upon his return from the Geneva summit, Reagan noted quite rightly that "the United States cannot afford illusions about the nature of the USSR. We cannot assume that their ideology and purpose will change." This illusion-free detente must be translated from the rhetorical to the practical level, however.

The USSR is a dogged and ruthless adversary, and Gorbachev has been described by Richard Nixon as the most dangerous Soviet leader the United States has ever confronted. Seventy years after the Bolshevik Revolution, Soviet foreign policy still operates on the Leninist maxim of *kto kogo?*—literally "who-whom." Politics from this perspective is a zero-sum game: the Communist camp is historically ordained to destroy the Free World. The only change is that the Soviets no longer theorize that war between the two opposing systems is inevitable. The advent of nuclear weapons meant that such a war would eradicate Communist as well as Western civilization. Thus, the USSR hopes to achieve victory without war through "salami tactics" coupled with an intensifying campaign of disinformation and strategic deception designed to erode Western military strength and political willpower. Advocates of detente who assail the United States for seeking "peace through strength" thus play directly into Soviet hands. They disregard the fact that the Kremlin still follows Lenin's dictum to "probe with a bayonet: If you encounter mush, proceed; if you encounter steel, withdraw."

The prevailing wisdom about the Soviet Union still perpetuates the myth that the Kremlin hierarchs are "just plain folks" and that the USSR is essentially a great power like any other, acting to ensure its strategic survival, territorial integrity, and a place in the global sun commensurate with its size and military prowess. This writer contends, however, that the USSR is still a revolutionary state determined to challenge and eventually overturn the status quo in order to bring about a Communist-style global order responsive to Soviet dictates. The author contends, further, that Soviet hostility and contempt toward the West are implacable and that Moscow's aggressive intentions are tempered only by the limitations of its capabilities. She would concur wholeheartedly with William Safire's observation that "we can hope both sides' means are peaceful, but we are sure that both sides' ends are antithetical."[54]

While some American opinion-molders may be regarded as "useful idiots" that, wittingly or otherwise, purvey the Soviet propaganda line to their audiences, more often the misunderstanding of Soviet intentions results from sheer ignorance. Then-Senator Dan Quayle (R.-Ind.), for example, admitted to astonishment over "the incredible lack of knowledge about the Soviet people and Soviet history" that pervades Congress. Sen. Richard Lugar complained that "we try to figure out where they're coming from, but it could well be the blind leading the blind." Rep. Jeff Bingaman (D.-N.M.) stated that lack of reliable data about the USSR "is one of the glaring inadequacies in our decisionmaking process." Thus, he lamented, Congressmen often "wind up making judgments on visceral reactions."[55] Former Sen. William Fulbright (who used to head the Foreign Relations Committee) did nothing to contribute to Congressional understanding of the Soviets in a recent comment he tendered: "I would like to see hearings by some Senate committee on why we think the Russians are such monsters. What have they ever done to us. . . . They have done some things to other people that we don't like, but so have we."[56] A more blatant statement of moral equivalence would be difficult to find.

The truth is that information about the USSR abounds; the problem lies in the unwillingness of many influential Americans in politics, the media, academe, and even Big Business to come to terms with the ominous trends that this information reveals. Richard Perle has pointed out that "Washington rhetoric" that labels as "pragmatists" those willing to compromise with the Soviet Union and as "ideologues" those who reject compromise is completely contrary to reality. "The preference for an easy cooperative relationship is easy to understand," he says. "But . . . despite the agreements of the early 1970's, there has been very little cooperation. . . . Those who would respeat the mistakes of 1972 are the ideologues" because they refuse to accept the facts of the situation and the conclusions flowing there-from.[57] The most dangerous species in the American political aviary is not the hawk but rather the ostrich, with its head buried in the sand.

Above and beyond the element of wishful thinking that many U.S. leaders harbor about the Soviet Union and the psychological mechanism of denying unpleasant facts that is at work, there appears to be a genuine incomprehension on the part of Americans about the nature of the "Evil Empire." The Soviets are quite open about proclaiming their intentions; too often, we dismiss their statements as mere propaganda. We have encountered the same phenomenon with regard to Hitler's Germany, which announced its plan to exterminate the Jews, with Ayatollah Khomeini's Iran, which regards the United States as the "Great Satan," and with some terrorist groups who relish the opportunity to achieve martyrdom in suicide attacks against Americans. The Soviet Union may not be Evil incarnate, but a state that liquidates millions of its own citizens in the name of a political credo and leaves hundreds of thousands of others to rot in the Gulag cannot reasonably be expected to conduct a foreign policy based on the moderation and restraint that U.S. politicians and diplomats value so highly. As Soviet emigre Vladimir Bukovsky has emphasized, there is no peaceful coexistence between the Soviet regime and its citizens and thus there can be none between the USSR and foreign powers.

The Soviet Union is a dogged and determined adversary but not an imprudent or irrational one. Thus, those who caution against provoking the Kremlin lest it unleash Armageddon misread the Soviet mindset. All evidence indicates that Moscow respects strength and firmness and disdains weakness and vacillation. Winston Churchill's remark in another context that "the malice of the wicked was reinforced by the weakness of the virtuous" applies in spades to the Soviet-American relationship.

The Reagan Administration was the most "hard-line" since Soviet-American diplomatic relations were established a half-century ago, and the President evidently had a gut instinct about the Soviet threat; but sometimes Reagan appeared schizophrenic in his attitude toward the USSR. Part of the explanation lay in his position in the midst of a tug of war between his dyed-in-the-wool conservative supporters who wanted him to adhere to their agenda and to be a "freedom President" and his political advisers (including, reportedly, the First Lady) who wanted him to be a "peace President." Evans and Novak have pointed to "the deep ideological fault over U.S. handling of the Soviets that has run down the middle of the Reagan Administration since [its] beginning."[58]

A second factor lay in the inability of a conservative, business-oriented Adminstration to "subordinate commerce to geopolitics."[59] Still another part of the explanation lay in Reagan's manifest reluctance to concede to an eternally optimistic electorate that U.S.-Soviet relations are unlikely to improve greatly in the foreseeable future. Finally, the President's humanitarian instincts often led him to unwise foreign-policy decisions. The Daniloff-Zakharov trade was a prime example in superpower relations of this phenomenon; the arms-for-hostages deal with Iran grew out of similar personal concerns, although other factors were involved.

Harvard Professor Stanley Hoffman has pointed to "a peculiar ambivalence" in Reagan's view of the Soviets:

> . . . his firm and fixed views about the "evil empire" somehow coexisted with a belief that Soviet misbehavior might in part result from a misplaced suspiciousness of Western intentions; his cheerful faith in America's moral superiority made him confident both about America's inevitable victory in a peaceful contest and about his capacity to convince his Soviet counterparts. [60]

In his own statements, the President reflected an ambiguous approach toward the Soviet Union. In the aftermath of the Daniloff affair, for instance, when some of his supporters were expressing dismay over his acquiescence to Soviet demands, Reagan recalled his postwar struggle with the Communists over control of the Screen Actors Guild in Hollywood. "It will be a cold day in Hades when I go soft on Communism," he said; "I was bloodied a long time ago in that battle, and I have never changed my view of them." Then he hastened to add that "as I said to [Gorbachev] in our meeting in Geneva, he and I are uniquely in a position today where we could bring about World War III, or we're also in a position that we could bring about peace in the world."[61]

On a number of occasions, Reagan displayed unwarranted solicitousness toward the Soviets. Like previous Presidents, he was overly concerned about either "embarrassing" or "provoking" Moscow. For example, in responding to journalists' queries about how he had handled the subject of human rights with Gorbachev at the Geneva summit, he emphasized the need for "quiet diplomacy," because " . . . in a world of politics, to try to push someone into a corner in which he must then publicly try to get out of that corner and, in doing that, appear to take orders from a figure in another government, that becomes an impossibility."[62]

If we could purge the word "embarrass" from our political vocabulary, our public discourse would be immeasurably clarified. The word, as outlined in Roget's Thesaurus, can be synonomous with "involve," "bewilder," "fluster," "impede," "give trouble," or "mortify." When we inveigh against embarrassing the USSR or making its leadership feel uncomfortable, we exhibit more concern about the Soviets' losing face than about the United States losing its political and moral bearings. We also tend too frequently to "blame America first," in Jeane Kirkpatrick's memorable phrase. One recent example of this phenomenon in U.S.—Soviet relations came in the aftermath of the nuclear power plant accident at Chernobyl. If Sweden, which was downwind from the radioactive fallout, had not raised its voice, the world probably would have waited a very long time for Soviet acknowledgment of the catastrophe. Nevertheless, liberals who urge the United States to be nice to the Soviets were eager to give Gorbachev the benefit of the doubt on his self-proclaimed policy of *glasnost*. Tom Wicker wrote, for example, that "it's not even certain that the original Soviet delay in warning other countries was callous and deliberate. . . . If adversity forced Mr. Gorbachev more toward Western ways of responding to crises, why not credit him for it?" Wicker was particularly critical of U.S. officials who extrapolated from the Chernobyl episode to question Moscow's trustworthiness in observing arms control agreements.[63]

Another example of Western solicitousness for Soviet feelings appeared in a 1983 article in *The Economist*, which stated that the Kremlin "has some fair complaints about American unpredictability."[64] In his New Year's message to the Soviet people in 1986, Reagan said that he "told Mr.Gorbachev [at the summit] of our deep desire for peace and that the American people do not wish the Soviet people any harm."[65]

Such actions as the downing of the KAL jetliner should not be regarded as mere blips on the radar screen of Soviet-American relations; rather, they reflect the fundamental differences between totalitarian and democratic systems. Moreover, as arms control negotiator Edward Rowny points out, "the Soviet Union did not come to occupy one-sixth of the world's landmass by fighting defensive actions."[66] Charles Krauthammer has commented,

We like to think of Soviet bloc leaders as hidebound thickheads whose addiction to ruthlessness undermines their diplomacy and injures their own interests. Addicted to ruthlessness they are. But the corollary—that this injures their interests—presupposes that ruthlessness is met with a significant Western riposte. It is not. [67]

Too often, our response is either hand-wringing—playing the role of the "pitiful, helpless giant" to borrow a Nixonian phrase—or a feeble gesture of accommodation shading into appeasement.

. . . One of the lessons learned from the 1970's is that the Soviets do not react to gestures of goodwill, kindness or consideration. Soviet leaders are well aware that their military buildup has brought them significant international advantages and it remains their most effective instrument in international affairs. [68]

Detentists adhere to the late John Lennon's exhortation to "give peace a chance." The Soviet Union, however, has a concept of peace that differs fundamentally from that in the West. *Mir* is a Russian word that means both "peace" and "world." It connotes a "Pax Sovietica"—a world in which capitalist societies and Western "imperialism" have been vanquished and the USSR presides over a community of Communist-style nations. In Soviet parlance, the "struggle for peace" is a multifaceted campaign to reduce Western—and especially U.S.—power in the global arena and enhance Soviet power proportionately. Or, as the Program of the Communist Party of the USA (a wholly owned subsidiary of the Kremlin) expresses it, " . . . the struggle for peace is objectively a struggle to facilitate the transition from capitalism to Socialism without the catastrophic devastation of nuclear war." Richard Shultz and Roy Godson, co-authors of the widely acclaimed book *Dezinformatsiya* (Disinformation), have pointed out that

. . . We in the West have a concept of war and peace. When there is peace, there is no war. The Soviets have a view of constant conflict. . . . We make this distinction that peace is the normal order of things and in peaceful relationships you don't go after the jugular and try to manipulate, you don't try to lie about something, you don't try to deceive someone. . . . [69]

These sentiments, however praiseworthy, render the United States an easy prey for the Soviet disinformation apparatus. As emigre Vladimir Bukovsky has written,

The combination of Soviet psychological warfare and Western willingness to be deceived has paralyzed the will of even the most resolute and wise leaders. Even the current American Administration has not learned how to resist it and is reluctantly sliding into detente. [70]

## 2. *Avoid mirror-imaging.*

A clearer insight into the nature of the Soviet adversary (including acknowledgment of unpleasant truths) should obviate the tendency toward mirror-imaging—the belief that Soviet leaders think and act as we do. Too often Americans attribute motivations and reactions to the Soviets that we ourselves would experience under a given set of circumstances. Charles Krauthammer devotes an entire collection of essays, *Cutting Edges*, to this theme. Noting that a patient with solipsism, a mental illness, believes that the whole world is himself, Krauthammer has coined the term "plural solipsism," which, as applied to detentists, says that the entire world is like the United States. Based upon this hypothesis that the superpowers (and others) share certain fundamental values and desires, conflicts can be explained primarily by a failure to communicate—or "to dialogue," in detentist parlance. Krauthammer labels this phenomenon "the broken-telephone theory of international conflict."

The Soviets do share some emotions with us—for example, a genuine horror of war that, in the Soviet case, grows out of first-hand experience. Nevertheless, as *The Economist* points out, "the snag is that the horror seems to produce a craving for security that is itself aggressive." This is why the moral symmetry that results from mirror-imaging is so dangerous and misleading. For example, the image of the superpowers as two scorpions in a bottle struggling to break out and attack each other does an injustice to the United States; while the USSR is not eager to start a war, it challenges the international status quo at every available oppurtunity.

Sometimes, the resort to mirror-imaging leads to nothing more than silly or amusing portrayals of the Soviet Union. For example, *The Washington Post* headlined an article by Soviet-affairs specialist Thane Gustafson "Mikhail's Malaise: The Honeymoon Is Over Back Home in the Kremlin."[71] Without wondering whether Mr. Gustafson himself may have chosen the title, one is struck by the facile assumption that a Soviet General Secretary, like a newly elected American President, enjoys a certain grace period before his critics declare open season on him. Another common example of mirror-imaging involves the portrayal of "hawks" vs. "doves" in the Kremlin, along the lines of what we call "hardliners" and "softliners" in the American political spectrum. Such an image might be harmless in itself, but it renders the U.S. government vulnerable to Soviet officials who peddle the line that if Washington doesn't accommodate Moscow's "doves," then the "hawks" will triumph in a Soviet power struggle.

One of the most common fallacies of the mirror-imagers is their contention that the Soviet leadership is a slave to public opinion—in the international arena if not at home. Thus, for exaple, a story in *U.S. News & World Report* on the Daniloff affair noted that it "did real damage to Gorbachev's image as a peacemaker and progressive."[72] Similarly, then-White House chief of staff Donald Regan declared that the Soviet Union lost "the public-relations battle" in the Daniloff case, and "now everyone knows what they are." Having already lost out in the popularity ratings with the KAL shootdown, the Soviets presumably were not unduly alarmed. George Will aptly noted that "Regan, a man from Wall Street, thinks the struggle of the 20th century is a matter for Madison Avenue."[73]

Surely the Soviets recognize the power of public opinion in the West; their propaganda and disinformation services are designed precisely for the manipulation and exploitation of Western perceptions. However, this is not the same thing as tailoring their policies to accommodate actual and potential critics abroad. On the contrary, as columnist Meg Greenfield has written, "one of the Soviets' principal weapons in getting their way has been a willingness to disregard the world opinion that we in the West are forever thinking they want to assuage."[74]

How do mirror-imagers deal with threats and bluster from the "Evil Empire?" Essentially, they ignore them. Khrushchev's famous and oft-repeated epithet that "we will bury you" was pushed out of our collective consciousness not only because it was perceived as bluff, but also because it was so alien to the political discourse employed in the West. Democracies still experience great difficulty coping with totalitarian states even after dealing with the USSR for 70 years. As Krauthammer writes in *Cutting Edges*, "when the comfortable encounter the unimaginable, the result is not only emotional but cognitive refusal." Perhaps we need a gutter mentality to comprehend the Soviets, just as we do to understand terrorists. An article by conservative columnist Joseph Sobran, entitled "Coping With Abu Nidal, makes this point:

We badly need to understand terrorism. . . . to put ourselves imaginatively in the place of the antagonist on the other side of the chessboard, who may see something we fail to see. Our leaders have a bad habit of talking as if the followers of Abu Nidal were Yuppies who shrink from disincentives. This appears not to be the case. These men don't think in terms of opinion polls and marginal tax rates. They think in terms of honor, revenge, blood, glory, maybe even salvation. Their violence is not "senseless"—not in their minds or in their universe. In a way, it's supremely rational, and we have nothing to offer them.[75]

The Soviets are not bloodthirsty terrorists, and they have a much greater stake in the intnernational system than do the stateless Palestinians. Nevertheless, their ideologically-driven quest for power and recognition places them outside the mainstream of the Western political heritage.

3. *Never underestimate the significance of ideology.*

A major reason why the Soviets do not think and act like we do is that they view the world through lenses tinted by Marxist-Leninist ideology. The ideology defines, inter alia, who are friends and who are enemies. Detente represents a tool by which the Soviet Union pursues its global objectives without frontally challenging the democratic world until the "correlation of forces" so warrants. Detente, like peaceful coexistence, is perceived by the Kremlin as a temporary phenomenon designed to last as long as capitalism and Socialism exist side by side on the earth.

The two superpowers have substantially different views of detente. The USSR understands the concept (whether it is called detente, peaceful coexistence, or relaxation of tension) in the negative sense of avoidance of nuclear war; thus, it functions as a deterrent to such war, much as the concept of mutual assured destruction (MAD) has done. Soviet-style detente does not rule out—indeed, it demands—intensification of the ideological struggle between the capitalist and Socialist camps and Soviet support of "national liberation movements." Thus, Moscow may advocate settlement of conflicts which, like Vietnam, have the potential to escalate into superpower confrontation—but the settlement must be on Communist terms. Washington, on the other hand, has regarded detente not only as a means of avoiding nuclear war, but also in terms of cooperation with the Soviet Union on a wide variety of fronts—in Ronald Reagan's words, to establish a peace "that goes well beyond the absence of war."[76] Behind the U.S. conception lies a desire to maintain international stability and the status quo; behind the Russian conception lies a desire to expand the boundaries of the Communist world by all means short of nuclear conflagration.

These sharply contrasting views naturally affect the expectations that each superpower holds of detente. Washington seems not to have abandoned hope that a mere show of goodwill and friendship eventually will melt the hearts of the Soviet leadership and extract rewards in the form of Soviet moderation abroad and liberalization at home. However, Soviet words and deeds indicate that Moscow has no intention of accommodating the United States on either count. Reagan's oft-repeated assurances that he means the Soviet Union "no harm" were essentially meaningless from the Kremlin's perspective. It is not physical harm (i.e., a military attack) that the Soviet regime fears, but rather the very existence of free democratic societies and the inability in this Age of Communications to seal off the Soviet population from Western values.

George Will has written that

> . . . the Soviet elite is devoted to its own continuity and wil not jeopardize itself by domestic reforms or a nonaggressive foreign policy that would call into question the Leninism that legitimizes its monopoly of power . . . [77]

Those who herald the "end of ideology" are far wide of the mark—although Soviet disinformation specialists cater to the Western belief that ideology is dead,, or, as former Ambassador to Moscow Jacob Beam opines, that "ideology is just dry bread."[78] As Will notes, "the point is not that a Gorbachev reads from 'Das Kapital' as from a breviary, any more than Richard Coeur de Lion was constantly studying theology. The point is that any Soviet leader has been thoroughly marinated in the ideology that legitimizes him."[79]

The "new generation" that Gorbachev represents is no less eager than its predecessors to retain power. Nor has it displayed any serious commitment to alter the fundamental priorities of the Kremlin, which traditionally has accorded preference to the "metal eaters" over those seeking improvements in the consumer sector. To quote George Will once more,

> Today's theory is that Gorbachev wants a respite from the arms race, and especially from one involving technologically exotic defense systems, so

he can "solve his economic problems." But it is absurd to say that military spending is causing the regime's economic problems. Military spending is the regime's raison d'etre. The regime has never given priority to the comforts of the masses. It has never made a serious effort to provide a Cuisinart in every apartment, or even a separate apartment for every family. . . . [80]

Even Paul Nitze, a longtime skeptic about Soviet intentions, appears to have fallen prey to the theory that the USSR finally may be amenable to transforming its swords into plowshares. In a recent issue of *Foreign Affairs*, Nitze, referring to Soviet economic and foeign policy setbacks, wrote that

> . . . internal and external factors would appear to call for Moscow to consider revisions in its policies. Moreover . . . it seems that many of the abler members of the younger generation realize that internal reforms are necessary. . . . and that it would be easier and safer to carry out such reforms under a foreign policy of "live and let live" than by pursuit of the Leninist goal of *mir* [Soviet global domination] and its concomitant exacerbation of international tensions.

Such wishful thinking aside, the new men in the Kremlin are not about to jettison the ideology that alone justifies their monopoly of power. They "are political figures, the majority of whom have led long careers as CPSU functionaries. They are not, as a group, 'technocrats,' if this term may be taken to imply, along with special expertise and concern for efficiency and rationalization, [an] absence of interest in symbols or substance of Marxist-Leninist ideology. . . . "[81] Proponents of "hard-headed detente" argue that the Soviet Union will be under increasing pressure to sustain a dialogue with the West because of economic difficulties and the "burden of empire." However, if the Western pursuit of detente does not take into account the continuing Soviet comitment to ideological and class struggle worldwide, there will be nothing more than a dialogue of the deaf between the superpowers.

4. *Do not engage in efforts at behavior modification.*

The ideological matrix in which Soviet foreign policy is molded militates against attempts at behavior modification. Set against the backdrop of a hoary Russian imperialist tradition, the Marxist-Leninist ideology renders the Soviet regime relatively impervious to Western attempts to use detente as a mellowing agent.

The U.S. approach in this regard takes two forms. One is carrot-and-stick diplomacy, a short-term, generally ad hoc policy aimed at increasing the incentives for Soviet moderation and restraint and administering penalties for misbehavior. This policy has failed for three main reasons. First, the United States and its Western allies usually have been reluctant to follow through on the penalties they threaten. A second, and related, reason for the failure was the glaring lack of consensus within the U.S. government on the issue of "linkage." Conservatives made it impossible for Washington to offer sufficient incentives to impress Moscow, while liberals made it impossible to sustain a credible threat of reprisals if the Soviets misbehaved. Finally, the carrot-and-stick routine failed because the Soviets have their own way of doing business. Former Sen. John Tower recalls that when he asked a Soviet negotiator how he would respond to a U.S. decision to forego deployment of the B-1 bomber, the Soviet replied, "Senator, I am neither a pacifist nor a philanthropist."[82] It is also instructive that the detente era of the 1970's, which witnessed an upswing in Soviet-American trade, was a period of Soviet aggressive behavior in the Third World and of increasing Soviet defense spending.

The other aspect of using detente to mellow the USSR involves a longer-term attempt to alter the very nature of the Soviet state—to draw it out of its xenophobia, obsession with secrecy, and habit of carrying to extremes the maxim that "the best defense is a good offense." Students of international affairs used to be divided roughly between "realists" and "idealists." During the 1960's, however, "behaviorism"—the attempt to render political science "scientific "—made its debut. Behaviorists, who cut across the realism-idealism dichotomy, hypothesized that the Soviet Union is paranoid and insecure and that the West must try to alleviate the causes.

Western behaviorists and their like-minded pundits in the media have woven some intricate constructs to further our "understanding" of the Soviet beast. Essentially, these constructs allege that Soviet policy is fundamentally defensive, reflective of a lack of self-confidence, and driven by fear of the West and by a yearning for genuine equality with the United States. Moscow allegedly is beset by an inferiority complex and is disappointed and resentful because detente hasn't brought a full measure of respect from Washington. It follows from these hypotheses that the Soviets are both appeasable and susceptible to envelopement in a Kissingerian web of mutually advantageous relations. Those in the West who are less certain of the basically defensive and reactive nature of Soviet policy may still argue for concessions, proffering detente "to assuage Soviet desperation that could result in a lunge for supremacy through aggression."[83] When the Soviet Union actually lunges, however, Western Kremlinologists resort to still other theories. Commenting on the invasion of Afghanistan, for example, William Hyland, a longtime Kissinger associate, speculated that the gerontocrats in Moscow were "nearing the end of their days and said, 'It's time to cash in the chips we've been accumulating.'"[84]

In fact, the application of psychotherapy to alleged Soviet neuroticism is not only useless; it is unnecessary. As George Will has pointed out, " . . . we can unilaterally change the atmosphere any time we decide not to care about Vietnam, Cambodia, Yemen, yellow rain, Angola, Ethiopia, Afghanistan, the Soviet arms buildup—all the things that characterized Soviet behavior in the '70's."[85] In the meantime, those advocating efforts at behavior modification should ask themselves this question: What course might Soviet history have taken if the United States had shown the USSR a full measure of "understanding"? Might-have-been scenarios on this score lack conviction.

5. *New personalities do not signify new policies.*

The inclination of many Soviet-watchers in the West to postulate the existence of a "hawk" vs. "dove" constellation in the Kremlin leads to an unwarranted emphasis on personalities. During the 1970's, U.S. observers commented extensively on Brezhnev's alleged personal stake in detente. Typical of this outlook was a *Newsweek* article of November 1971 contending that "it was Brezhnev . . . who swung the decision to invite President Nixon to visit Moscow [for the 1972 summit]. And it was Brezhnev who shepherded the crucial decisions on East-West detente through the ruling Politburo." The implication was that Brezhnev moved forward in the face of resistance from the "metal eaters," who, for their part, were engaged in an intraparty struggle with the "goulash faction."[86] Peter Tarnoff, President of the Council on Foreign Relations, recently urged us to place all our eggs in Gorbachev's dovish basket in order to give peace and detente a chance:

> Without doubt, the President is now heeding his senior advisers who want to explore actively the chances for significant arms control agreements. These circles believe—correctly, in my view—that we can exact better arms control terms from Moscow today than at any previous time in the two Reagan Administrations, and that waiting longer for greater Soviet concessions runs the serious risk of having an exasperated Mikhail S. Gorbachev back away from compromise under pressure from his own hard-liners. [87]

Americans are prone to mistake changes in style for changes in substance (it is worth noting in this regard that Ronald Reagan's bark is worse than his bite), and Gorbachev (the first General Secretary with a career background in the propaganda apparatus) is peculiarly well placed to exploit this weakness. West German Chancellor Helmut Kohl was right on the mark when he said that Gorbachev "is a modern Communist who understands public relations."[88] What a *Washington Post* correspondent wrote about Foreign Minister Shevardnadze applies in spades to his boss: i.e., "his ability to deliver a hard-line policy with a smile and a tone of flexibility. . . . "[89]

Paeans to the "new generation" in the Soviet leadership have flowed copiously since Gorbachev acceded to power. After meeting with the General Secretary, Denis Healey, deputy chief of the British Labor Party, mused that "emotions flicker over a face of unusual sensitivity, like summer breezes on a pond. We know he's the candidate of all the forward-looking elements within the Soviet system. . . . "[90] Dwayne O. Andreas, chairman of Archer-Daniels-Midlands Co. and of the U.S.-USSR Trade and Economic Council, likened Gorbachev to "a Methodist minister that I knew out in a little town in Iowa. He's gentle. He looked me right in the eye—pleasant, good voice, smile—and after 10 seconds of that, the thought crossed my mind, 'Well, the man has a sense of humor.'"[91] The new General Secretary has been judged by the firmness of his handshake and the fact that he maintained good eye contact—an alleged sign of sincerity. According to one Western pundit, the fact that Gorbachev was the first Kremlin leader with a wife who weighed less than he seemed to connote a modesty in his political ambitions (corresponding to Raisa's modest bodily volume). Furthermore, her attractiveness allegedly signaled that Gorbachev would refrain not only from sexual philandering but also from political hanky-panky! Gorbachev's own well-tailored appearance has given rise to what Brzezinski labels "sartorial determinism"—a tendency to equate pinstriped suits with civilized policies. "Actuarial determinism" allegedly is another positive trait in the new Soviet leader—his "youth and relative energy quotient" offer hope for the USSR (and for us). Wrap all of these supposedly favorable characteristics in a nice public relations package and the result is surface affability that allegedly reflects inner liberalism.

Other observers take such analysis a step further and purport to read Gorbachev's mind. As Jeane Kirkpatrick has written,

> These scenarios feature an altogether likable Gorbachev and his beautiful wife. Though the product of [a] . . . bureaucratic regime that stifles freedom . . . "our" Gorbachev knows there is a better way to live. Therefore, we are told, he "longs" for a return to detente. Our Gorbachev "needs" to negotiate an end to the arms race because his priority is a better life for the Soviet people and development of the Soviet economy. . . . Our Gorbachev not only "wants" to negotiate deep arms cuts; many commentators suspect he probably would like to relax internal repression, release dissidents, and permit Jewish emigration as well but is "prevented" from doing so by his Politburo colleagues. Our Gorbachev has a special need to prove to those colleagues that he is as tough as they expect him to be. . . . [92]

From such attempts at psychoanalysis, it is only a short step to prescribing positive reinforcement so that Gorbachev's allegedly generous instincts can come to the fore. Give the General Secretary a break, these therapists suggest. Kissinger has noted that "Western media and the pronouncements of Western leaders reflect a rapt fascination with the new Soviet personality, coupled with suggestions that he is entitled to some unilateral concessions to reassure him."[93] Archie Brown, a scholar from Oxford, wrote that "though the fate of Gorbachev's policy innovation will be determined essentially within the Soviet Union itself, it requires something more from the West than a stock response."[94]

These behavioral specialists spurn the wisdom of some of Gorbachev's own countrymen, who, it would seem, have a better claim to insights into their leader. Anatoly Shcharansky has warned the West to "beware of Gorbachev's new face." Andrei Gromyko, who cannot be accused of having an axe to grind as might Shcharansky after seven years as a political prisoner, has remarked that Gorbachev has "a nice smile and iron teeth."

"New-generation" theories notwithstanding, Gorbachev is cut from the same ideological cloth as his predecessor. Insofar as the "doves" with leadership potential have been sent to the Gulag or otherwise coerced into silence, Gorbachev is a "hawk":

> . . . It is theoretically possible that Mr. Gorbachev is dedicated to achieving true arms reductions and creating an atmosphere which will nurture peaceful coexistence between the two superpowers. If such is the case, however, Mr. Gorbachev would be a mutation in the Soviet leadership system. For within that system it has always been those who were most repressive who rose to the top—including Josef Stalin, who brutally murdered millions of his own countrymen; Leonid Brezhnev, who, as a young

officer, was linked to the imprisonment of Raoul Wallenberg; Yuri Andropov, who, as ambassador to Hungary, assured the Hungarian people during their revolt in 1956 that there would be no intervention in their affairs by his country—while he knew Soviet troops and tanks were on their way to crush the uprising; and Konstantin Chernenko, who is believed to have been involved in the mass killings of Ukrainians at Dnepropetrovsk. . . . [95]

Moreover, Gorbachev's American admirers would do well to remember that the new General Secretary was a protege of the late Mikhail Suslov, a top Comintern official and ideological watchdog, and of Andropov and his KGB cohorts, as well as of the military-industrial complex. As former CIA official Donald Jameson emphasized during an interview with *Human Events,*

> It's important to bear in mind that Gorbachev got into the party apparatus and began to attract notice in 1952, the last full year of Stalin's reign and when Stalin was engaged in organizing . . . the last great purge, whose first step looked like it was going to be the incarceration of virtually the entire Jewish population of the Soviet Union.
>
> Gorbachev was in the Party Comittee at Moscow University and within Moscow itself while he was a student at the University. During this period, he obviously made a good name for himself, so one can legitimately conclude he was part of the agitprop system, talking about the threat of "international Zionism." It was a time of openly anti-Semitic cartoons and one when many leading Jewish actors and artists were killed and imprisoned by Stalin. . . . A man who had scruples about being an anti-Semite and the propriety thereof would not have made it to the top. . . .

So much for Gorbachev's purported interest in advancing human rights and Jewish emigration.

Leaving aside the speculation about Gorbachev's personal background and motives, two caveats should be applied to any discussion of the role of personalities in the Soviet system. First, as Bukovsky has noted, "it is not an autocracy but a totalitarian regime, where the death of a leader doesn't mean anything at all. And that is exactly why the Soviet system is so dangerous: autocracies disappear with the death of autocrats; a Communist system continues."[96] Secondly, collective leadership has become institutionalized in the USSR. The General Secretary is *primus inter pares* but no longer is empowered to wield his authority in a totally arbitrary manner. Thus, the importance of individual personalities in the Kremlin has diminished.

Ultimately, the obstacles to genuine detente lie in the political and ideological realms, not in the interpersonal. As journalist·David Satter, a veteran commentator on Soviet affairs, has observed,

> Mr. Gorbachev has shown a friendly face to the West, but his readiness to exchange pleasantries with Western leaders, repeat inane propaganda to Western journalists, and grant marginal freedom to his wife are . . . unrelated to the real problems in East-West relations. . . . [97]

Similarly, Kissinger notes that

> Gorbachev . . . has cultivated the appearance of a new type of Soviet leader—appealing to Western predilections to reduce historical conflicts to a clash of personalities. . . . Common sense suggests that the principal causes of tensions are political. Chief among them is the Soviet proposition embodied in the Brezhnev Doctrine that proclaims all Soviet possessions as sacrosanct and everything else as subject to pressure or subversion. . . . [98]

What we have witnessed since Gorbachev's accession to power is Teflon transfer from Ronald Reagan to the Soviet leader. Neither Gorbachev's past nor more recent misdeeds appear to have tarnished his image. His Teflon coating is particularly formidable when viewed in conjunction with the durable and resilient structure he is building underneath. As Soviet-watcher Dimitri Simes cautions, "If your adversary becomes more capable and can conduct your rivalry more effectively, that's bad news."[99]

6. *Do not place excessive faith in summits.*

Summitry, of course, is an area in which interpersonal relations assume peculiar importance. From this perspective, a summit is regarded above all as a forum for communication. John F. Kennedy stressed that "it is far better that we meet at the summit than at the brink."[100] Winston Churchill, who emphasized that it's better to "jaw-jaw" than "waw-waw," first called for "a parley at the summit" in 1950. He also pointed out the need to avoid a meeting "overhung by a ponderous, rigid agenda . . . zealously contested by hordes of experts and offficials drawn up in vast cumbrous array." Presumably, such an array would spoil the good vibrations between the men at the top.

The difficulty with such a mindset lies in its supposition that East-West tensions result from garbled communications (Krauthammer's "broken telephone" theory). However, George Will rightly observes that

> . . . We are communicating constantly with the Soviets: in Washington, Moscow, Geneva, Vienna, Madrid. Faith in the inevitable efficacy of "communication" suggests that the conflict between the United States and the Soviet Union is some sort of misunderstanding, rather than a clear understanding of differences that cannot be split. [101]

Similarly, Jeane Kirkpatrick has commented that

> . . . if there is progress [at the summit], it will be because the Soviet goals have changed, not because greater interpersonal understanding has been achieved. . . . Problems between the United States and the Soviets are not interpersonal problems. . . . What is not caused by a misunderstanding between rulers cannot be cured by understanding, nor by personal affinity, nor by a diplomatic marriage counselor.
>
> Problems between the Soviet Union and the United States were caused by a clash of goals. . . . This is one of the reasons that no summit meeting . . . has brought significant improvement in Soviet-U.S. relations—and a few seem to have sparked dangerous occurrences. [102]

Although good personal rapport may be achieved at a summit and may lead to a temporary easing of tensions, it is unlikely to overcome the political and ideological differences that contribute so heavily to international tensions. A commentary on the Arab-Israeli conflict bears relevance for Soviet-Americn relations as well:

> Encounters, meetings, and conferences of various types are being held to advance mutual understanding and cooperation between Jews and Arabs [in Israel]. . . . Might these efforts clarify not converging interests and shared values, but polarized interests and conflicting values? [103]

Even more important than the interpersonal factor in summitry, however, are the pressures generated in Western democracies by public opinion and the media for concrete progress at a summit. This phenomenon leads, in turn, to a search for agreement at any price—to "treaty entreating" in the words of one wag. This is a phenomenon that besets only the United States and other democratic societies—the Soviet Union can rather easily justify to its population the lack of a summit accord by blaming alleged U.S. obstructionism. At the same time, Moscow exploits to the hilt Western eagerness for agreements. For example, during 1986, virtually up to the eve of Reykjavik, Soviet spokesmen cautioned against holding an "empty" summit; this was their way of coaxing greater concessions from the U.S. government prior to the meeting.

For many detentists in the State Department, Congress, the media and academe, the most significant outcome of the 1985 Reagan-Gorbachev summit was the agreement of the two leaders to continue meeting on an annual basis. After the Reykjavik summit of 1986, however, a note of caution crept into post mortems among American liberals. Reagan nearly acceded to a cleverly crafted Soviet plan to divest the United States of its nuclear deterrence capability (nor has the danger yet passed). The institutionalization of a summit "process" would hold many of the same perils as the arms control, Contadora, Middle East peace, and other assorted "processes."

Despite the pitfalls, detente fever is likely to keep raging in Washington and other Western capitals. Soviet-American summits are public relations bonanzas, the media are the sherpas, and Ronald Reagan seemed to possess "an irresistible urge to be photographed in the smiling presence of an Evil Emperor" en route to securing his place in history.[104] Reagan's political and biological clocks were ticking inexorably. He hastened to climb aboard the "peace" train before it left the station. The President, who once reminded the Kremlin that "it takes two to tango," proved increasingly ready to dance to the beat of the Soviet orchestra. In his eagerness to reach agreements with Gorbachev, especially on arms control, he often appeared to have forgotten that agreements cannot substitute for an adequate power balance. They reflect rather than shape the power balance in the broadest sense of that term—what the Soviets call the "correlation of forces." A summit, no matter how successful, is an ephemeral event; the correlation of forces is a permanently operating factor, to borrow a phrase from Stalin, that we dare not let shift too far in favor of the Soviet Union.

## 7. *Beware of the Soviets as negotiating partners.*

Entire volumes have been devoted to the subject of negotiations with the USSR and other Communist countries. Let it suffice here to relate the issue of negotiations to Point 1 above (knowing your adversary) and Point 3 (Communist ideology). The Soviets, after all, pioneered the "talk-fight" strategy that their Vietnamese allies employed so brilliantly in "peace" talks with the United States. (The strategy in fact may derive from Napoleon's maxim to "talk peace and act war.") A study prepared by the Congressional Research Service observes quite rightly that "negotiation is an instrument of Soviet diplomacy founded on Leninist tactics of exploiting the contradictions of interests among the class enemies and used to achieve the goals and purposes of the Soviet Union."[105] American historian Gordon Craig writes that

> . . . Soviet negotiators have always had a fundamentally different approach toward diplomacy from that of their Western colleagues. To them, diplomacy is . . . a weapon in the unremitting war against capitalist society. Diplomatic negotiations, therefore, cannot aim at real understanding and agreement. . . . [106]

Even before he came to power, Adolph Hitler, an astute observer of human behavior, noticed a fundamental incompatibility between Soviet- and Western-style diplomacy. In 1932 he wrote that "I look upon Soviet diplomacy not only as being unreliable but, above all, as being incapable of being considered of the same nature as the foreign political activity of other nations and, in consequence, as being something with which one cannot negotiate or conclude treaties."[107] Former Secretary of State Dean Acheson once told a press conference that

> . . . in Western tradition, negotiation was bargaining to achieve a mutually desired agreement. In Communist doctrine, it was war by political means to achieve an end unacceptable to the other side. In both cases, it was a means to an end, but in the latter case the ends were, if understood, mutually exclusive. [108]

Lenin reputedly always preceded the noun "compromise" with the adjective "putrid." This attitude is part and parcel of the zero-sum game that the Soviets play in the international arena. Leaders schooled in the Western democratic tradition, by contrast, believe that two sides at a bargaining table can split their differences and that the truth lies roughly midway between their competing positions.

It is worth noting that both President Reagan and Secretary Shultz prided themselves on their skills as negotiators. On the eve of the 1985 Geneva summit, Reagan reminisced about his days as head of the Screen Actors Guild in Hollywood and told a group of West European journalists that the experience would serve him well in his encounter with Gorbachev:

> . . . Long before I ever thought I would be in public life in this way . . . I did the negotiating for the union of which I was president. I am the first President of the United States who was ever president of a labor union. And I think I know something about negotiating. And I intend to go at it in the same manner [at the summit]. [109]

In a pre-summit interview with *U.S. News & World Reprt*, Reagan stated that "I've always believed you go in with your proposal, there's a counterproposal, and you keep on going until someplace between the two proposals you arrive at something mutually satisfactory."[110]

Shultz, who has served as a mediator in labor negotiations and as Secretary of Labor, told a meeting of the Rand-UCLA Center for the Study of Soviet International Behavior: "Some argue that if you cannot trust the Soviets, you should not negotiate with them. But the truth is, successful negotiations aren't based on trust."[111] They are based, said the Secretary, on such fundamental factors as a strong national defense, domestic unity and bipartisan consensus at home, and close cooperation with allies abroad. Unfortunately, these commodities appear to be in rather short supply in the United States today.

Even on occasions—admittedly rare—when U.S. negotiators adopt a tough stance and refuse to be swayed by Soviet blandishments, the United States is at a disadvantage because of the pressures of public opinion, the media, Congress, and the West European allies. At this particular juncture in history, the United States is doubly burdened—first, because, as Stalin's Foreign Minister Vyacheslav Molotov once said, "Democrats talk peace but make war, while Republicans talk war but make peace," and secondly because Reagan was so concerned about how historians will judge him. "When at the table with the Russians, never negotiate with a clock," warns Charles Krauthammer. "Reagan's clock is his age and the 22nd Amendment [ruling out his reelection]. Aware of both, the Soviets are demanding a price."[112]

Reagan's personal situation also should be viewed against the backdrop of the impatience that characterizes most Americans. As START negotiator Edward Rowny has cautioned,

> . . . The Russians are prepared to wait for shifts in . . . the "correlation of forces" that serve their political ends. Americans are not patient . . . The Russians play chess; we play video games. They like the well-thought-through results of step-by-step reasoning; we like the instant results of electronic machines. [113]

Gorbachev may appear at a disadvantage vis-a-vis Reagan because of the backward Soviet economy, the war in Afghanistan, instability in Eastern Europe, and anti-reform elements in the CPSU who may challenge his policies. These drawbacks need not have a negative impact on

Soviet negotiating positions, however. As Adam Ulam, director of the Russian Research Center at Harvard, points out, the Soviets " . . . don't only look at the moment, and a failure might not be a catastrophe for them. They can wait for another meeting or [another] President."[114]

Moscow's obsession with secrecy also confers an advantage over Washington at the bargaining table. As Rowny notes, "Soviet society is closed and secretive. The United States is an open society. In negotiations, the Russians always play their cards close to the chest; we mostly play ours face up on the table. . . . "[115] The problems posed for American negotiators by the Soviet passion for secrecy is compounded by the practice of Soviet strategic deception. This is a stratagem of disinformation and "semantic infiltration" to mislead the adversary about the true nature of Soviet intentions and goals. For the USSR, strategic deception is an integral part of the negotiating process. Kissinger evidently recognized this phenomenon in action when he told North Vietnamese negotiator Le Duc Tho that "I admire your ability to change impossible demands to merely intolerable demands and call this progress."

In view of the well known Soviet intransigence and duplicity, is it advisable to negotiate—"to dialogue"—at all? Is "jaw-jaw" the only alternative to "waw-waw"? Rep. Charles McC. Mathias Jr. (R.- Md.), whose views probably reflect widespread perceptions in the liberal community, wrote that

> . . . [not to negotiate] would be a mistake. We would run two major risks in refusing. First, we would risk locking the Soviet leadership into a position of permanent hostility that could encourage rather than discourage the aggressive tendencies we are trying to curtail. . . . Second, we would feed the propaganda effort in Europe that is painting us, with some success, as the enemy of dialogue. . . . [116]

Perhaps one solution to the problem is to broaden the channels of U.S.-Soviet communication at every opportunity while reducing the number of set-piece negotiations. Informal conversations and discussions allow each side to put forth proposals without anticipating that they will be implemented immediately and to air grievances without expecting them to be resolved at the table. In the case of formal negotiations, by contrast, the government bureaucracy swings into action, mountains of memoranda are written, hordes of advance men swarm over the proposed site, and media representatives raise public expectations of "progress" or the actual signing of an agreement. To smooth the way for an accord under such circumstances, the United States may proffer concessions, which the Soviet Union is likely to pocket in preparation to tabling demands for further concessions. The Soviets abide by their usual maxim that "what is mine is mine—what is yours is negotiable." They also may resort to stimulating U.S. fears of going home empty-handed if further concessions are not put forth. Frequently, the outcome is an agreement that is disadvantageous to Washington or the lack of an agreement, which Soviet propaganda skillfully attributes to U.S. intransigence.

The negotiations game, as it is currently played, seems to constitute a "no-lose" situation for the Soviets. Unless and until the United States can formulate its objectives on a particular issue in terms that transcend political convenience and address the national interest, formal Soviet-American negotiations on that issue should be deferred. Attempting to bank Russian goodwill in the meantime by offering gratuitous concessions is futile—if not counterproductive in terms of making the United States appear weak. Perhaps the most important thing to keep in mind when dealing with the Soviets is that, in the words of a European diplomat, "they take what you give them—and then they demand more."[117]

### Conclusions.

The collapse of detente brought a cry in some U.S. circles for a return to containment. However, as noted above, the geopolitical landscape has changed so drastically since the "Cold War" era that to apply countervailing military pressure at every point of Soviet expansion would be virtually impossible—and exceedingly dangerous to boot. To emphasize this fact is not to condone Soviet or Soviet-sponsored aggression. Nor is it to suggest that we should remain passively optimistic about detente in the face of Soviet adventurism and hope that the USSR will overextend and exhaust itself.

An editorial in *The Washington Times* has noted that

speculation about Mr. Gorbachev's wanting to concentrate on "economc reforms" is probably no more reliable than fanciful yarns about Andropov's fondness for scotch and jazz. It's the way some Americans drug themselves into seeing neo-Stalinists as plain politicians whom one can "do business with." [118]

It should be clear by now that the Soviets will not be deterred from foreign policy opportunities because of domestic problems—particularly if such opportunities entail low-risk, low-cost activities in the Third World that reap maximum returns. So long as Washington shies away from protracted involvement in regional and sub-regional conflicts and vacillates in its commitments to Third-World friends and allies, Moscow will have a green light to expand its presence abroad— the "burdens of empire" notwithstanding. Under these circumstances, detente will proceed along an asymmetrical course, with the Soviets writing the rules of the game.

In closing, let us make a plea for entertaining worst-case assumptions about the Soviet Union. Let us forsake Pollyanna for Cassandra. Not only will such a switch help us guard against unpleasant surprises; it will also put us on the same wavelength as the Soviets themselves (who attribute the darkest motives to the United States) and thus might even help to promote mutual understanding. Finally, we would do well to heed the advice of Rep. Jim Courter, who has written that "our long-term policy should not be based on specific incidents—it should respond to the permanently hostile nature of Soviet foreign policy itself."[119]

The fact that the United States and the Soviet Union lack a common code of international morality and have fundamentally different political traditions and ideologies renders chimerical the pursuit of a genuine detente. The Americans have had their Watergate, and a modicum of venality and corruption is inescapable in even the most advanced democratic societies. The Soviets, however, have a political culture of which rampant corruption and obsessive secrecy are hallmarks. In the international arena, this culture manifests itself by what the late "Scoop" Jackson called a Soviet tendency to tiptoe down the corridors and examine every door to see whether it is unlocked.

Our Soviet adversary is, in short, not inscrutable. In fact, a strong case can be made for the contention that the Soviet Union is more predictable in its foreign policy behavior than is the United States. Let history be our guide in this respect. As conservative columnist M. Stanton Evans has written,

> . . . We are repeatedly invited to wonder whether some new assertion from the Kremlin, some radar blip from within the Soviet empire, some quirk of personality in a newly chosen leader, offers the prospect for constructive change or a negotiated peace. Our inability to learn from history where the Soviets are concerned, and our compulsion to ruminate the same primordial questions as if we had no experience to go by, paralyzes thought and inhibits action. . . .

If the question of Soviet goals and methods is to be held permanently open, regardless of the massive data base, then we will never have a coherent strategy for dealing with the problem.

We have a solid body of knowledge about the way the Soviets behave, compiled over more than half a century and uncontradicted by any credible evidence. The course of wisdom is to build a policy on that knowledge, rather than trying to reinvent our understanding of the subject every time there is a summit. [120]

# Epilogue

Has *The Deceptive Lure of Detente* been overtaken by events (O.B.E. in bureaucratic jargon)? It's very unlikely. The continuing success of the USSR's appeal to Western rope-sellers is well documented in a 1988 *Washington Post* report that "European businessmen and bankers, waving checkbooks and order blanks, are rushing to Moscow to answer the siren song of *perestroika.*"

Gorbachev's "new" Russia appears to be proffering major concessions in the interest of detente: permission for Andrei Sakharov to visit the West for the first time; an offer to release all political prisoners (numbering only a few dozen by Mocow's calculations!); tantalizing hints that Western participants in joint economic ventures can obtain majority control; assurances that the USSR will play a constructive role in the settlement of regional conflicts; and pledges to negotiate in good faith on conventional as well as strategic arms reductions in order to maintain the arms control momentum generated by the INF treaty. In exchange for these purported concessions, the Soviets unabashedly seek Western assistance for *perestroika* in the form of trade, technology transfer, cheap loans and credits, and restraint in the modernization of Western nuclear and conventional arsenals. Foreign Minister Eduard Shevardnadze typified the current approach during a press conference in Copenhagen when he claimed that "the COCOM list [of items banned for export to the Soviet bloc] should, in a time of cooperation, be revised and shortened. Real secrets are becoming very rare."[1]

Nevertheless, as Richard Perle observed, "there is not a shred of evidence that Mr. Gorbachev's restructuring has diminished by a single kopeck the resources flowing to the military, the KGB, or the worldwide program of subversion that flourished under the last detente and since."[2] As before, Western largesse is helping Moscow avoid the difficult choice between producing guns and butter. A French commentator has written quite accurately that

> . . . Foreign policy once again offers a compensatory avenue of hope. Several times ... in the course of its history, the Soviet regime has tottered on the edge of collapse; each time, Western aid has come to the rescue and provided a new lease on life. In large part, the entire thrust of Soviet foreign policy today is aimed at securing those means of survival which the West has hitherto afforded periodically and .... may be persuaded to provide permanently and as if by obligation. A race is thus on between the ... deepening process of internal decomposition ... and the so-far successful policy of external diplomacy which may yet procure a lengthy reprieve, if not ... eventual triumph.[3]

Western Europe and, to a lesser extent, the United States indeed are responding favorably to Gorbachev's diplomacy of smiles—even though the Soviet leader has offered more on the rhetorical than on the practical level to date. Gorbachev may shun a cult of personality at home as uncomfortably reminiscent of the Stalinist era; but he is busily developing one abroad. He is a virtual folk hero in Western Europe, where many public opinion polls indicate that he is regarded as more sincere in his desire for peace than is Ronald Reagan. Moreover, many West Europeans seem to have taken to heart the Kremlin line that if they don't "help" Gorbachev, he may be ousted by "hardliners."

"Iron Lady" Margaret Thatcher of Britain surprised the Reagan Administration in 1984 when she announced that Gorbachev (then Number 2 behind General Secretary Konstantin Chernenko) was a man that she could do business with. Since that time, several West

European governments have climbed eagerly aboard the *perestroika* bandwagon. Between 1982 and 1984, for example, loans by Western banks to the Soviet Union (in constant dollars) totalled $2.3 billion. Between the beginning of 1985 and the third quarter of 1987, the figure was $8.4 billion.[4] This amount was exceeded in the single year of 1988, when West Germany alone proffered more than $2 billion in credits to the USSR. In October, Chancellor Helmut Kohl made an official visit to Moscow, where six government-to-government agreements and some 30 contracts between West German businesses and Soviet agencies were signed. Kohl was the last of the major Western leaders to receive an invitation to meet with Gorbachev in the Soviet capital. In the aftermath of the visit, Gorbachev declared that "the ice has been broken" in a relationship that was beset with friction over INF deployments and other issues. The General Secretary reportedly urged Kohl to oppose arms modernization in Western Europe—notably deployment of a new generation of short-range nuclear weapons that would be placed on West German territory.

West German Foreign Minister Hans-Dietrich Genscher has been a leading proponent in the West of "taking Gorbachev at his word" on security matters and of helping him to build a "common European home" stretching from the Urals to the Atlantic. This concept, in Gorbachev's formulation, invokes a peaceful, prosperous Continent devoid of American troops and "cowboy" culture. It does *not* provide for the dissolution of the Warsaw Pact or for German reunification and thus stands at odds with Genscher's intonation of "an historical duty" to assist *perestroika* and reunite Europe.[5] The influential Swiss newspaper *Neue Zuercher Zeitung* observed that "Gorbachev's 'European home' is walled up on the inside to prevent residents in the East wing from moving to the West wing."

The Italian government, like the West German, has expressed support for *perestroika*. Prime Minister Ciriaco de Mita proffered loans during his visit to Moscow in 1988, and he has advocated a Marshall Plan to ease the Soviet bloc's economic plight. France also is lending money to the Soviet Union, and British banks have renewed their support for loans to the East after a period of retrenchment. Shevardnadze's visit to Paris in October boosted Franco-Soviet relations to "the highest level," according to French Foreign Minister Roland Dumas.[6] French President Francois Mitterrand visited Moscow in the autumn of 1988, as did Austrian Chancellor Franz Vranitzky. Meanwhile, NATO plans to modernize short-range nuclear systems in Western Europe, once accepted willingly by the allies, are increasingly controversial. West Germany and Belgium are among the holdouts in voicing support—perhaps because they are reluctant to "provoke" the Kremlin.

By successfully procuring West European financial help for *perestroika,* Gorbachev kills two birds with one stone: He obtains material assistance and simultaneously exacerbates disputes between some West European nations and the United States over the wisdom of furnishing untied loans and other economic goodies to the Soviet Union (although President Reagan himself represented an unsteady model for resisting Soviet blandishments). In media interviews, Defense Secretary Frank Carlucci and some other Reagan Administration officials expressed concern that West Germany or other U.S. allies may be willing to help build nuclear reactors and powerful computers for the USSR. However, Commerce Secretary William Verity encouraged pilgrimages by U.S. corporate executives to the Soviet Union in search of business deals. A study by the U.S. Global Strategy Council (a private group) on *The Dangers of Detente II* remarks that "the U.S. Government, multinational corporations, and many scientific and legal associations are signing economic, scientific, educational and cultural agreements with the Soviet Union without requiring any prior Soviet compliance with past human rights accords." A pervasive sense of déja vu hovers in the air.

Meanwhile, Jim Hoagland of *The Washington Post* urged the West to proffer "an arms-control rescue for *perestroika,*" lest a blocked arms control agenda result in the "Brezhnevization of Gorbachev."[7] Deputy Secretary of State John Whitehead stated that "it would be completely out of character" for Gorbachev the peacemaker to quell any East European rebellion through the use of Soviet troops.[8] And Ronald Reagan remarked that "it would be a great setback" if reform-minded Gorbachev were replaced.[9]

In short, detente is in full bloom once again. But what has changed since its previous incarnations? In contrast to the Lenin, Stalin and Brezhnev periods, the Soviet Union seems to be seeking a more protracted period of *razryadka* (relaxation of tensions) to concentrate on putting its domestic house in order. However, no opportunity for a significant expansion of Soviet influence in the international arena has arisen since Gorbachev's accession to power. Would Gorbachev abandon detente in favor of making major strategic gains if a war or revolution erupted in such volatile places as the Middle East or South Africa? Would he support a Communist takeover in such important pro-Western countries as the Philippines or Chile if Communist movements there seemed on the brink of ousting the incumbent governments? Nikita Krushchev's rule represents a sober lesson for those in the West who apparently believe that attempts at domestic reform are incompatible with Soviet expansion and adventurism abroad.

Meanwhile, on the home front, Andrei Sakharov has thrown some cold water on Western illusions about Gorbachev's enlightened reign. "Democratization" is a term for Western consumption, Sakharov suggests. He warns that the planned electoral, legal and constitutional changes in the Soviet political system would provide a veneer of pluralism while actually bolstering the authority of the Communist Party and giving Gorbachev a virtual monopoly of power. "Today it will be Gorbachev. Tomorrow it may be somebody else, and there are no guarantees," he intones, implying that a return to Stalin-type dictatorship cannot be ruled out.[10] Gorbachev's reforms—both political and economic—stand squarely in the tradition of Peter the Great and Tsar Alexander II, whose policies were designed to strengthen the autocracy by making the system more efficient and responsive to direction from the top. The wholesale reshuffling of the Kremlin leadership that Gorbachev carried out on 30 September 1988 in the course of about an hour and without a visible sign of dissent was a performance worthy of the Tsarist—and Stalinist—tradition. If Gorbachev is fostering democratization, it is democracy by dictat.

Repression of political dissidents continues apace, as typified by the arrest in October 1988 of some 50 people in Moscow and Leningrad "for holding candles and reading poetry" during a rally to demand freedom for hundreds of political prisoners held in the Gulag or in psychiatric institutions.[11] Gorbachev certainly has not leashed the secret police—a pillar of his regime. Moreover, he chose KGB chief Viktor Chebrikov to head the Communist Party Central Committee's new commission on legal policy. "It's like naming Al Capone the Attorney General," said U.S. Sovietologist Marshall Goldman, noting that the commission's tasks include the formulation of human rights policies.[12]

On the arms control front, the Soviet Union has done little to alleviate U.S. concerns about the Krasnoyarsk radar installation. Moreover, behind Moscow's threats and bluster about "Star Wars," the Soviets continue to pursue work on their own anti-missile defenses.

Many Western experts voice concern about a potential Soviet "break-out" from the ABM treaty.

The current period of neo-detente has witnessed a noticeable increase in the Kremlin's anti-Western propaganda, disinformation, "active measures," and intelligence and counter-intelligence operations abroad. One alarming development in this regard was the elevation of Vladimir Kryuchkov to head the KGB. His previous position as head of the agency's First Chief Directorate, which is responsible for the collection and assessment of foreign intelligence, suggests that the KGB will focus its energies increasingly on foreign targets, especially in the United States and Western Europe. During periods of detente, when human contacts and the flow of information between East and West expand, the Soviets traditionally have intensified their intelligence and espionage activities—ranging from the cultivation of potential agents of influence and recruits to the illegal acquisition of Western technology. The current period is no exception. In this dimension at least, the Soviet threat to the West is growing rather than declining.

Even a gradual evolution of the USSR from a totalitarian to an authoritarian state, as Jeane Kirkpatrick and others suggest might occur, and a decline in ideological fervor would not necessarily curb Soviet aggressive and expansionistic tendencies. Relentless overland conquests by the Tsars made Russia the vast multi-ethnic and multinational empire that it is today.

Soviet propagandists and disinformation specialists are working overtime vis-a-vis the West to "demolish the enemy image" of the USSR (in the words of Foreign Minister Shevardnadze). That Moscow succeeded in converting Ronald Reagan, a "hardline" anti-Communist, from a critic of the "Evil Empire" to an apostle of detente suggests that future U.S. administrations may fail to muster the political will to withstand the Soviet Union's charm offensive. As in past periods of detente, the Soviet perception managers are projecting the image of a benign USSR, interested only in peaceful competition with the West and in achieving a degree of prestige and respect commensurate with its power and sheer size. The Kremlin is well versed in lulling the West into a false sense of security while acquiring—by fair means or foul—the wherewithal to strengthen the Soviet economy and military machine. It is instructive to recall the words of Dmitri Manuilsky, a Comintern operative, in this regard. Speaking to the Lenin School of Political Warfare in Moscow in 1931, Manuilsky said:

War to the hilt between Communism and capitalism is inevitable. Today, of course, we are not strong enough to attack. Our time will come in 20 or 30 years. To win, we shall need the element of surprise. The bourgeoisie will have to be put to sleep, so we shall begin by launching the most spectacular peace movement on record. There will be electrifying overtures and unheard-of concessions. The capitalist countries, stupid and decadent, will rejoice in their own destruction. They will leap at another chance to be friends. As soon as their guard is down, we shall smash them with our clenched fist.

Skepticism about *perestroika* and *glasnost* is politically unfashionable today; but if one acknowledges that Western firmness is as important as Soviet economic stagnation in restraining the Kremlin's foreign policy adventurism, it will be possible to reap our own benefits from detente while husbanding the strength that we will need in the event of a new East-West crisis.

# Notes

## Chapter 1

1. *Pravda, 25 February 1976.*
2. *The New York Times,* 23 September 1981.
3. Graham D. Vernon, "Controlled Conflict: Soviet Perceptions of Peaceful Coexistence," *Orbis,* Summer 1979, p. 292.
4. Quoted in E.H. Carr, *The Bolshevik Revolution,* Vol. III (London, 1966), p. 277.
5. Quoted in *Soviet Analyst,* 26, July 1979, p. 3.
6. George F. Kennan, *Russia and the West Under Lenin and Stalin* (Little, Brown, 1960), p. 197.
7. Cord Meyer, "Thinking About the Worst," *Washington Star,* 6 February 1980.
8. As an historical footnote, it is worth pointing out that Nixon arrived in Moscow 25 years to the day after he voted as a Congressman in favor of the Truman Doctrine symbolizing global confrontation with communism.
9. Richard Lowenthal, "The Shattered Balance," *Encounter,* November 1980, p. 10.
10. Quoted in Allan E. Goodman, *The Lost Peace* (Hoover Institution Press, 1978), p. 124.
11. See, e.g., *Izvestia,* 10 June 1976, and "K itogam vyborov v SSha," *Mezhdunarodnaya zhizn,'* 12 November 1976, p. 102.
12. *Pravda,* 26 October 1976.
13. Interview with Arnaud deBorchgrave and Michael Ledeen, *The New Republic,* 7 February 1981.
14. Statement to Senate Foreign Relations Committee, 19 September 1974.

Chapter 2

1. *The Wall Street Journal,* 28 August 1978.
2. In mid-1986 it was reported that Viktor Karpov, currently head of the Soviet delegation at the Geneva arms-control talks, was heading a new disarmament agency in the Foreign Ministry. See *The Washington Post,* 8 June 1986.
3. See., e.g., Sen. Henry M. Jackson, "We Must Not Mismanage SALT II," *Freedom at Issue* (May-June 1973), p. 2.
4. The American ICBM's included 52 obsolescent Titan missiles that were scheduled for retirement.
5. Samuel Cohen & Joseph Douglass, Jr., "Into the Valley of Arms Control," *The Washington Times,* 28 February 1985.
6. Josef Joffe, "Why Germans Support SALT," *Survival,* September/October 1979, p. 209.
7. The treaty was approved by the Senate Foreign Relations Committee, but it never reached the Senate floor because Carter withdrew his support in the wake of the Afghan crisis.
8. *The New York Times,* 21 May 1979.
9. See *Newsweek,* 28 May 1979, p. 104.
10. *The New York Times,* 7 June 1980.
11. *The Wall Street Journal,* 15 June 1979.
12. It should be noted that the 200 MX's were to form the basis for a new nuclear warfighting doctrine—the so-called PD-59—which was announced in August 1980. The MX's, by virtue of their mobility, were supposed to survive a Soviet first strike and be capable of striking back to destroy the silo-based missiles that the USSR would hold in reserve.
13. Other important elements of Reagan's defense program included the manufacture of 100 B-1 bombers by 1986; pending development of the "Stealth" radar-evading bomber by 1990; the production and stockpiling of neutron bombs in the United States (with the implication that they could be transferred rapidly to Europe in a crisis); deployment of the Trident II submarine; the production of several hundred nuclear-armed submarine-launched cruise missiles; the improvement of the command, control and communications network needed to direct and counter a nuclear attack; the upgrading of continental air defense; and the study of an ABM system—perhaps using space-based killer satellites—to destroy incoming enemy warheads.
14. Article I of the Protocol to the SALT II treaty states: "Each party undertakes not to deploy mobile ICBM launchers or to flight-test ICBM's from such launchers." See the text of the treaty in *The New York Times,* 19 June 1979. The protocol expired in 1981.
15. One proposed remedy floated in the Pentagon was dubbed "carry hard." It called for rotating 40 to 50 missiles among 100 hardened silos, in an attempt to convince the Soviet Union that the silos were temporary shelters rather than additional launchers banned under SALT. See *The Washington Post,* 8 May 1982. Moreover, Weinberger and other Administration officials argued that the new underground silos would not be launchers because the launch equipment for the MX was contained in a cannister surrounding the missile and would be transported with the missile from one silo to another. See *The Washington Post,* 27 November 1982. As a *Wall Street Journal* editorial pointed out (9 December 1982), "this silly argument serves only to underline that the [SALT] treaty limited launchers without ever defining launchers."
16. *The Wall Street Journal,* editorial, 4 June 1984. Another potential problem was that Dense Pack probably would be unworkable without an ABM system to protect it, and such a system would necessitate the abdication or amendment of the 1972 ABM treaty.
17. *The Wall Street Journal,* editorial, 30 August 1984.
18. *The New York Times,* 20 April 1983.

19. See Angelo Codevilla's review of the book *Arms Control: Myths Versus Reality*, edited by Richard F. Staar, *Strategic Review*, Winter 1985, p. 62.
20. *The Washington Post*, 2 June 1982.
21. The first public mention of the change in nomenclature appeared in Reagan's address to the National Press Club on 18 November 1981. See the text of the speech in *The New York Times*, 19 November 1981.
22. *The Washington Post*, 13 April 1983; *The Economist*, 18 June 1983.
23. *The Washington Post*, 13 April 1983.
24. *The Washington Post*, 29 August 1982.
25. *The New York Times*, 31 October 1982.
26. *The New York Times*, 10 January 1983. One such proposal issued from a Warsaw Pact summit meeting in January 1983.
27. The Supreme Allied Commander Europe has at his disposal about 6,000 short-range nuclear devices—warheads, bombs and howitzer projectiles—for battlefield use. They can strike targets in Eastern Europe but none can reach Soviet territory. The British and French have independent nuclear arsenals, but they are numerically insignificant in the overall nuclear balance in Europe.
28. *The New York Times*, 21 March 1982.
29. The SALT II treaty sets 3,400 miles (5,500 km) as the threshold for an intercontinental missile.
30. See "What Next in Arms Control?" The Heritage Foundation, *National Security Record*, No. 75, January 1985, p. 2.
31. *IBID.*
32. See James Hackett, "Risky Arms Dealings," *The Washington Times*, 16 January 1986.
33. See *The Washington Post*, 9 April 1985.
34. Manfred Hamm, "The Umbrella Talks?" *The Washington Quarterly*, Spring 1985, p. 136.
35. Richard Lowenthal, "The Shattered Balance," *Encounter*, November 1980.
36. Kvitsinsky was a major behind-the-scenes player in constructing the four-power agreement on Berlin in the early 1970's. He has served in the Soviet embassy in East Berlin and received a doctor of laws degree with a thesis on West Berlin. See *The New York Times*, 1 December 1981.
37. Each SS-20 launcher has at least one re-fire missile, and each missile has three warheads. Each Pershing missile launcher can be reloaded after the first missile is fired, but the United States announced that only 108 launchers and a few spares—no complete extra missiles with nuclear warheads—would be sent to West Germany. See *The Washington Post*, 27 November 1982.
38. *Pravda*, 24 November 1981.
39. *The New York Times*, 24 November 1981 and 21 January 1982.
40. See *Pravda*, 4 and 10 February 1982.
41. The British have four nuclear submarines with 16 missiles each; the French have five subs with 16 missiles each, as well as 18 land-based, single-warhead missiles.
42. "Brezhnev's Moratorium: An Analysis," Radio Liberty Research, 126/82, 17 March 1982.
43. See Raymond L. Garthoff, "That SS-20 Moratorium: Who is Telling the Truth?" *The Washington Post*, 26 April 1983.
44. Mr. Kvitsinsky recounts his version of the "walks in the woods" in a *New York Times* Op. Ed. article ("Soviet View of Geneva") on 12 January 1984. He writes, inter alia, that "Washington created a false impression that the talks were making progress, while proceeding with plans to deploy new missiles in Europe. It deliberately led Western Europeans to believe that the walk in the woods proposal had originally been acceptable to both sides. In reality, it was a blind alley from the start."
45. *The New York Times*, 16 January 1983.
46. See the text of Andropov's speech in *The New York Times*, 22 December 1982. Britain has 64 Polaris A missiles aboard four nuclear submarines. France has 80 similar missiles aboard five submarines and 18 medium-range rockets on land.

47. *Newsweek,* 3 January 1983.
48. *The Wall Street Journal,* 22 December 1982.
49. *The Washington Post,* 1 February 1983.
50. *The Wall Street Journal,* 23 March 1983.
51. Tom Wicker, "A Bird in the Hand," *The New York Times,* 12 July 1983.
52. *The Washington Times,* 19 October 1983.
53. *Stern,* 17 October 1983.
54. See Lawrence T. Caldwell, "Soviet Policy on Nuclear Weapons and Arms Control," in Dan Caldwell, ed., *Soviet International Behavior and U.S. Policy Options* (Lexington, Mass.: Lexington Books, 1985), p. 216.
55. *Ibid.,* 21 November 1983.
56. Quoted in *The Washington Times,* 9 December 1983.
57. For the text of the SDI speech, see press release from the White House, "Address by the President to the Nation," 23 March 1983.
58. See *The New York Times,* 8 January 1985.
59. *The Washington Post,* 3 April 1983.
60. *The Washington Times,* 18 November 1985.
61. Keith B. Payne, "The Soviet Union and Strategic Defense: The Failure and Future of Arms Control," *Orbis,* Winter 1986, p. 674.
62. *The Washington Post,* 4 November 1985.
63. *The New York Times,* 27 December 1984.
64. According to many knowledgeable observers, Reagan's hope to use SDI for population defense may be unrealistic—at least in the short run. Even if the system were 99% effective, it is likely that enough enemy missiles could get through to render the U.S. uninhabitable. However, "Star Wars" could be highly effective in protecting the country's second-strike capability, in that only a fraction of the nuclear missile force would have to survive in order to retaliate against a Soviet attack.
65. See "SDI: The 'Star Wars' Project," The George C. Marshall Institute, New York, 1985, p. 9.
66. Dimitri K. Simes, "Are the Soviets Interested in Arms Control?" *The Washington Quarterly,* Spring 1985, p. 154.
67. Quoted by Edward Teller, "Making the Shield Stronger Than the Sword," *The Washington Times,* 25 October 1985.
68. See *The Washington Times,* 10 May 1985.
69. Edward Teller, "Making the Shield Stronger Than the Sword," *The Washington Times,* 25 October 1985.
70. *The Washington Times,* 9 January 1985.
71. Dimitri Simes, "Are the Soviets Interested in Arms Control?" *The Washington Quarterly,* Spring 1985, p. 151.
72. *The New York Times,* 8 April 1985.
73. *The New York Times,* 11 June 1985.
74. In order to remain within the bounds of SALT II, the United States had to destroy a Poseidon submarine, which carries 16 missiles, or 14 Minuteman single-warhead missiles.
75. *The New York Times,* 11 June 1985.
76. George Will, "The Case for Abandoning SALT II," *The Citizen* (Ottawa), 7 June 1985.
77. Marshall D. Shulman, "A Coming Tornado in U.S.-Soviet Relations," *The New York Times,* 2 June 1985.
78. *The Economist,* 6 July 1985, p. 11.
79. *The New York Times,* 31 July 1985.
80. At that time, the U.S. government generally cited a figure of 11,500 for the number of nuclear warheads in the Soviet arsenal. This figure, higher than previously, included the warheads on the new SS-24 and SS-25 ICBM's. For excerpts from Gorbachev's speech, see, e.g., AP (Paris), 3 October 1985 and *The Washington Post,* 4 October 1985.
81. *The Washington Post,* 7 October 1985.

82. "The Numbers Game," *The New York Times,* 2 October 1985.
83. *IBID.* During an interview with *The New York Times* on 12 October, Soviet Chief of Staff Akhromeyev attempted to offset Western concern on this issue by stating that "the missiles withdrawn from combat alert are concentrated within one area. It is quite verifiable by space means. They will not be moved to Asia. See *The New York Times,* 8 October 1985.
84. *The Washington Post,* 25 October 1985.
85. See *The Washington Post,* 25 October 1985.
86. *The New York Times,* 5 October 1985.
87. *Newsweek,* 14 October 1985, p. 30.
88. See, e.g., *The Washington Times,* 7 November 1985.
89. Barry Schneider & Michael Ennis, "Confusing Times for Strategic Planners," *The Washington Times,* 29 January 1986.
90. See William Rusher, "Beating Drums of Surrender," *The Washington Times,* 2 October 1985.
91. Gerard C. Smith & Paul C. Warnke, "Hope for the Summit," *The New York Times,* 26 September 1985.
92. *The New York Times,* 25 November 1985.
93. Excerpts from Gorbachev's news conference are published in *The New York Times,* 22 November 1985.
94. The President's objections to a comprehensive nuclear test ban are essentially threefold: He believes the United States is still behind the Soviets in nuclear arms building and must test its new weapons as they come onstream; he contends that testing is necessary to maintain the reliability of the nation's nuclear arsenal; and he feels that testing helps the United States to retain its technological edge over the USSR.
95. M. Stanton Evans, "Carter's Statement on SALT Is Not True," *Human Events,* 19 May 1979.
96. See Evans & Novak, "A 'Smoking Gun' in Siberia?" *The Washington Post,* 17 August 1983.
97. Quoted in *The New York Times,* 23 April 1983.
98. Ambassador Seymour Weiss, quoted in *Human Events,* 19 June 1982.
99. Rep. Jim Courter, "What If We've Verified Soviet Treaty Violations?" *The Wall Street Journal,* 14 December 1983.
100. See *Pravda,* 16 January 1986.
101. Colin Gray, "Snake Oil From Moscow," *The Wall Street Journal,* 27 January 1986.
102. *Izvestia,* 16 Januar 1986. The Soviets even took out a full-page ad in *The New York Times* to publicize the no-nukes plan.
103. *The New York Times,* 17 January 1986.
104. *The Wall Street Journal,* 15 January 1986.
105. Mary McGrory, "The Insult of Silence," *The Washington Post,* 23 January 1986.
106. *The New York Times,* 19 January 1986.
107. At the time the U.S. plan was introduced, the Soviets had deployed 441 SS-20's, of which about 270 were targeted on Western Europe. The United States had deployed all of its planned 108 Pershing 2 missiles in West Germany and 60 of its planned total of 116 cruise missile launchers in England, Italy, West Germany, and Belgium; no deployments had taken place yet in the Netherlands. See *The Washington Post,* 25 February 1986.
108. *The Washington Post,* 25 February 1986.
109. *IBID.*
110. See *The Washington Post,* 9 February 1986.
111. See Dimitri Simes, "What's So Great About Gorbachev? Nothing—Yet," *The Washington Post,* 24 February 1986.
112. *The Washington Post,* 22 April 1986.
113. For the text of Gorbachev's speech at the party congress, see *Pravda,* 25 February 1986.
114. *The Washington Post,* 14 March 1986.

115. Opposition to a nuclear test ban, in isolation from other arms control measures, has been widespread across the American political spectrum. *The New York Times,* for example, editorialized that "a test ban now, without other agreements, would appear to do a great deal more for the Soviet Union than it has yet admitted: it would kill development of the nuclear-powered X-ray laser, a device that some see as the most promising technical component of President Reagan's antimissile defense initiative. However misconceived the "Star Wars" program, the Administration isn't obliged to kill it for free. It should be bargained away . . . for sizable reductions in nuclear stockpiles.

   "'Star Wars' aside, why should a test ban be a prepayment for a major arms control agreement? The Administration is pursuing arms talks with the Soviet Union across a wide front; to hang toughest on the items the Russians want most is not a bad tactic, provided the negotiations are sincerely pursued. . . ." See *The New York Times,* 31 March 1986.
116. Quoted in *The Washington Times,* 31 March 1986.
117. *The New York Times,* 3 April 1986.
118. *The Washington Post,* 8 April 1986.
119. *The Economist,* 26 April 1986, p. 51.
120. See *The Washington Post,* 30 May 1986.
121. *The Washington Post,* 1 June 1986.
122. *The New York Times,* 30 May 1986.
123. Weinberger was questioned on CBS' "Face the Nation" about what the Soviets would have to do to induce the President to reconsider his position. The Secretary of Defense replied that, inter alia, they would have to remove their SS-25 missiles and permit the United States to verify effectively overall Soviet compliance with SALT. See *The Washington Times,* 2 June 1986.
124. *The Washington Post,* 29 May 1986.
125. *IBID.*
126. *IBID.*
127. *The Washington Post,* 14 June 1986.
128. *The New York Times,* 31 May 1986 & *The Washington Post,* 31 May 1986.
129. *The Washington Post,* 13 June 1986.
130. *IBID.*
131. *The Washington Post,* 14 June 1986.
132. *IBID.*
133. *The Washington Times,* 30 May 1986.
134. *The Washington Post,* 4 June 1986; emphasis added.
135. *The Washington Post,* 29 May 1986.
136. *The Washington Times,* 30 May 1986.
137. Anthony Lewis, "What Is the Sense?" *The New York Times,* 9 June 1986; emphasis added.
138. "Half Right and All Wrong on SALT," *The New York Times,* 1 June 1986.
139. *The Washington Post,* 30 May 1986.
140. Albert Gore Jr., "Why Mr. Reagan Blundered on SALT," *The New York Times,* 1 June 1986; emphasis added. The three treaties that the senator referred to were SALT II, the 1974 Threshold Test Ban Treaty, and the 1976 Treaty of Peaceful Nuclear Explosives.
141. *The Washington Post,* 30 May 1986.
142. Letter to the Editor of *The New York Times,* 17 June 1986.
143. *The New York Times,* 1 June 1986. The ABM accord is of indefinite duration, but it provides for the withdrawal of either party (on six months' notice) if it deems the treaty has "jeopardized its supreme interests."
144. *The Washington Post,* 19 June 1986.
145. *The Wall Street Journal,* 20 June 1986.
146. Quoted in *The Washington Times,* 18 April 1986.
147. See *The Washington Post,* 27 June 1985.
148. *The Washington Times,* 18 April 1986.

149. See *The Washington Times,* 27 June 1985. Albert Weeks, a Sovietologist, has emphasized "the ease with which both missiles and warheads may be concealed, particularly warheads, which stand only a bit taller than a man. Let us not forget that during World War II, the Russians were able to bury whole defense factories underground. . . ." See Weeks' Letter to the Editor of *The New York Times,* 20 June 1986.
150. Quoted in *The Washington Times,* 27 June 1985.
151. *IBID.*
152. See *U.S. News & World Report,* 10 June 1985, p. 38.
153. *The Washington Post,* 9 June 1986.
154. See *The Washington Post,* 12 August 1986.
155. *IBID.,* pp. 25-26.
156. *The New York Times,* 11 April 1986.
157. See the article by Leslie Gelb in *The New York Times Magazine,* 5 June 1983, p. 34.
158. Keith B. Payne, "The Soviet Union and Strategic Defense: The Failure and Future of Arms Control," *Orbis,* Winter 1986, p. 675.
159. "Soviet Freeze Warning," *The Washington Post,* 5 April 1982.
160. James Reston, "The Protection Game," *The New York Times,* 1 June 1986.
161. Lou Cannon, "A Chance for a Serious Summit," *The Washington Post,* 30 June 1986.
162. Seymoure Weiss, "The Case Against Arms Control," *Commentary,* November 1984, p. 20.
163. *IBID.*
164. *The Washington Post,* 23 October 1985.
165. *The Wall Street Journal,* 30 December 1981 & 11 June 1982.
166. Flora Lewis, "Soviet-American Crossroads," *The New York Times,* 6 July 1986.
167. Henry Kissinger, "An Opportunity for a Breakthrough," *The Washington Post,* 17 November 1985.

## Chapter 3

1. Among the items that the United States buys from the Soviet Union are anhydrous ammonia, chemicals, nickel, fuels and lubricants, palladium, platinum, sponge, gold, beverages, and occasionally, uranium.
2. Juliana Geran Pilon, "Strategic Trade With Moscow," The Heritage Foundation, Washington, D.C., 2 January 1982, p. 11.
3. *The Christian Science Monitor,* 1 August 1979.
4. *The Wall Street Journal,* 29 January 1985.
5. See *U.S. News & World Report,* 9 May 1983, p. 48.
6. Carl Gershman, "Selling Them the Rope," *Commentary,* April 1979, p. 39.
7. Gershman, p. 42.
8. Zygmunt Nagorski, "The Deal Goes Against the Grain," *The New York Times,* 31 August 1983.
9. Gershman, p. 36.
10. Quoted in E.H. Carr, *The Bolshevik Revolution,* Vol. 3 (London: 1966), p. 277.
11. Edward Jay Epstein, "Petropower and Soviet Expansion," *Commentary,* July 1986, p. 23.
12. Gershman, p. 36.
13. Gershman, p. 37.
14. Gershman, p. 37.
15. *IBID.,* 10 December 1972.
16. *Human Events,* 12 March 1983.
17. Pilon, *op. cit.,* p. 11.
18. See, e.g., *Renmin Ribao* (Beijing), 9 February 1982.

19. Arnaud de Borchgrave & Michael Ledeen, "Selling Russia the Rope," *The New Republic*, 13 December 1980, p. 14. According to Miles Costick, Sweden gave a contractual promise to the United States not to re-export critical components of the air-traffic control system. However, Datasaab, which is owned by the Swedish government, conspired to sell critical circuits to the USSR for about $100 million. The Swedes removed the American markings from the circuits and substituted markings in the Cryillic alphabet so that they could not be traced to their U.S. manufacturer. When Swedish technicians arrived in Moscow to install the coveted equipment, the Soviet Union displayed its "gratitude" by blindfolding them during the journey to and from the underground facility where the installation took place.

20. *IBID*.

21. *The Daily Telegraph* (London), 25 January 1982.

22. A *Wall Street Journal* correspondent painted a lively picture of the grain-trading game: "Mr. Carter said he was confident that other major grain exporters would not replace the 17 million tons that the U.S. was not going to ship. It turned out that he was more than somewhat over-confident. Argentina didn't have enough excess grain to make a major dent in Russia's needs, but that problem was easily solved. Argentina simply cut off some of its traditional customers in Latin America. What happened to those traditional customers? That was no problem at all; the U.S. took care of their needs. . . . East Germany never had been a major importer of grain from the U.S., and yet it suddenly became one. Other East European nations also increased their grain purchases from the U.S. and elsewhere. The assumption is that the Soviet Union, a traditional supplier to its satellites, cut them off to use its own grain at home. The U.S. could then fill the gap. See Lindley H. Clark Jr., "Grain Embargo: Let's Declare Victory and Quit," *The Wall Street Journal*, 10 February 1981.

23. *The Economist*, 1 November 1980, p. 45.

24. *The Washington Post*, 23 October 1980.

25. William Safire, "Selling the Rope," *The New York Times*, 9 October 1983.

26. *The Washington Post*, 21 May 1985.

27. "Trade Mission-itis," *The Wall Street Journal*, editorial, 25 February 1985.

28. *IBID*.

29. *The Washington Post*, 23 August 1985.

30. *IBID*.

31. Judy Shelton, "Reagan Signals Business-as-Usual," *The Wall Street Journal*, 26 December 1985.

32. *The Wall Street Journal*, 9 December 1985.

33. *The Washington Post*, 11 December 1985.

34. *IBID*.

35. *Bu siness Week*, 23 December 1985, p. 39.

36. *The Washington Post*, 10 December 1985.

37. *Pravda*, 9 December 1985.

38. *The Wall Street Journal*, 2 October 1985.

39. *The Washington Post*, 5 August 1986.

40. *The Wall Street Journal*, 13 August 1986.

41. Quoted in *The Wall Street Journal*, 29 January 1985.

42. *IBID*.

43. *IBID*.

44. Quoted in *The New York Times*, 14 January 1982.

45. De Borchgrave & Ledeen, "Selling Russia the Rope," 13 December 1980, p. 14.

46. See, e.g., the CIA's massive 1982 report entitled "USSR: Measures of Economic Growth and Development, 1950-80" for a thorough assessment of Soviet economic performance.

47. Joseph Finder, "Trade Won't Soften an Adversary," *The Wall Street Journal*, 31 May 1985.

48. *The Economist*, 6 July 1980.

49. *The Washington Post*, 26 December 1982.

50. Herbert E. Meyer, "This Communist Intternationale Has a Capitalist Accent," *Fortune Magazine,* February 1977, p. 148.
51. Marshall Goldman, "Cooperation in the Field of Economics: The Soviet Side and Basket Two," *Radio Liberty Research,* 10 January 1977, p. 1.
52. Gershman, *op. cit.,* p. 39.
53. See *Pravda,* 26 February 1986 and *The Wall Street Journal,* 26 February 1986.
54. De Borchgrave and Ledeen, *op. cit.,* p. 14.
55. Quoted in Robert W. Kasten, Jr., "Repaying the Polish Loans," *The Wall Street Journal,* 28 July 1983.
56. Marshall Goldman, *Detente and Dollars: Doing Business With the Soviets* (Basic Books, 1975), p. 5.
57. George Will, "Trading With the Enemy," *The Washington Post,* 4 May 1979.
58. *Human Events,* 21 December 1985, p. 5.
59. *The New York Times,* 7 December 1978.
60. *The Washington Post,* 3 Marchh 1982.
61. Epstein, "The Riddle of Armand Hammer," p. 122.
62. Samuel Pisar, "Gorbachev's Pragmatic Generation," *The Wall Street Journal,* 26 December 1985.
63. George F. Will, "Statesmanship and the Profit Motive," *The Washington Post,* 25 November 1982.
64. *IBID.*
65. Carl Gershman, *op. cit.,* p. 42. A provision of the Smoot-Hawley Tariff Act of 1930 prohibits the importation into the United States of "all goods, wares, articles and merchandise mined, produced or manufactured wholly or in part in any foreign country by convict labor and/orforced labor." The only time the law was enforced against the USSR was from 1951 and 1961, when canned crabmeat was banned. In 1983 William van Raab, commissioner of the Customs Department, moved to implement the law but collided with the immovable force of bureaucratic inertia. See George Will, "What, Enforce the Law?" *The Washington Post,* 27 November 1983.
66. Gershman, p. 42.
67. Jim Courter, "Where Are Our Afghanistan Sanctions"? *The Washington Times,* 17 January 1985.
68. Lawrence Brady, "Technology Transfers: Do Crackdowns Work"? *The Wall Street Journal,* 1 October 1985.

## Chapter 4

1. Walter Laqueur, "Poland and the Crisis of the Alliance," *The Wall Street Journal,* 4 January 1982.
2. *The Washington Post,* 11 September 1984.
3. Max Jakobson, "Eurocommunism's Beneficial Decline," *The New York Times,* 16 April 1986.
4. James O. Goldsborough, "The Roots of Western Disunity," *The New York Times Magazine,* 9 May 1982, p. 49.
5. *The Manchester Guardian,* 29 May 1980.
6. Quoted in Arthur Schlesinger Jr., "NATO: Time for a Divorce?" *The Wall Street Journal,* 5 Marchh 1984.
7. Goldsborough, "The Roots of Disunity," p. 60.
8. Walter Laqueur, "Poland and the Crisis of the Alliance," *The Wall Street Journal,* 4 January 1982. Willy Brandt, the former West German Chancellor, was an architect of *Ostpolitik.* Bruno Kreisky is the detente-minded former Chancellor of Austria. Andreas Papandreou, Greece's prime minister, has adopted a markedly "soft" policy toward the Soviet Union.
9. Henry Kissinger, "A Plan to Reshape NATO," *Time,* 5 March 1984, pp. 22-23.
10. "C.I.A. Study: Soviet Action and Propaganda," Hearings Before the Subcommit-

tee on Oversight of the Permanent Select Committee on Intelligence, House of Representatives, 96th Congress, 2nd session, 6 & 9 February 1980, pp. 75-76.

11. Bruce Porter, "The Euromissile Dispute and the Tactics of Soviet Foreign Policy," Radio Liberty Research, 26 April 1983.
12. Edwin M. Yoder Jr., "Europe's Choice: The Missiles," *The Washington Post*, 18 November 1983.
13. See, e.g., Jeffrey Record, ". . . And NATO's Impending Collapse," *The Washington Post*, 25 September 1981.
14. *The Washington Post*, 18 November 1981.
15. Francois de Rose, "European Concerns and SALT II," *Survival*, September/October 1979, p. 206.
16. Quoted in *The Wall Street Journal*, 16 May 1983.
17. See the article by Irving Kristol in *The New York Times Magazine*, 25 September 1983.
18. Henry Kissinger, "Arms Control and Europe's Nuclear Missiles," *The Wall Street Journal*, 31 January 1984.
19. Quoted in *U.S. News & World Report*, 4 April 1983.
20. *The New York Times*, 22 March 1981.
21. Wynfred Joshua, "Soviet Manipulation of the European Peace Movement," *Strategic Review*, Winter 1983, p. 13.
22. See Joshua, p. 14.
23. See Joshua, p. 15.
24. *The New York Times*, 4 November 1981.
25. Quoted in *The Washington Post*, 25 October 1981.
26. Mark Helprin, "Drawing the Line in Europe," *The New York Times Magazine*, 4 December 1983, p. 104.
27. See Joshua, p. 16, and *The New York Times*, 6 April 1982.
28. *The Washington Post*, 11 June 1982.
29. *The Washington Post*, 10 June 1982.
30. *The New York Times*, 25 October 1981.
31. *IBID*.
32. Bruce Porter, "The Euromissile Dispute and the Tactics of Soviet Foreign Policy," *Radio Liberty Research*, RL 169/83, 26 April 1983, p. 5.
33. *The Washington Post*, 9 April 1985.
34. *IBID*.
35. In a gesture to the Dutch peace movement (and perhaps to the Soviets too), the government decided to terminate two nuclear roles that NATO had assigned to the Netherlands in case of war. These involved the use of F-16 fighter bombers to deliver nuclear payloads and the use of P-3 Orion aircraft to drop nuclear depth charges against enemy submarines. The Dutch committed themselves to retain two other nuclear systems—the Lance short-range missile and a nuclear-capable howitzer.
36. See *The Wall Street Journal*, 2 December 1985.
37. See *The New York Times*, 6 March 1986.
38. See *The New York Times*, 26 January 1986.
39. Evan Galbraith, "Europe's Security Depends on Enhanced French Nuclear Force," *The Wall Street Journal*, 16 July 1986.
40. Jeane Kirkpatrick, "SS-20's and Europe," *The Washington Post*, 23 February 1986.
41. Graham T. Allison and Albert Carnesale, "Is Europe Contrary?" *The New York Times*, 26 March 1986.
42. *The New York Times*, 2 March 1986. Henry Kissinger wrote in early 1984 that "the basic European attitude toward the missiles is that of a host toward a now-unwanted guest whose invitation to dinner it would be too awkward to withdraw" (see *Time*, 5 March 1984, p. 20). If this were indeed the general attitude of that time, a change for the positive appears to have occurred since then.
43. *The Washington Post*, 14 March 1986.
44. Quoted in *The Wall Street Journal*, 2 December 1985.

45. Pierre Lellouche, "SDI and the Atlantic Alliance," *SAIS Review*, Summer/Fall 1985, pp. 67-68.
46. Karen Elliott House, "Europe's Escapism Makes it Balk at Accepting Star Wars," *The Wall Street Journal*, 24 June 1985.
47. See *The Washington Times*, 9 July 1985.
48. Lellouche, *op.cit.*, pp. 73-74.
49. *The Wall Street Journal*, 31 August 1982.
50. *The Wall Street Journal*, 2 November 1982.
51. *IBID*.
52. Gordon Crovitz, "Europe Pays for Its Pipe Dream," *The Wall Street Journal*, 13 December 1983.
53. See *Newsweek*, 5 July 1982.
54. "Pipeline Basics," *The Wall Street Journal*, 11 August 1982.
55. Sen. Jake Garn, "Questions About the Soviet Gas Pipeline," *The Wall Street Journal*, 20 May 1982.
56. According to Polish defector Col. Wlodzimierz Kuklinski, who had attended top-level planning meetings, the Soviet Union ordered Poland in September to prepare for martial law. He tipped off the West before the actual imposition of martial law occurred in December.
57. See Jack Anderson, "How Reagan Was Foiled on Soviet Sanctions," *The Washington Post*, 27 May 1983.
58. *The Wall Street Journal*, 13 December 1983.
59. "Pipeline Basics," *The Wall Street Journal*, 11 August 1982.
60. *The Wall Street Journal*, 31 August 1982.
61. See *The Wall Street Journal*, 31 August 1982.
62. *The Wall Street Journal*, 23 June 1982.
63. Quoted in *The New York Times*, 3 January 1982.
64. See *Business Week*, 1 February 1982, p. 34.
65. "Our Grain, Their Pipeline," *The Washington Times*, 21 July 1982.
66. See *The Wall Street Journal*, 23 July 1982.
67. *The New York Times*, 17 January 1982.
68. Jack Anderson, "How Reagan Was Foiled on Soviet Sanctions," *The Washington Post*, 27 May 1983.
69. Jake Garn, "Questions About the Soviet Gas Pipeline," *The Wall Street Journal*, 20 May 1982.
70. Quoted in *The New World* (New York), 4 August 1982.
71. See *The Wall Street Journal*, 13 December 1983.
72. *The Wall Street Journal*, 6 June 1986.
73. *The Wall Street Journal*, 20 November 1984.
74. See *The Washington Times* and *The Wall Street Journal*, 6 June 1986.
75. See, e.g., *Business Week*, 8 March 1982.
76. *The Washington Post*, 7 June 1982.
77. *The Washington Post*, 7 June 1982.
78. This fascinating case if described in detail in *The KGB in France*, by French writer Thierry Wolton.
79. See *The New York Times*, 27 January 1985.
80. Quoted in *The New York Times*, 27 October 1985.
81. Evans & Novak, "Reaping the Benefits of Geneva," *The Washington Post*, 27 November 1985.
82. *The Washington Post*, 30 May 1986.
83. *The Washington Post*, 30 May 1986.
84. *The New York Times*, 1 July 1986.
85. See G. Lokshin, "Peace Movement and Ideological Struggle," *International Affairs* (Moscow), June 1984, p. 59.
86. James O. Goldsborough, "The Roots of Western Disunity," *op. cit.*
87. *IBID*.
88. Quoted in John Vinocur, "The German Malaise," *The New York Times Magazine*, 15 November 1981, p. 120.

89. Wettig, *op. cit.*, pp. 91-92.
90. *Newsweek,* 7 February 1977, p. 36.
91. Gerhard Wettig, "Europe and the Idea of Common Security," *The Washington Quarterly,* Spring 1985, pp. 88-90.
92. Radio Moscow, 20 May 1979.
93. See *Soviet World Outlook,* 15 June 1979, p. 4.
94. Quoted in James O. Goldsborough, "Europe Cashes in on Carter's Cold War," *The New York Times Magazine,* 27 April 1980, p. 42.
95. *IBID.*
96. *IBID* .
97. Goldsborough, p. 42.
98. Goldsborough, p. 42.
99. Goldsborough, p. 46.
100. *The New York Times,* 15 January 1982.
101. *The New York Times,* 19 January 1986.
102. *Sovetskaya Rossiya,* 13 January 1982.
103. *Pravda,* 16 November 1985.
104. *The Wall Street Journal,* 18 December 1984.
105. *The New York Times,* 24 January 1983.
106. *IBID.*
107. Josef Joffe, "Why Germans Support SALT," *Survival,* September/October 1979, p. 209.
108. Jan Sejna, *We Will Bury You* (London: Sidgwick & Jackson, 1982), p. 117.
109. Joffe, *Survival,* p. 210.
110. Radio Moscow, 30 June 1980.
111. Joffe, p. 210.
112. K. Karagezyan, "USSR-FRG: A Dialogue in the Interests of Detente," *Novoye Vremya,* 4 July 1980, pp. 6-7.
113. *Newsweek,* 11 January 1982, p. 29.
114. "Ostpolitik or Illusion?" *The New York Times,* 28 December 1981.
115. *The Washington Post,* 14 October 1981.
116. Radio Prague, domestic, 16 September 1981.
117. *The Washington Post,* 11 October 1981; emphasis added.
118. *IBID.,* p. 118.
119. *IBID.,* p. 117.
120. *IBID.,* p. 123.
121. *The Wall Street Journal,* 14 January 1982; emphasis added.
122. *Newsweek,* 11 January 1982, p. 30.
123. *The New York Times,* 3 January 1982.
124. *IBID.*
125. *IBID.,* p. 29.
126. Evans & Novak, "A Warning From West Germany on Detente," *The Washington Post,* 16 June 1982.
127. *IBID.*
128. *The Washington Post,* 25 February 1983.
129. Morton M. Kondracke, "German Showdown: Reagan Sweeps, Andropov Weeps," *The Wall Street Journal,* 10 March 1983.
130. *The Washington Post,* 6 February 1983.
131. *The Washington Post,* 6 February 1983.
132. "A Finlandized Germany?" *The Wall Street Journal,* 2 March 1983.
133. *The Washington Post,* 26 February 1983.
134. *The Washington Post,* 26 February 1983.
135. *The Washington Post,* 26 February 1983.
136. "German Showdown," *op. cit., The Wall Street Journal,* 10 March 1983.
137. "The Kohl Mandate," *The Wall Street Journal,* 8 March 1983.
138. *The New York Times,* 7 March 1983.
139. *La Stampa* (Turin), 7 July 1983. Kohl also made a hastily arranged trip to East

Germany in June for talks with Erich Honecker. See *Business Week,* 27 June 1983, p. 44.
140. *The New York Times,* 5 July 1983.
141. *The Washington Post,* 21 September 1983.
142. *The Washington Post,* 23 July 1983.
143. *The Washington Post,* 22 July 1986.
144. Melvin J. Lasky, "Tremors on Germany's Political Seismograph," *The Wall Street Journal,* 21 October 1981.
145. Josef Joffe, "Why Germans Support SALT," *Survival,* September/October 1979, p. 211.
146. "Germany Uber Alles," *The New York Times,* 27 November 1983.
147. Mark Helprin, "Drawing the Line in Europe," *The New York Times Magazine,* 4 December 1983, p. 56.
148. *The New York Times,* 30 October 1985.
150. James O. Goldsborough, "The Roots of Western Disunity," *The New York Times Magazine,* 9 May 1982, p. 56.
151. Reuter, 22 February 1981.
152. "Combatting the Eurowedge," *The Wall Street Journal,* 20 May 1983.
153. "Who Is This Mitterrand?" *The Washington Post,* 24 June 1984.
154. Evan Galbraith, "Europe's Security Depends on Enhanced French Nuclear Force," *The Wall Street Journal,* 16 July 1986.

## Chapter 5

1. See a review of the book in *Kommunist,* No. 5, 1980.
2. U.S. Department of State, "The Meaning of Detente" (Washington, D.C.: Government Printing Office), June 1974, p. 4.
3. The Soviet Union was one of eight countries that abstained in voting on the Declaration, which was adopted by a vote of 48 to 0. The Soviet Union is a party to the International Covenant on Civil and Political Rights; Article 12 of the Covenant stipulates that "every one shall be free to leave any country, including his own."
4. *A Chronicle of Current Events,* No. 60 (1980), p. 77.
5. See Chapter 2.
6. David Satter, "The Kremlin Tortures a Psychiatrist," *The Wall Street Journal,* 29 December 1983.
7. Khrushchev equated political dissent with mental illness by declaring: "We can say that . . . there are people who struggle against Communism . . . but clearly the mental state of such people is not normal." *Pravda,* 24 May 1959.
8. *A Chronicle of Current Events,* No. 44, Amnesty International Publications, p. 185.
9. *International Herald-Tribune,* 28 September 1978.
10. *The New York Times,* 12 May 1979.
11. See *The News World* (New York), 10 March 1981.
12. Ben Wattenberg, "Can We Deal With Such People?" *The Washington Post,* 12 October 1982.
13. The small number of Soviets who returned home from the United States—usually because they had been obliged to leave family members behind in the Soviet Union or could not adjust to the freewheeling American lifestyle—were cited in Soviet propaganda campaigns as "proof" that living conditions in the West were intolerable.
14. There are about half a million Baptists in the USSR, many of whom belong to "unregistered"—and thus illegal—congregations. Moscow's official Baptist community has about 5,000 members. See *The Washington Post,* 10 May 1982.
15. *The Washington Post,* 10 May 1982.
16. Peter Reddaway, "KGB Purging Human Rights Activists," *The Guardian* (London), 27 July 1983.

17. *The New York Times*, 17 July 1983.
18. "Return to Madrid," *The Wall Street Journal*, 9 February 1981.
19. See *The Washington Post*, 22 November 1985.
20. *Newsweek*, 2 December 1985, p. 33.
21. *IBID*.
22. See *The New York Times*, 23 August 1986.
23. See Serge Schmemann, "Soviet Union Lists Formal New Rules on Who May Leave," *The New York Times*, 9 November 1986.
24. Quoted in William Korey, "A Human Rights Meeting in Moscow?" *The New York Times*, 26 January 1987.
25. Cited by Secretary of State George Schultz in his address to the Los Angeles World Affairs Council on 31 October 1986.
26. Quoted in *The New York Times*, 17 October 1986.
27. "Trade Mission-ites," *The Wall Street Journal*, 25 February 1985.
28. Melvyn Krauss, "Stop Rewarding the Soviets for Human-Rights Improvements," *The Wall Street Journal*, 24 June 1986.
29. Letter to the Editor of *The New York Times*, 5 July 1983.
30. George Will, "Luckily, Little 'Progress,'" *The Washington Post*, 22 November 1985.
31. *The Christian Science Monitor*, 15 June 1983.
32. *IBID*.
33. Stanley Hoffmann, "Rights and Democracy," *The New York Times*, 31 December 1978.
34. *The Washington Post*, 22 November 1985; emphasis added.

## Chapter 6

1. William Safire, *Safire's Political Dictionary* (New York: Ballantine Books, 1978), p. 167.
2. *Pravda*, 22 August 1973.
3. Quoted by Dimitri K. Simes, "What's So Great About Gorbachev? Nothing—Yet," *The Washington Post*, 24 February 1986.
4. John Lewis Gaddis, "The Rise, Fall and Future of Detente," *Foreign Affairs*, Winter 1983-84, pp. 359-40.
5. *IBID*.
6. William Safire, *The New York Times*, 31 December 1975.
7. *Pravda*, 4 January 1976.
8. *The Guardian Weekly*, 11 January 1976.
9. Interview with *The New Republic*, 7 February 1981, p. 20.
10. During his pre-election interview with *U.S. News & World Report*, Reagan said: "My criticism of the embargo was not that I objected to sanctions against the Soviet Union, but that the embargo was mere window-dressing. The embargo was really the only thing that Carter did. At the same time that we were boycotting grain, we were selling the Soviets an assembly line to build V-12 tank engines. . . ."
11. Radio Moscow, 1 March 1981.
12. *Pravda*, 9 March 1981.
13. Quoted in Hedrick Smith, "Geneva: A Test of Two Wills," *The New York Times Magazine, op. cit.*
14. The transcript of Reagan's speech to the National Press Club (the speech in which he introduced the "zero option" on intermediate-range missiles in Europe) appears in *The New York Times*, 19 November 1981.
15. See Chapter 3.
16. See, e.g., John Barron, "A KGB Blueprint for the Disarming of America," *The News World* (New York), 20 October 1982.
17. *The Washington Times*, 24 April 1985.

18. *Newsweek,* 29 August 1983, p. 26.
19. *The Economist,* 20 November 1982, p. 9.
20. Quoted in George Will, "The 'New Generation Theory'—Again," *The Washington Post,* 14 March 1985.
21. *IBID.*
22. *Pravda,* 3 March 1984.
23. The Soviets also forged letters purporting to be from the Ku Klux Klan to the Olympic committees of South Korea, Sri Lanka, Malaysia, and Zimbabwe. The letters proclaimed that only whites would be welcomed at the Games and others might risk their lives by participating.
24. For excerpts from the President's speech, see *The New York Times,* 24 September 1984.
25. *IBID.*
26. *The New York Times,* 30 September 1984.
27. "Trying to Be Mr. Nice Guy," *The Washington Times,* 26 September 1984.
28. *Newsweek,* 24 September 1984, p. 37.
29. *The New York Times,* 24 September 1984.
30. *Newsweek,* 31 December 1984, p. 40.
31. *Newsweek,* 31 December 1984, pp. 40-41.
32. *Business Week,* 25 March 1985, p. 42.
33. Hedrick Smith, "Geneva: A Test of Two Wills," *The New York Times Magazine,* 17 November 1985.
34. *The New York Times,* 28 March 1985.
35. *The New York Times,* 13 November 1985.
36. Hedrick Smith, "Geneva: A Test of Two Wills," *op. cit.*
37. Richard Cohen, "Gorbachev: On Target," *The Washington Post,* 13 November 1985.
38. Hedrick Smith, "Geneva: A Test of Two Wills," *op. cit.*
39. Henry Kissinger, "An Opportunity for a Breakthrough," *The Washington Post,* 17 November 1985.
40. Fred Barnes, "Summit Scorecard," *The New Republic,* 2 December 1985, p. 11.
41. *IBID.*
42. *The Washington Post,* 15 November 1985.
43. *The Washington Post,* 2 December 1985.
44. *U.S News & World Report,* 21 December 1985, p. 20.
45. *The New York Times,* 23 November 1985.
46. *The Washington Times,* 25 November 1985.
47. *The Washington Post,* 15 December 1985.
48. *The Washington Times,* 22 November 1985.
49. For the text of the joint statement, see *The Washington Post,* 22 November 1985.
50. *The Washington Post,* 3 October 1986.
51. Charles Krauthammer, "A Bad Deal Gets Worst," *The Washington Post,* 3 October 1986.
52. "Ronald Reagan's Killer Rabbit," *The Wall Street Journal,* 6 October 1986.
53. William F. Buckley, "The GOP and Reykjavik," *The Washington Post,* 17 October 1986.
54. William Safire, "Are They for Real?" *The New York Times,* 24 November 1985.
55. *The New York Times,* 4 June 1983.
56. Paul Greenberg, "How Fulbright Reads History," *The Washington Times,* 9 January 1987.
57. *The Washington Times,* 29 July 1985.
58. Evans & Novak, "The White House Blink," *The Washington Post,* 10 September 1986.
59. George Will, "When Murder Becomes an 'Episode,'" *The Washington Post,* 4 April 1985.
60. Stanley Hoffman, "Fog Over the Summit," *The New York Review,* 16 January 1986, p. 22.

61. "A Cold Day in Iceland," *The Washington Times,* 6 October 1986.
62. *The New York Times,* 22 November 1985.
63. See Tom Wicker, "Following Up Chernobyl," *The New York Times,* 16 May 1986.
64. *The Economist,* 24 December 1983.
65. For the text of Reagan's message, see *The Washington Post,* 2 January 1986.
66. Edward L. Rowny, "10 'Commandments' for Negotiating With the Soviet Union," *The New York Times,* 12 January 1986.
67. Charles Krauthammer, "Those 'Blundering' Russians," *The Washington Post,* 19 September 1986.
68. Col. James B. Motley, "Soviets and Arms Control: Rhetoric and Exploitation," *Army Magazine,* June 1983, p. 20.
69. See the interview with Shultz and Godson in *Human Events,* 19 January 1985.
70. Quoted in *The Washington Times,* 27 May 1986.
71. *The Washington Post,* 5 October 1986.
72. *U.S. News & World Report,* 15 September 1986.
73. George Will, "Reeling Toward Reykjavik," *The Washington Post,* 3 October 1986.
74. Meg Greenfield, "Gorbachev vs. the Computer Age," *The Washington Post,* 29 October 1985.
75. Joseph Sobran, "Coping With Abu Nidal," *The Washington Times,* 7 January 1986.
76. *The New York Times,* 18 November 1981.
77. *Newsweek,* 9 December 1985, p. 104.
78. *Soviet Diplomacy and Negotiating Behavior: Emerging New Context for U.S. Diplomacy,* Special Studies Series on Foreign Affairs Issues, Vol. I, Prepared by the Senior Specialists Division, Congressional Research Service, Library of Congress (Washington, D.C.: Government Printing Office, 1979), p. 527.
79. George Will, "Abolishing the 20th Century," *Newsweek,* 9 December 1985, p. 104.
80. George Will, "All Lenin's Children," *The Washington Post,* 17 November 1985.
81. Herbert S. Levine, Francis W. Rushing, and Charles H. Movit, "Potential for U.S. Economic Leverage on the USSR," *Comparative Strategy,* Vol. 1, No. 4, 1979, p. 400.
82. See Morton Kondracks, "Reagan's Soviet Success," *The Washington Times,* 4 October 1984.
83. See *The Washington Post,* 9 March 1986.
84. Quoted in *The Guardian,* 3 February 1980.
85. George Will, "Statesmanship and the Profit Motive," *The Washington Post,* 25 November 1982.
86. See *Newsweek,* 1 November 1971, p. 29.
87. Peter Tarnoff, "A Chance at Arms Control," *The New York Times,* 24 November 1986.
88. Quoted in *The Washington Times,* 29 December 1986.
89. *The Washington Post,* 10 November 1986.
90. Quoted in Zbigniew Brzezinski, "Overview of East-West Relations," *The Washington Quarterly,* Fall 1985, p. 31.
91. *The Washington Times,* 12 January 1987.
92. Jeane J. Kirkpatrick, "Who Knows What Gorbachev Wants?" *The Washington Post,* 17 November 1985.
93. Henry Kissinger, "An Opportunity for a Breakthrough," *The Washington Post,* 17 November 1985.
94. Archie Brown, "Change in the Soviet Union," *Foreign Affairs,* Summer 1986, p. 1065.
95. Elmo Zumwalt, "Beware of Soviets Bearing Gifts," *The Washington Times,* 2 December 1985.
96. Vladimir Bukovsky, "Mesmerized by the Bear," *The Washington Times,* 27 May 1986.
97. David Satter, "'New Openness' and Other Illusions," *The Washington Post,* 15 November 1985.
98. Quoted in *Newsweek,* 23 February 1987, p. 33.

100. Quoted in William Safire, "Begging for a Summit," *The New York Times*, 28 March 1985.
101. George Will, "Statesmanship and the Profit Motive," *The Washington Post*, 25 November 1982.
102. See *Human Events*, 23 November 1985.
103. *Counterpoint* (Israel), January 1987.
104. Charles Krauthammer, "Drug Fever, Cory Fever, Summit Fever," *The Washington Post*, 26 September 1986.
105. *Soviet Diplomacy and Negotiating Behavior: Emerging New Context for U.S. Diplomacy, op. cit.*, p. 7.
106. *IBID.*, p. 6.
107. Gordon Craig, "Totalitarian Approaches to Diplomatic Negotiation," in A.O. Sarkissian (ed.), *Studies in Diplomatic History and Historiography in Honour of G.P. Gooch* (London: Longmans, Green, 1961), p. 119.
108. *IBID.*
109. *The New York Times*, 13 November 1985.
110. *U.S. News & World Report*, 9 November 1985.
111. Quoted in *The Washington Times*, 19 October 1984.
112. Charles Krauthammer, "Drug Fever, Cory Fever, Summit Fever," *The Washington Post*, 26 September 1986.
113. Edward Rowny, "'10 Commandments' for Negotiating With the Soviet Union," *The New York Times*, 12 January 1986.
114. *The Wall Street Journal*, 15 November 1985.
115. Rowny, "'10 Commandments,'" *op. cit.*
116. Charles McC. Mathias, "Gromyko and Haig," *The New York Times*, 21 September 1981.
117. *The Washington Post*, 17 May 1979.
118. "Pruning the Politburo," *The Washington Times*, 3 July 1985.
119. Jim Courter, "Where Are Our Afghanistan Sanctions?" *The Washington Times*, 17 January 1985.
120. M. Stanton Evans, "Back to Square One?" *The Washington Times*, 2 December 1985.

# Epilogue

1. *The Washington Post*, 1 November 1988.
2. *The Washington Times*, 18 November 1987.
3. Alain Besancon, "Gorbachev Without Illusions," *Commentary*, April 1988, p. 57.
4. Bank for International Settlements.
5. *The New York Times*, 30 October 1988.
6. *Agence France-Presse*, 12 October 1988.
7. Jim Hoagland, "*Perestroika* in Peril," *The Washington Post*, 2 August 1988.
8. *The Washington Post*, 28 October 1988.
9. *Ibid.*, 29 October 1988.
10. *The New York Times*, 2 November 1988.
11. See *The Washington Times*, 31 October 1988.
12. *The New York Times*, 5 October 1988.

# Index